This book is provided to you by the volunteers of the
Assistance League® of Minneapolis/St. Paul

It is our sincere hope that it will be of help to you.
We want you to know that somebody cares.

Assistance League® of Minneapolis/ St. Paul
6416 Penn Avenue S., Richfield, MN 55423
(612) 866-2135

Recovering from Rape

RECOVERING FROM RAPE

SECOND EDITION

Linda E. Ledray,
R.N., Ph.D., L. P., F.A.A.N.

A Holt Paperback · Henry Holt and Company · New York

Holt Paperbacks
Henry Holt and Company, LLC
Publishers since 1866
175 Fifth Avenue
New York, New York 10010
www.henryholt.com

A Holt Paperback® and ⓗⓟ® are registered trademarks of
Henry Holt and Company, LLC.

Library of Congress Cataloging-in-Publication Data
Ledray, Linda E.
Recovering from rape / Linda E. Ledray—2nd ed.
p.   cm.
Includes index.
ISBN-13: 978-0-8050-2928-4
ISBN-10: 0-8050-2928-1
1. Rape victims—United States—Life skills guides.
2. Rape victims—United States—Psychology.   I. Title.
HV6250.4.W65L42   1994
362.88'3—dc20   CIP

Henry Holt books are available for special promotions and
premiums. For details contact: Director, Special Markets.

Originally published in 1986 by
Henry Holt and Company

Second Holt Paperbacks Edition 1994

Designed by Paula R. Szafranski

Printed in the United States of America
23   25   24   22

This book is dedicated to the thousands of rape survivors seen by me and my staff in the past, and to those we will see in the years to come. Thank you for allowing us to be a part of your recovery.

Contents

Acknowledgments

I have been fortunate throughout my life that many of the people with whom I have lived and worked have allowed me to step outside the usual roles for women and encouraged me to try to do what others have not yet done. They have been tolerant of my impatience with the way things are and have accepted my need to try to make things different. They have defended me against many an attack by those resistant to change or disapproving of my methods. They have been friends when it would have been easier not to be. To these people I am truly indebted and always will be. I wish to thank Mr. and Mrs. J. A. Majeski (my mom and dad), Mark Hartsch, Tom Kiresuk, Teresa Ledray, Patrick Ledray, Zig Stelmachers, and Susan Valentine.

I wish to thank the staff at the Sexual Assault Resource Service (SARS) in Minneapolis—Mary Cody, Jan Kraft, Chris Lewis, Maureen Malloy, Maggie Pharris, Barb Rolland, Julie Sherber, Pam Smith, and Nancy Uber. I greatly appreciate not only their critique of the manuscript but also their dedication and their belief in the work that we are doing with survivors of rape.

I also wish to thank the hundreds of survivors of rape from whom I continue to learn so much as they allow me to work with them through their process of recovery.

Recovering from Rape

Introduction

What Is Rape, and What Can We Do About It?

I was a gifted girl, I was meant to live up to a high standard, to expect much of myself, and to do great things. I could have played a great part. I could have been the wife of a king, the beloved of a revolutionary, the sister of a genius, the mother of a martyr.

—HERMAN HESSE, *Steppenwolf*

For generations women have been socialized to defer their worth, power, and authority to men, to play a secondary, supplemental role in a male-dominated world. Rape represents the ultimate surrender of any remaining power, autonomy, and control. The surrender is not by choice but is usually necessary to ensure survival, or in the hope of survival. Through this destruction of a woman's feelings of personal power and self-worth, the rapist hopes to gain a sense of his own power and worth, to take from the woman what he does not already feel in himself.

In our culture sex is often used by both men and women to exert power or control over each other—by offering it, withholding it, or even having it. However, rape is the taking of sex without consent, the violation of one person by another. Rather than an act of sexual gratification, rape is an angry and violent expression of the rapist's desire to dominate someone else. Sex becomes a weapon. Unfortunately, many people, including those in decision-making positions in this country, still do not understand that rape is a crime of violence, the expression of anger, not a crime of passion motivated by sexual desire.

In the fall of 1983, in Anderson, South Carolina, three men who pled guilty to raping and torturing a woman for more than six hours were given the choice of thirty years in jail or surgical castration. In the spring of 1993, in Minneapolis, Minnesota, a repeat sex offender also facing a twenty-year sentence for yet another sexual assault of a child asked to have his sentence shortened and be surgically castrated. He admitted to raping fifty young girls over twenty-five years. He sought castration and then the reduction of his sentence to ten years in jail and probation.

On both occasions, an emotional debate followed. The logic of the option of castration for rape depends to a great extent on what we consider the purpose of our criminal justice system, as well as our belief in the motive for rape. If the purpose of our courts is to ensure revenge, or to see that an eye-for-an-eye, tooth-for-a-tooth justice is carried out, then castration could be just punishment for rape. Does this mean that thieves should have the option of having a hand cut off instead of going to jail?

If, on the other hand, the purpose of our criminal justice system is to ensure our safety from criminals and to prevent further crime, then there is no logic whatsoever in castrating rapists, except in the minds of those who believe the myth that sex is the primary motivation for rape. In the South Carolina case, intimidation was an obvious motive for the rape. The woman knew one of the three men and had threatened to name him in a paternity suit. Castration will not keep this woman safe from this man. It may even increase his anger and his violence toward her and other women and make him want revenge. However, if these men are imprisoned, the survivor and other women will be safe from them at least until they are paroled.

The decision of the judge in the 1983 case demonstrates a very serious misunderstanding of why men commit rape. Rapists will not be stopped or controlled because their testicles have been removed, which is what surgical castration involves. It may prevent them from having sexual intercourse in the future, but rape and torture have nothing to do with their ability to have intercourse or to procreate. In fact, with testosterone injections or a prosthetic implant, some surgically castrated men will be able to resume having intercourse, and they will be able to rape again. They all probably will be even more angry and a greater threat to society.

Nor will rapists be stopped by giving them Depo-provera, a female hormone. Inaccurately called "chemical castration," this drug treatment is another choice that has recently been presented to rapists as an option to jail. Some men choosing Depo-provera still will be able to have erections. Like those who are surgically castrated, they certainly will be able to torture and kill. Some people believe that the threat of castration or drug treatment will act as a deterrent to rape. Perhaps it will. However, it will not protect women from being victims of other forms of violence. The 1993 case in Minneapolis, where the convicted serial rapist requested castration in lieu of thirty years in jail, seems to indicate that longer jail sentences are a more effective deterrent to rape as well as a more effective means of protecting women. Fortunately, the judge denied his request and sent him to jail. A primary issue was, however, his being able to give consent to the castration, without coercion. The state was concerned that he would later claim the jail sentence was a form of coercion. The judge wrote: "Given the permanent nature of surgical castration, as well as the bodily mutilation, surgical castration as an option for probation would be unconstitutional." Yet this judge also ruled against allowing the castration because he found there to be no evidence that castration changes the behavior of habitual sex offenders.

The most that castration of assailants can do is change the weapon they use against women. In place of sex and a penis, they may instead more often use a knife, a gun, or a lead pipe. Rape will not be stopped until the myths about it are recognized as myths, until we, and the people in positions of power and influence, understand the real meaning of and motives behind rape, until we all work toward true equality and respect for women and their value in our society.

• • •

Once a rape has ended and the woman has survived, an intensely personal second struggle begins for her: to recover, to take back control of her body and her life, and even to forge a stronger identity as a result of what has happened. This is a time for her to evaluate her vulnerabilities and weaknesses, to set new goals that maximize her strengths, and to develop strategies that utilize her abilities to attain these goals. She has been victimized, yes, but she is also a survivor who can turn the outrage of her assault into an opportunity for recovery, change, and growth.

This book is first and foremost a self-help manual designed not only to provide further support for women who report being raped but also for the 60 to 90 percent of survivors who do not report. Too many women do not seek help because they fear involvement with "the system," because they fear the threats of the assailant "if you report," because appropriate resources are not available in their area, or because they are attempting to deny the severity of the crime. Those who decide not to report need somewhere to turn so they can understand what they are going through and what their choices are. It is estimated that almost 4 million adult American women have suffered from long-term rape-induced psychological distress, now referred to as post-traumatic stress disorder; 1.3 million of them still suffer from this disorder.

Survivors need information to resolve the initial fears and anxieties that most experience and to help them avoid developing many of the long-term problems associated with rape. These women—and some men (see chapter 9)—must learn to identify their inner strengths and resources and to mobilize themselves to guide their own lives and more fully recognize their potential. They do not need to remain victims, immobilized by the trauma, resigned to a life of quiet desperation. They must decide if they want to get professional help in working through the often painful stages of emotional and physical recovery. *If you've been raped, you're not alone, and you don't need to suffer alone.*

Only within the last ten years or so has any thought been given to the impact of rape on the family and friends of the survivor. These people often also experience a significant emotional response to the assault. Often they too deal with feelings of vulnerability, fear, and guilt for somehow not having protected the survivor or prevented the rape. They are, however, much more likely than the rape survivor to deal with these traumatic and difficult events in isolation, not knowing that these feelings are shared by others and are a normal response to the situation. Either they don't know where to turn for help in understanding and dealing with their feelings, or they are reluctant to do so.

In this book these people—lovers, husbands, parents, siblings, children, friends, coworkers, roommates—are referred to as "significant others." Their responses to the survivor are crucial to how she copes with negative feelings resulting from the rape and how long it takes for her to recover. *If you know someone who has been raped, you can help pull her through, and you can learn to better understand your own responses to the rape.*

This book also will be useful to the many volunteer rape crisis counselors across the country. Although a few professionally staffed programs have become available since the development of the first rape crisis centers in the early 1970s, dedicated volunteers serve the largest group of rape survivors in the numerous centers across the nation.

The volunteers, often rape survivors themselves, have given unlimited time, energy, and personal resources to see that survivors of rape have someone to turn to who understands, cares, and believes them. Volunteers recognized and responded to the needs of this vast population long before the professional human services community even acknowledged the extent of the problem.

The professional community has given little information to these volunteers that would help them to accomplish their goals. There are few training manuals for rape crisis counselors. Many counselors have expressed a desire to learn more about rape. *If you want to help someone who has been raped, you can learn more.*

Considerable research data have been generated since the development in 1976 of the National Center for the Prevention and Control of Rape in Washington, D.C. Professional counselors and researchers have taken major strides in understanding the issues involved in rape, its impact, and the treatment needs of the survivors and their significant others. The information in this book is based in part on the research findings that have been gathered in work with rape survivors in centers across the United States. However, it is to a great extent also based on my experience in treating survivors and their families and doing research with this group for more than fifteen years at the Sexual Assault Resource Service (SARS) in Minneapolis, Minnesota.

In the following pages I provide information from national and local studies for survivors and their significant others to allow them to understand better their responses and to begin to rebuild their lives. Numerous personal accounts and case studies are included. Although the names in these accounts have been changed, the cases presented all involve real events or feelings that have been expressed by real survivors and significant others.

The first part of each of the first eight chapters is especially for the rape survivor. By having more information, by knowing that other rape survivors have felt the same way, and by knowing how these other women have dealt successfully with the same problems, the survivor will find that the process of recovery can be less traumatic and more easily resolved than if she tries to cope alone.

The second part of these chapters is for her family, friends, and associates, the other people affected by the rape. This second portion deals with the things they need to know to understand their own feelings about the rape and what they can do to resolve these feelings. They too are victims of the assault—secondary victims.

Most of the information in this book is based on the experiences and needs of female survivors, and feminine pronouns are used throughout to refer to survivors. However, male rape survivors also will benefit from the information provided. Although there are unique aspects of the rape of men by other men (see "Men Who Are Raped" in chapter 9), many of the experiences of the male rape survivor are similar to those of the female survivor.

Only a short time ago, our society did not recognize rape as a real problem. There were few rape centers or other services for survivors. Having intercourse with a woman, whether she wanted it or not, was seen as a man's right, particularly if he was married to the woman. Today we are becoming conscious of the fact that a woman has the right to give her body when she decides. We are therefore in a better position to help rape survivors resolve the problems that result from a rape. Unfortunately, we have not yet reached the point where we have learned to prevent the crime.

1

It's Not Your Fault

Our identity is a dream. We are process, not reality,
for reality is an illusion of the daylight, the light of
our particular day.

—LOREN EISELEY, *The Star Thrower*

TO THE SURVIVOR

Whatever you did—accepted a ride from a stranger, wore a low-cut blouse, had too much to drink with someone you met in a bar, invited a man you did not know well to your home, forgot to lock the door, were out late, took a walk alone—*you did not deserve to be raped*. In retrospect, we are all aware of things we would not have done if we could have known the results ahead of time. But we cannot always know the results of our actions in advance, and we do not usually get hurt. Yes, you were hurt this time, but that does not mean you should have known better and done things differently. You are not to blame. You were the *victim* of a violent crime, not the person responsible.

Unfortunately, rape is not something that happens to only a few women. On the average, one woman is being raped somewhere in the United States every minute of every day. One out of every four women born in this country will be raped at some point in her life. According to FBI statistics, in the United States alone, more than 100,000 women report being raped each year, and an estimated additional 400,000 to 900,000 women are raped but do not report the crime. Because most rapes go unreported, and fewer than 10 percent of the reported rapists go to jail, most rapists are still out walking the streets, free to rape again, having suffered no negative consequences as a result of their crime.

Rape occurs any time a person is forced or coerced, physically or through verbal threats, into any type of sexual contact with another person, whether the assailant is a friend, an acquaintance, an employer or a fellow employee, a husband, or a stranger. Although we may not be aware of it, each of us probably knows at least one other person who has been raped. Like many of these women, you may feel as if you should or could have done something to avoid being raped. But no matter what you did or didn't do, you should not feel foolish or stupid. You should not chastise yourself with thoughts like "I shouldn't have walked down that street," or "I should have known better than to trust him." The rape is over now, and you survived. It's time to move ahead.

At first you may find it difficult not to blame yourself, especially since other people may blame you too or not believe you were raped. Often, unintentionally upsetting comments come from boyfriends, roommates, friends, parents—those closest to you and whose opinions you value the most. People may say things without considering the implications of their words. You should be prepared for this. You must understand the dynamics involved and know not to accept the myths about rape that you may hear from others.

Janet, an eighteen-year-old woman, was out for a late-afternoon walk in the early spring.

He came out of nowhere and grabbed me from behind. I froze. He had a gun. I didn't know what to do or what he wanted. It was early, but at that moment there was no one else around.

He grabbed my hair and stuck the gun in my ribs, jerking me sideways into the alley. He was holding me up by my hair as I stumbled sideways. It all happened so quickly. He raped me in back of some garbage cans. It was so dirty and so humiliating. I can still smell that terrible odor. The police brought me into the hospital and called my parents. My father came down to the emergency room. The first thing he asked me was "Can you defend yourself against a man with a gun?" I told him I couldn't, and he had been much bigger than I am too. So my father said, "That's right, so you should know better than to go out of the house alone. If you can't defend yourself, you should never go out of the house alone, day or night."

Janet felt completely deflated and helpless. She did not know how to respond. She knew somehow that what her father had said was illogical, but how could it be? She *had* been unable to defend herself, and in a similar situation in the future she also would be unlikely to be able to do so. Did that mean that she should become a prisoner in her own home or dependent on the "protection" of a man who could defend her? Was her father suggesting that the rape was her fault because she was "foolish" enough to go out of the house alone?

Her father, a large man himself, had not been there to "protect" Janet and "prevent" the rape. Nor had anyone else been there to protect her. But few women or men can protect themselves from someone with a gun, and it is unrealistic to become prisoners in our own homes, afraid to go out alone, day or night, for fear of being raped. Besides, women are raped when they are out with their friends and when they are home with their families. In fact, more women are raped in their own home than any other single place. In a study I conducted in Minneapolis in 1984 on the impact and treatment needs of rape victims and their families, 29 percent of the women were raped in their own homes.* The next most frequent place was in a car, where 28 percent of the women were raped. While only 2 percent were actually raped on the street, another 34 percent were first ap-

---

*Study funded by the National Institute of Mental Health.

proached by the rapist while they were on the street, coming and going to work, visiting friends, or waiting for a bus.

According to these statistics, if you stay off the streets, out of cars, and out of your home, you may reduce your chance of being raped by more than 90 percent. Unfortunately, even being with a man "for protection" does not always prevent rape.

My boyfriend and I decided to see a late movie after having dinner downtown. I always thought I was safe out with him. I still can't believe it really happened. We were in the parking lot when all of a sudden two men were forcing us into a car. A third guy got into the backseat. They drove us to a deserted lot, somewhere on the edge of town, all the while saying, "If you just sit quiet and cooperate we won't hurt you." The only thing worse they could have done was to kill us both. I thought they might. They made my boyfriend watch while one raped me and they forced me to have oral sex with one of the others. Then he urinated on me. When they were done with me, they raped my boyfriend.

Should Peggy and her boyfriend have known better than to stay out late or to park in the restaurant parking lot? Does the fact that they parked there mean that they deserved to be raped or that they were asking for it? The initial response of one of Peggy's friends was "You should have known better than to have parked there."

Gloria, the mother of two teenage sons, was spending a quiet evening at her suburban home with her family. She went to answer the door and was overpowered by three men with a shotgun. They tied up her husband and her eighteen-year-old son and dragged her around the house looking for valuables, then they raped her before they left.

Should Gloria have known better than to have answered the door? Does the fact that she answered the door and that these men then got in make her responsible? Her neighbor told her, "You should never have opened your front door without knowing who was there."

No matter what you could have done differently, the rapist—not you—is to blame for the assault. So, why do so many otherwise-intelligent, rational people blame the survivor? Why do survivors blame themselves? Why have the many myths about rape been kept alive for so long? In order to put these detrimental myths to rest, we must understand why certain beliefs are accepted.

The Function of Rape Myths

Myths about rape have survived in our culture so tenaciously for so long because they have a number of social functions. Rape myths allow people to feel safe by letting them believe that rape rarely happens, and that when it does, it is because the woman secretly wanted to be raped. The myths enable us to maintain our belief that we live in a just world. They allow us to believe we can prevent future rapes. They keep women unequal to men, living under their control and in need of their protection from harm, and they maintain the Adam-and-Eve tradition of our culture, in which man is believed to be the innocent victim of the evil temptress—woman.

Myths Provide False Security

When we are confronted with the story of a rape, the easiest way to maintain our feelings of safety and invulnerability is to believe that what we are hearing is indeed a work of fiction, not a true story. If we believe that "many rape reports are false," then we significantly lower our perceived chance of becoming a victim too. In 1978 a survey evaluating the acceptance of rape myths was conducted at the University of Minnesota School for Social Research. Most participants believed that more than half of the women who claim to be raped lie about it because they are "angry at the man and want to get even," or "they are pregnant and want to protect their reputation." More than 49 percent reported believing that women who say they are raped are "lying to call attention to themselves."

There have been a few cases where women have recanted their stories, as happened in the widely publicized 1985 Gary Dotson/

Cathleen Webb case in Illinois. However, the vast majority of women who report being raped are telling the truth. Even a woman who recants may not have lied about being raped. She may have decided to change her story for a number of reasons, such as to end threats from the rapist's family or because of pressure from a religious leader who urges her to forgive and forget. Battered women often recant to the police in order to get the assailant out of jail, after he begs for their forgiveness and perhaps even offers marriage or to change his ways to prove his real love.

The implication behind many myths is that there may have been sexual intercourse, but it was not rape. For example, the myth that "a woman can run faster with her skirt up than a man can with his pants down" is simple enough. People who believe this myth think that a woman should be able to run away from a rapist, and if she does not, then she really must not have wanted to get away. This does not, however, take into consideration the immobility that results when you are faced with a threatening, angry man, with or without a weapon, and are afraid of being hurt or killed if you don't do what he tells you.

Many people, especially men, are unwilling to believe that a rape has occurred unless the woman fights to the point of exhaustion and sustains physical injuries, such as cuts or bruises, or torn clothing, as proof of her resistance. A 1979 study completed at Iowa State University found an interesting difference between male and female students' attitudes toward rape survivors who did or did not fight back. In cases in which the survivor resisted more forcefully, male students believed that the woman was more intelligent and less to blame for the rape. Female students, on the other hand, believed survivors who had resisted more forcefully were less intelligent and more at fault. According to researchers, the findings supported established societal norms. The students interpreted the survivors' behavior according to norms for their own sex: Men are taught to fight back and defend themselves, and see this as the intelligent, responsible thing to do; women are taught that men will be good to them and won't hurt them if they do as they are told. The result is that many women believe if a woman is foolish enough not to follow a man's directions, she "deserves what she gets." The Iowa State University study also found that, because they expect women to resist physical aggression, the men were less likely to believe a crime—a rape—had really been committed when the woman did not fight back. They were more likely to blame the nonresisting woman and to believe the rape was her own fault. After all, if she had really wanted to get away, she would have fought back—as these men felt they would do—when attacked.

Pauline met a very attractive man in one of the classier bars in town while out one Friday night. The man bought her a couple of drinks, then suggested they go to another bar just a short distance away. His car was in the parking lot, so he said he would drive. As soon as she got into his car, he grabbed her hair and forced her down on the seat. Then he took out a pair of handcuffs and put them on her. He drove to a deserted street not far away, raped her both vaginally and anally, and forced her to perform oral sex.

The police would not make an arrest in the case because they did not think it would hold up in court. Pauline had been seen drinking with this man, and she had willingly left the bar with him. She had not fought back, so she had no cuts, bruises, or torn clothing to indicate there had been a struggle. He claimed consent and there was no physical proof to indicate he was lying. Too many people still believe the old myths, so this man went free. Unfortunately, this is not an unusual situation.

In reality, less than 30 percent of all rape survivors are cut or bruised as a result of the rape. Only 23 percent of the women I interviewed in a Minneapolis study completed in 1984 used physical means such as hitting, biting, kicking, or pushing to resist the assailant. An additional 24 percent screamed. More than half of the women were too frightened or intimidated to use any physical means of resistance. But they did *not* consent. It was still rape.

Women, for the most part, are not taught to resist physical attacks. We are taught to submit to physical force, and we usually do. In fact, we usually submit even before we are confronted with threats of physical harm. While aggressiveness is an expected and approved trait in boys, it is strongly discouraged in girls. Even today advocates are still fighting for equality of sports activities in the schools, and they have a long way to go.

Women are expected to respond with fear to the same situations to which men are expected to respond with anger. In a 1976 study completed at Cornell University, subjects were shown a videotape of a small baby seeing a jack-in-the-box for the first time and were asked to describe the baby's reaction. When the subjects were told that the baby was a girl, they interpreted her response as being frightened. When other subjects saw the same tape of the same baby but were told it was a boy, they described the response as anger.

Some people concede that a man accused of rape may have used force, but they still maintain that the woman "really wanted it anyway." While some women may fantasize about being raped, there is a big difference between what people want in fantasy and what they want in reality. No woman wants to be brutally raped by anyone. Both men and women fantasize about many things they would never actually want to have happen.

More than 70 percent of the general public responding in a 1978 survey carried out by the University of Minnesota Center for Social Research believed that women are raped because, out of an unconscious wish to be raped, they do such things as dress provocatively. Rapists, however, know that this is not true. Only 6 percent of the rapists questioned in the same survey said that rape was the survivor's fault.

There are also many myths about how women are supposed to act after a rape—that is, if they were "really raped." One of these beliefs is that "after a woman is raped, she will be hysterical"; she will be extremely upset, crying, afraid, angry, or very sad.

Nina had been raped at knifepoint. Here's her story.

He acted like a lunatic. He was real nice when I first met him, and insisted on walking me home so I would be safe, of all things. My apartment was close, only a few blocks away, but he insisted and he seemed so nice. When we got to my apartment door, he suddenly forced his way in and took out a knife and started talking about how he was going to kill me. I was so scared I couldn't move or speak. I did exactly what he wanted.

When Nina got to the hospital emergency department, she was genuinely ecstatic. She was bright, cheerful, smiling, and joking with the staff. The doctor and nurse who were working that evening were both relatively new and had not worked with many rape survivors. When the sexual assault nurse clinician on call came in to see the woman, they told her about Nina's behavior and said they did not know if she had really been raped because "she's just too happy." How could she be so happy after being raped? But Nina had lived through the rape, something she did not expect to happen. As Nina told the counselor a number of times, "I'm just so happy to be alive. I truly believed he was going to kill me."

Although most rape victims are afraid of being killed during the rape, few respond to this fear as Nina did after the assault. Yet police, emergency department staff, and counselors who have worked with a number of survivors realize this variation of response is normal and do not question whether a rape occurred.

Myths Maintain Our Belief in a Just World

We all would like to believe we live in a just world in which people get what they deserve. It would be nice to think that if we are good people and do the "right" things, bad things will not happen to us. However, following this line of reasoning, if a woman is raped, then it can only mean that she is bad or that she has done something wrong that makes her deserve it. Maybe she hitchhiked, was promiscuous, went around braless, or was a prostitute—in other words, she must be a "bad woman" who was asking for trouble, unlike any of us. Many of the myths believed today are based on our need to maintain this assumption. But rapists know that women's reputations or previous sexual behavior have nothing to do with why they picked them as their victim. All women, no matter how "good," are vulnerable to rape and other bad things. It may be difficult for you to accept this, because then you must see yourself as vulnerable. Even if you are relatively careful and do nothing terribly wrong, you too could be hurt.

Some women feel that if they can find what they did wrong to "cause" the rape and never do it again, they will not be vulnerable to being raped in the future. It is, however, important to separate the issue of vulnerability from blame. Indeed, there may be something you or someone else did that made you more vulnerable, or an easier target, such as leaving a door unlocked. However, that does not mean that you are to blame for the rape. Only the rapist is to blame for the rape. The fact that he took advantage of your vulnerability does not make you to blame.

> Angela dropped her keys as she reached her apartment door. When she bent down to pick them up, a man grabbed her, forced her into her apartment, then raped her. Ever since, she has been extremely careful about having her keys securely in her hand because, she says, "If I hadn't dropped my keys, he wouldn't have raped me, and I don't want it to happen again."

Finding "the thing" that you did "wrong" and not doing it again may actually provide a false sense of security. While no one is ever entirely safe from being raped, there *are* things we can do to make ourselves less vulnerable. (See chapter 10.) Recognizing and being aware that you always are vulnerable is one of those things.

Myths Keep Women Unequal and Controlled by Men

We are more likely to blame women for being raped when it happens when they are engaged in actions not socially sanctioned for women— activities such as hitchhiking, being out in bars alone, or walking alone at night. These are acceptable activities for men, but the possibility of rape makes them dangerous for women. Fear of rape is an accepted means for men to keep women out of male-dominated areas, such as bars, and in their homes with their children, "where they belong." Women have no defense against this tactic if we accept these rules. Even other women often blame survivors when they are raped while not adhering to these restrictions.

As a result, women continue to be controlled by men, without equal freedom of activity. They live in fear of stepping outside their socially accepted roles and being punished by rape.

Myths Perpetuate the Adam-and-Eve Syndrome

According to the story of Adam and Eve, man was good until the seductive temptress, Eve, came along and he succumbed to her evil powers.

Rape myths perpetuate the idea of the evil woman tempting the innocent man. We blame women for rape if they are not wearing a bra or if they are wearing a short skirt. We accept the myth that, much like Adam, the poor innocent man simply cannot control his sexual desire when confronted by a woman he finds attractive.

Sue was waiting for a bus one hot summer afternoon when a van with two men in it pulled up and offered her a ride. She refused. The men got out and forced her into the van, then raped her. When the case went to trial, the defendant's attorney held up Sue's white shorts to indicate that she had provoked these men. "Why else would she be standing on the corner, wearing white shorts?" the lawyer wondered. The men were found not guilty.

The outcome of this case was based on the premise that the rape was the survivor's fault, that she was guilty and the rapists innocent. We've all heard the myth that men need sex more than women and that if a man is sexually excited but is not allowed to ejaculate, he will get the excruciatingly painful "blue balls."

Men do not need sex any more than women, and it is not true that rape is a "crime of passion." It is a crime of violence. It is a means of controlling women, of degrading, humiliating, and using them. While sex is a part of rape, it is not the primary motivation for rape. The woman who is raped becomes the target of the rapist's anger. It is no wonder that women are afraid of being killed, even when no weapon is used. They are sensing and responding to this anger. Since rape is believed to be a crime of passion, provoked by young, attractive, sexually provocative women, when an older or un-attractive woman reports being raped, some people believe she just wants attention or a free test for sexually transmitted diseases or pregnancy. Often the survivor was just the first available or the most vulnerable woman to the rapist. Vulnerability is not dependent on age, attractiveness, or the type of clothes a woman happens to be wearing. Sue was vulnerable because she was waiting for a bus, not because she was wearing shorts. Sometimes rape is not even dependent on the survivor's sex. If a woman is not available, a man will do.

Rapists are not "oversexed, strong, 'macho' men." They are more likely to be angry men, unable to deal with their anger effectively. They are often ineffectual in other relationships as well. They may be married and have children, or they may be single. They are often divorced. While a small percentage of them could be considered mentally ill or criminally insane, most of them appear to be basically "normal." They may be fat or thin, old or young, hairy or clean shaven, employed or unemployed, rich or poor, and of any race. You cannot pick them out in a crowd. However, no matter how they appear, they are not normal, healthy men or they would not be raping women.

Different Kinds of Rape

You may have been raped, but while the experience was frightening and upsetting, you may not have labeled it rape. This is because there are many kinds of rape and many circumstances in which it occurs. Some of these are clear-cut cases of rape and others are not.

While all states and most individuals recognize that rape is indeed a crime, the definitions vary from state to state and individual to individual, leading to much confusion and ambiguity. In the past, the legal definition of rape was for the most part limited to vaginal penetration by a penis. This meant that men could not prosecute if they were raped, that forced anal and oral sex were not legally rape, and that vaginal penetration by an object or manipulation of the genitals was not legally rape. Fortunately, as a result of the women's movement and the entrance of more women into the legal profession, these limitations have been recognized and addressed. Now everything from manual manipulation of the genitals to penetration by an object is legally considered sexual assault in most states. Men can prosecute after being raped, women raped by their husbands or lovers can press charges, and charges can be brought against an assailant even if he or she is the same sex as the survivor.

Today the terms *criminal sexual conduct, sexual assault,* and *rape* are often used interchangeably. These terms all refer to any type of sexual contact without consent between two or more people, regardless of their sex or marital status. The sexual contact may involve the sex organs of one or both, including any penetration, however slight, of the vagina or anus by a penis, hand, or object.

Stranger Rape

By far the easiest to identify as rape is rape by the absolute stranger who "jumps out of the bushes." This is sometimes referred to as the "blitz rape" because the rapist seems to come from nowhere and, after the rape, is quickly gone. In such a situation other people, such as friends, the police, and medical personnel, are unlikely to blame you, and you are less likely to blame yourself. You were clearly an innocent victim. When most people think of rape, it is the stranger rape that they usually picture and are the most comfortable with as "really being rape." Although as many as 60 percent of rape survivors report being raped by a stranger, this figure is certainly inflated; a higher percentage of stranger rape cases are reported, because they are more clearly rape to everyone involved.

Date Rape

A type of sexual abuse that has emerged more recently as a widespread phenomenon is date rape. At some point during a planned meeting, the male becomes interested in sex and starts attempting to "seduce" his date. When she resists, he becomes verbally and/or physically threatening. The amount of physical force or coercion the date rapist is willing to use to attempt to get sex varies, although with each new victim, the violence escalates. Victims of date rape are often less able to resist because their reflexes are impaired by drug or alcohol intoxication, making them easier targets.

In a 1982 study done at Kent State University, one in four of more than 2,000 female students reported experiencing sexual aggression in the form of threats, physical coercion, or violence. Even more appalling is that they did not label the experience rape. An additional one in eight stated that they had been raped. In the same study, more than 30 percent of the male students admitted to using force of threats and coercion to get sex when the woman they were with was unwilling to consent, and 4 percent more admitted to using physical violence. This 4 percent thought the violence was normal and acceptable. They did not label it rape; nor did they consider themselves rapists.

In a 1988 study from the University of Arizona in Tucson, more than half of the junior high students surveyed reported that there are circumstances in which forced sex is acceptable, such as when a boy spends a lot of money (more than ten dollars) on a girl. Among a younger group of adolescents, a Rhode Island Rape Crisis Center in 1988 found that more than half of those interviewed thought it was okay for the boy to rape the girl if they had been dating for more than six months. Nearly half also agreed that rape was okay if "he had spent a lot of money" on her. Because of these attitudes, often other people as well as the woman herself blame survivors of date rape: The women were with the men willingly and perhaps even allowed the men to pay. But even if you choose to go out with a man, agree to let him buy you dinner, or drinks, agree to go to his apartment or invite him to yours, and even if you have had sex with him in the past, it's still rape if he forces you to have sex with him and you don't want to now. Whether he uses physical force or not, he may try to make you feel as if you led him on—by inviting him home or wearing an attractive dress—and that you therefore "owe" him sex. You "owe" him nothing. It's still rape.

Acquaintance Rape

Acquaintance rape includes all situations in which you have met the assailant prior to the assault or have seen him on several occasions but do not know him well. He may live in your building or be a friend of a friend, or you may ride the same bus to work every day.

Acquaintance rape often involves men whom survivors met by chance at local bars or parties. At the end of the evening the man offers to drive the woman home. She accepts, eager to save the cab fare. Then he either rapes her in his car or in his apartment, or when he gets to her home he insists on coming in for "a minute for a drink" and rapes her there. Regardless of how or where the assault occurs, if you are coerced or physically forced to have sex with someone against your will, it is rape, no matter how "foolish" you may feel for having trusted him. How many times did you, and other women, really just get a ride home when one was offered? You couldn't have known what would happen.

Marital Rape

Until 1975, when reform of rape laws began, most state rape statutes included a spousal exception, making rape by a husband legal. Some states (Oregon and Colorado, for example) even excluded individuals living together in common-law marriages from the rape statutes. As of January 1990, forty-three out of fifty states had changed their laws to provide legal protection for married women who are sexually victimized by their husbands.

The word *rape* comes from the Latin term *raptus*, meaning "carrying off, abduction, or plunder." The term referred to the damaging of one man's property—his wife or daughter—by another man. This belief by men and the legal system that the wife and children are the man's "property," that they belong to him and that he essentially can do as he pleases with them, lingers on even today. This fact is not only apparent in rape laws, but in enforcement of wife-battering and child abuse laws as well.

Ritualistic Abuse

Children, adolescents, and adults are all victims of ritualistic abuse—brutal physical, psychological, and sexual abuse involving rituals, sometimes satanic ones, and sometimes by members of organized cults. Ritualistic abuse rarely is a one-time experience, but instead involves multiple instances over an extended period of time. The purpose is sometimes to induct victims into satanic beliefs and practices and gain dominance over them through the use of pain, humiliation, and torture. The psychological abuse is devastating and often includes mind control and terror with the threat of death for disclosure. Because the ritualistic aspects of the abuse seem so unbelievable to those unfamiliar with the practices, the credibility of survivors who report such abuse is often called into question.

Unfortunately, ritualistic abuse is widespread today. It has perpetuated and grown in silence due to the abusers' dominance over and terror inflicted in the victims. Major networks of "family" cults whose practices include sexual abuse have developed and are difficult to prosecute.

Sexual Harassment

Still another form of sexual abuse occurs to many of us on an almost daily basis. This category of "small rapes" includes the verbal, sexual comments you hear from men you pass while walking down the street and the looks that undress. It also includes the so-called compliments from men you know ("You have a great body," "Nice ass") that make you feel uncomfortable. The unwanted, unappreciated arm around your shoulder or waist is another example.

The most widely publicized and scandalous account, which brought to the public's attention the widespread nature of sexual harassment, was the 1991 navy Tailhook incident in which twenty-six females and several males were groped, fondled, and sexually harassed as they walked through the halls of a Las Vegas, Nevada, hotel where navy aviators were having their annual convention. It wasn't the first time this had happened, it was just the worst. This incident resulted because of the navy's history of looking the other way and allowing "boys to be boys."

It doesn't matter if the things men say or do might be appreciated in another context or situation, or if they had come from another person. The important thing to note and respond to is the way these words and actions make you feel. Even though we are taught to be polite, women must also learn that it's okay and even important to be aware of the double messages men give us and let them know the behavior is unacceptable.

These "small rapes" are more important than they seem. In many cases they are the way potential rapists size you up, see how easily you can be intimidated and controlled, and see how much they can get away with without your saying no. Your response may determine what happens next. (See chapter 10.)

Office Rape

Another form of rape that is seldom reported is office rape. The assailant in this case may be the woman's boss, coworker, client, or any combination of these. Office rape is an especially upsetting situation for most women, because they likely have so much to lose whatever they choose to do. It also carries the most implications of guilt, shame, and self-blame and is the most blatant abuse of power by men in positions of authority. Also, unfortunately, many women who are raped by their bosses are so intimidated that they don't label it rape, or if they do they are too afraid to do anything about it. Because of the often-subtle intimidation used, people may find it difficult to believe that a woman could have been in a situation like this.

Mary was twenty-six at the time of the incident and had been working as a secretary for a small sales company a little less than a year. It had really begun weeks earlier when her boss, an older, conservative-looking man of fifty-seven, told her how attractive she was. At first she liked the extra attention he gave her, and she was especially pleased to have been selected over two other women to be his private secretary. A small salary increase resulted as well. Then he began putting his arm around her shoulder—in a "fatherly" way at first. A few days later when he called her into his office, he put his hand on her knee and up her leg just a little while he talked about routine matters. She felt uncomfortable, confused, and wasn't sure what to do. This was her boss, and she had always trusted him and done what he told her. She was convinced that she must be misinterpreting a simple friendly gesture. This occurred again on a couple of occasions until one day he began rubbing her crotch. When she tried to stop him, he insisted she take her clothes off and have sex with him. He promised it would be "just this once." Mary was frightened and confused. All she could think about was how much she needed the job. He forced her to the floor and had sex with her. She went home and said nothing to anyone.

About a week later, toward the end of the day, her boss called her into his office. As he introduced her to the client he had with him, he put his arm around her shoulder and began to tell the client what a good secretary she was, how she always tried to please him and do her job well. As he talked he began to unbutton her blouse. When she resisted, he said he wouldn't want to have to tell anyone about the time she had "willingly" had sex with him the week before. He said he wanted to share her with his friend "just this once." He undressed her and forced her to have oral and vaginal sex with both of them. Before she left that day he reminded her how good she was and reminded her that she had been willing to participate and had not resisted. "You probably enjoyed it too," he added.

When she got home that night she was so distraught that she finally told her husband what had happened. She had always been told that being "good" meant obeying people in positions of authority and doing as she was told. She had done this. She had submitted under coercion the first time, hoping it would end his behavior. He had promised her it would. Now she was certain it would happen again. She had no idea what to do. Quitting her job was not even an option, as far as she was concerned, because her husband had been laid off recently. They were both dependent on her paycheck to pay the rent.

Mary's husband called the local rape crisis center, even though he and Mary were not certain this was rape. No force had been used, and she had not fought to get away; she had only resisted verbally, and her boss had coerced her verbally. She could have screamed or run out of his office, but she had not. Surprisingly, her husband was not blaming her. He knew she had not wanted to have sex with her boss and the client. He was supportive, although confused and fearful himself.

Both occasions were clearly rape. Many rape laws specifically state that consent shall not be construed to include coerced submission.

Physical force or violence need not occur. Coerced submission is rape, not consenting sex.

Few women will report office rape right away. Often they wait until long after the incident or until they have been raped several times and can no longer deal with the emotional trauma. Guilt and self-blame keep them from thinking of it as rape because they have been verbally coerced, not physically forced to have sex.

In some ways it may feel like an extension of the "favors" you are asked to perform, such as being "asked" to make and get coffee for the boss, or buy cards and gifts for his wife, and the numerous other favors that really are not part of the job. Perhaps the boss also sees sex as an extra bonus of being the boss and having a female secretary around to take care of him and meet all of his needs.

Some women quit without telling anyone what happened. They feel they were to blame and carry the guilt and shame for years. Few prosecute. More must do so if such intolerable abuse of women by men in positions of power is ever to be stopped. These cases most typically come to the attention of professionals after the woman tells someone she is close to, who in turn gets help.

TO THE SIGNIFICANT OTHER

Don't Blame Her

There are times when it is difficult for the family and friends not to blame the survivor. This is especially true when she was raped doing something you told her not to do, or when she was raped doing something you and perhaps others "know" is quite risky. Thus you feel "she should have known better." The more adamantly you tried to keep her from doing something, the more difficult these infractions are to deal with, and the more likely you will be to fall into the I-told-you-so position.

Debbie's boyfriend didn't want her to go out drinking with "the girls." Before she left their apartment he told her, "You can get raped doing that," but she had gone out with her friends a number of times before and had had a great time. She knew her boyfriend didn't really like it, but she went anyway. While walking over to one friend's house, a man forced Debbie into a car and raped her. The first thing Debbie's boyfriend said when he came down to the hospital to take her home was "I told you you'd get raped."

A number of situations appear quite risky and often do result in rape. Some women engage in these activities frequently and do not want to believe that they are as risky as everyone says, because they don't want to give them up. Some of these risky activities are convenient, others are simply fun. Hitchhiking is a good example of an extremely risky activity that women and men continue to engage in because it is convenient.

Terri often hitchhiked to her university, about a mile from her home. She did not like walking or riding her bike when it was cold out and did not want to spend the money for a taxi. One morning she was raped at gunpoint and beat up by a man who had picked her up.

No matter how often you may have warned someone in Terri's situation not to hitchhike, it won't help her now for you to berate her with comments like "How could you have been so foolish?" or "What did you expect?" Terri had hitchhiked twice a day, four days a week, for three years during cold weather and had never been raped before. The risk had seemed minimal. Instead of blaming her, she needs you to be supportive while she recovers from the attack. For instance, you might want to help her figure out a safer way for her to get to classes. She, more than anyone, now knows what a bad decision it was to hitchhike. Terri now says that if she had known beforehand the fear and trauma associated with rape, she never would have taken the chance.

In a 1978 study done at the University of Illinois in Chicago, both male and female college students indicated that they thought women who were raped while hitchhiking were responsible for the assault. These students believed that by accepting a ride from a stranger, they had "provoked" the crime and should have foreseen the possibility of an attack. The students felt that because the victims should have foreseen the consequences of their actions, they were to a significant extent deserving of the outcome.

That women are raped by men they meet in bars, amusement parks, or parties does not mean that they should be prisoners in their own homes or that they are responsible for an assault that occurs. It does not mean that they deserve to be raped when they do frequent such places.

Don't Blame Yourself

One of the most important things for you to remember is that whatever you did or did not do, you are not to blame for someone else's rape. It is not her fault, and it is not your fault. The rapist is the one who committed the crime. However, families and friends of survivors often spend time blaming themselves or the survivor instead of concentrating on the positive things they can do to help her cope with the effects of the rape.

There are essentially three types of situations in which families and friends of survivors tend to blame themselves. These include situations in which something they did or did not do directly contributed to the assault, situations in which their actions were tangentially related to the assault, and situations in which they had no involvement.

The first type of situation, in which the assault was directly related to the actions of a family member or friend, is often the most guilt producing.

Cindy and her husband had spent the past five years without incident living in areas that were considered high-crime areas. Then they moved to the quiet suburbs, where they felt quite safe. One day, at about one o'clock in the afternoon, while Cindy was ironing clothes before going to work, a man walked into their home through an unlocked door and raped and robbed her. When her husband had left earlier that day, he had not thought it necessary to lock the door behind him.

On her way to her friend's house, Barbara gave her mother a ride to the bank. Her mother did not lock the car door when she got out. At a stoplight down the road, a man got in the unlocked car door, abducted Barbara, then raped her at knifepoint.

Martha was in her bedroom just starting to get dressed for work, when a man appeared at her bedroom door. He had a gun. He wanted to know if she had a car. She told him, "It's in the garage and the keys are on the kitchen table. Take it." Instead of leaving, he threw Martha her robe, which was on the bed, and said, "You're coming with me." He drove to the other side of town, then raped her brutally before letting her go. When she asked why he had picked her out, he told her that he and a friend had robbed a small store in the neighborhood. In an attempt to evade the police, they had separated, and his friend had left with the car. He was planning to escape on foot until he saw her front door wide open. She later learned that her eight-year-old son had let the dog out and had left the door open.

In these three situations, the husband, mother, and son all expressed considerable guilt and blamed themselves for the rape. While it is true that each played a role in making their loved one more vulnerable to the assault, they did not know, nor could they have known, that a rapist would be out there on that particular day and that he would rape their wife, daughter, or mother. We cannot live our lives in fear of a rapist being outside our door.

In situations where the actions of family and friends are less directly related to the assault, the self-blame is often less apparent and may be overlooked. The following is an example.

Judy's boyfriend borrowed her car one evening while she was at work. She often took the bus and did so that evening. When she got home at one o'clock in the morning, her boyfriend called to tell her he'd had a minor accident with the car. She was somewhat concerned and decided that, rather than wait until morning, she would walk the short distance to his house to see him and her car. On the way, she was attacked and raped by two men.

Judy was confused by her boyfriend's feelings of guilt and responsibility for what happened. Granted, his actions were one link in the chain of events that led up to the assault, but that does not make him responsible for the rape.

What If She Blames You?

If a survivor becomes angry at you, or blames you for the rape or the circumstances leading to it, it is important for you to understand what she is going through before you react.

> Luann was sleeping in her upper-middle-class suburban condominium when a man climbed through her bedroom window. She had left it open for the first time that summer because it was a hot night and the breeze was refreshing. Her two roommates were asleep in their bedrooms. She awoke with the man on top of her with a gun to her head. He told her to cover her face and not look at him. She was afraid to scream. He raped her, then left. When she woke her roommates, they called the police.
>
> In the emergency department Luann let everyone she came into contact with know how angry she was that she had been raped. The rape counselor tried to comfort her by commenting on how lucky she was to have such supportive roommates who were concerned enough to have come to the hospital with her. She shouted angrily, "They only came down here because they were afraid to stay in the condo alone. They don't really want to help."

Luann had generalized her anger to include everyone she was in contact with, regardless of their real concern for her. Very often rape survivors do generalize their anger, which really should be directed at the rapist. Like Luann, they feel angry at everyone or, more often, at all men. If the rapist was of a racial group different from their own, they will be angry at all men and possibly all women of that racial group as well. If he was young, they will be angry at all young men. This may include young male physicians, nurses, or friends. The more similar a man is to the rapist in race, age, appearance, or mannerisms, the more likely he will incur the survivor's rage.

Betty was grabbed by a man in her garage as she was coming home from work. He made her bend over and hold onto a dirty shelf while he raped her from behind. When he was finished, he carefully wiped between her legs and said, "You're a nice lady." The next day, after Betty had made a police report, a sympathetic officer told her, "I'm really sorry this happened to you. You're such a nice lady." Betty became livid. She immediately flashed back to the rape and to her anger at the rapist's audacity in trying to be nice to her after committing such a degrading crime. She was also furious at the insinuation that if she hadn't been "a nice lady" she would have deserved to be raped.

Fortunately, the police officer had worked with many survivors during their initial crisis phase and understood Betty's outraged response to him as generalized anger toward men. The officer kept calm as she blew up at him. When the rapist had been present, Betty was too afraid to show any anger. The officer was a safe target for her to express some of her anger and fear.

You too may become a "safe target" of a survivor's generalized anger and fear. It is extremely important for you to understand this and not take what she is saying personally. Becoming defensive and angry will only aggravate the situation. Responding as the officer did works best. Just sit quietly until she is finished, then tell her you understand that she is angry she was raped, that you are angry at the rapist too, but that you are not the rapist. You are on her side.

As time passes, the generalization of anger should diminish. Typically, a woman such as Luann would move from her anger at everyone for anything, to anger at all men, to anger at all men who resemble the rapist, to more appropriately focused anger at the rapist. Sometimes women need help in this process of resolution of their unrealistic, generalized anger. At times we all have trouble focusing our anger at the appropriate target. We do, however, need to focus this anger, so we can deal more effectively with our feelings and their results. (See chapter 2.)

Why Blame Yourself or the Survivor?

There are four common reasons you may blame yourself or the survivor for the rape: a desire to maintain your belief in a just world; to avoid self-blame; a desire to maintain future control; or your socially expected role as protector. Rape also touches off personal issues in many of us. It is important for you too to understand why you may blame yourself or the survivor, so you can choose not to.

To Continue Believing the World Is Just

You have even more at stake in maintaining the belief that people get what they deserve than the survivor does. She was already raped and may have faced her vulnerability. You still need to find a way to protect your sense of invulnerability. To do this, you need to find ways in which you are different from the survivor, so you can feel safe and invulnerable to rape. There are two ways for you to do this and maintain your belief that this is a just world. The first is to find something wrong with the survivor's behavior, something she did that you believe you would never even consider doing. If you, like the college students in the hitchhiking survey, really believe that the survivor deserved to be raped because she should have foreseen the likelihood of rape, then you are safe. *You* would never even *consider* hitchhiking, you tell yourself. This allows you to distance yourself from the survivor and the events that led to her rape.

Another way to maintain your belief in a just world is to find something wrong with the survivor's character. If you cannot find something she did wrong that led to her being raped, then maybe you can find something wrong with her personality—something that, of course, is not true about you. Maybe she is too naive, or not too smart. Even worse, perhaps she has done something terribly wrong in the past that makes her a "bad" person who "deserves" to be raped. However, no one—not even women who have done things they or others regret—deserves to be raped.

To Avoid Self-Blame

You may blame the survivor to avoid feeling guilty yourself. If it was her fault, then it cannot be your fault. If she is responsible, then you cannot be responsible for the assault. It is true that you are not responsible, but neither is she. The rapist is the only one to blame. You too must keep your anger focused on him. Since he is not available, you also may tend to take your anger out on yourself, other people, or even the survivor. But doing so is not fair to them or helpful to yourself.

To Maintain Future Control

Another reason why you may attempt to find "the thing" the survivor did wrong or "the thing" you did that "caused" the rape is that finding it may make you feel as if you can once again be in control. If you do not do that particular thing again, you may feel that you can prevent a rape in the future. Barbara's mother now always locks the car door when she gets out and leaves her daughter waiting in the car. She keeps the doors locked when she is in the car alone as well, so that she will be safe, and she has her daughter do the same. As was mentioned in the section of this chapter addressed to the survivor, while these actions may indeed lower our vulnerability and the vulnerability of others, it is important to keep them in perspective. The fact that we *did not* do them in the past does not make us to blame for the rape. The fact that we *do* them in the future will not keep us entirely safe from rape. Believing that they will can only result in a false sense of security and possibly even a higher vulnerability.

Because You're Supposed to Protect Her

You may blame yourself because you think it was your duty to protect her, especially if you are the survivor's parent, husband, boyfriend, or brother. While parents do indeed have a responsibility to try to protect their children, there are limits to this responsibility and to their ability to provide total protection. It is unrealistic for you or other people to expect that you can, or should, always be there to protect your daughter, wife, girlfriend, or sister. It is unrealistic to expect husbands, brothers, or boyfriends to be parentlike to women or to be available all the time to be strong and able to stop bad things from happening. Your trying to do so may even be harmful for you and for the survivor. It would limit both of your freedom. If she is an adult, she must be allowed to be responsible for her own life.

Your response to the survivor and the things that you do now can make a difference to both of you. You must respond to her in a positive way that helps her not only alleviate her anxiety temporarily but also take back control over her life, feelings, and actions in the future. To better understand what she is going through, ask yourself with each situation that arises or each problem that must be resolved: How would you feel if you were in her position?

2

Your Next Move Can Make a Difference

Experience is not what happens to a [woman]. It is what [she] does with what happens to [her].

—ALDOUS HUXLEY

TO THE SURVIVOR

It was dark and cold and I was alone again—finally. I wasn't sure where I was. I had tried to see where he was taking me, until he grabbed my hair and forced my head down onto the front seat. I was freezing. He had driven away with my coat still in his car, and my shirt was ripped. A car pulled up. I was terrified that it was him again. But it was another man, and he was offering me a ride. I called out, "No, no, leave me alone," and I started walking faster. He shrugged his shoulders and drove off. I knew I'd never be able to get into a car with a strange man again.

While Ann is still confused and disoriented, a normal response after such a serious life crisis, her primary need and concern at this point is finding out where she is and getting to a safe place with people she can trust. Then she will need to make some important decisions about getting medical attention and contacting her local rape crisis center.

You may or may not have already considered and made decisions about these matters yourself. You may or may not be satisfied with the results. This chapter should answer any remaining questions as well as help you understand what your own experience was all about. It will be especially helpful if you have not taken the initial steps yet.

Dealing with the Police

One of the most important decisions you may still be struggling with is whether to report the crime to the police. While the number of reports is rising, unfortunately only about one out of every four women who have been raped decides to make a police report.

Why You Should Report

FOR YOUR SAFETY. The police can get you to a safe place and will know the resources available in your community to help you, and they will know the best place to take you for treatment and for an evidentiary exam, a physical exam to collect evidence of the crime. They also will provide safe transportation.

While some survivors do get to the hospital on their own or on rare occasions are dropped off by the rapist, most are brought by the police. They play a key role in getting you to where there are people specially trained to provide the emotional and medical care you need. In most communities this is the emergency department of a major medical center. The police will know which hospitals have established a protocol and have identified dedicated staff who will make treating you a priority so you do not have to wait. They will know which facilities recognize that the emotional trauma of rape is every bit as urgent as the physical trauma of an accident.

On more than one occasion the Minneapolis police have spent many additional hours with a survivor seeing that she was home safe and a locksmith was available to change her locks before they left her alone. If the rapist has your keys and knows your address, you must have your locks changed immediately. Even if he doesn't use your keys himself, he may sell them to others who might.

FOR THE SAFETY OF OTHER WOMEN. Even if a substantial amount of time has passed and little evidence is available that could lead to an arrest and conviction in your case, reporting may provide useful information to aid the police in finding a man who has raped other women. All rapists are really serial rapists. If a man raped you, likely he has raped other women in the past and will continue to rape others in the future until he is arrested. If he is finally arrested for another rape, you may be asked to testify in that case to help corroborate the other survivor's story. Your testimony could make the crucial difference in the court's finding the man who raped you guilty of another rape.

The county attorney had decided not to take Arlene's case to court. It was her word against the two men who raped her, until Hazel decided to call and report her rape to the police. Arlene had met the men at a neighborhood bar and had had a few drinks with them. They offered her a ride home. She accepted and was raped by both of them in their car. It turned out that Hazel had been raped by the same two men, in much the same manner, after meeting them at the same bar one week earlier. They pled guilty.

FOR YOUR OWN MENTAL HEALTH. While right after the rape you may feel afraid and intimidated by the rapist, later you are going to be angry that he did this to you. That's when you are going to want the police to do something. If you didn't make an early report, there will be little they can do and little chance he will go to jail. If you don't report now you also will have to deal with the role you played in letting him stay free, something he does not deserve. Reporting is an important step in reaffirming to yourself that the rape was not your fault and you are not to blame. We at the Sexual Assault Resource Service (SARS) have found over and over again that women who report are more likely to be believed by other people and less likely to be blamed for the rape. Unfortunately, when you choose not to report, uninformed people always assume it's because there was something else you're not telling that really made it your fault, or that it really never happened, "Because if you were really raped you would report it to the police. Rape is a crime."

IT'S YOUR RIGHT AND RESPONSIBILITY. Reporting the crime of rape is both a right and a responsibility. Today there are many treatment programs for survivors of rape. (See the representative selection of rape crisis centers in major U.S. cities on pages 259–73.) These centers did not exist before the early 1970s, when women began to demand that something be done about rape. Federal and local governments began allocating money to develop treatment programs only after large numbers of women who had been raped were brave enough to come forward and be identified as survivors whose lives had been altered dramatically as a result of the anger of the men who attacked them.

While we have indeed made progress during the past twenty years, we are still a long way from having a just or objective legal system. As women, we must continue to play a role in defining rape by reporting rape. If we don't report coercive sex, rape by an acquaintance, date rape, or marital rape, we are accepting rape. We are allowing others to decide what is and is not rape, what is and is not okay. We are sitting back and choosing to remain victims instead of standing up and being heard and taking the risk necessary to effect change.

It is true that today only a small percentage of all rapists go to prison, about 10 percent of those reported to the police. However, only if a rape is reported can the rapist be caught and prosecuted. If you choose not to report the crime committed against you, you will be ensuring that the man who raped you will suffer no consequences for his crime and reinforcing the impression that rape is less common than it in fact is. Deceptively low statistics on rape give us all a false sense of security. Unless more women report what has been done to them, little will be done to improve the legal system so that more rapists go to prison. And the person who raped you will be free to rape again.

YOU MAY BE ELIGIBLE FOR COMPENSATION. In many areas, legislation allows the county or state to pay the cost of the evidentiary exam if you report the rape to the police. Payment is contingent on reporting because the exam provides the state with important evidence necessary to prosecute the case. In some places, you must report the crime within a specified period of time, ranging from thirty-six hours to one week. The exam must be done quickly because most of the medical evidence is present only for about thirty-six hours after the assault. If more time has passed, the exam may be worthless. In most areas, the complete exam (which may include testing for and prevention of sexually transmitted diseases, pregnancy testing and prevention, and care of minor injuries) will be paid for as long as you file a police report within a week of the attack. Payment of medical fees is usually contingent only on reporting and doesn't depend on your proceeding with the entire prosecution. That is a separate decision you can make at a later date. Your local rape center can provide you with the most up-to-date information about the policy in your area.

Many areas now also have crime victim compensation programs. These programs provide a variety of types of compensation, depending on their resources and philosophies. They range from compensation for medical costs resulting from violent crimes, such as rape, to compensation for material loss or theft, to compensation for the cost of counseling for the psychological turmoil that often results when you have been victimized. Once again, your local rape center or your county attorney's office is a good resource for further information about such programs in your area.

Why You May Not Have Reported

THE RAPIST THREATENED YOU. You may have decided not to report because the rapist threatened you with retaliation if you told anyone. In more than 75 percent of all rapes, threats are the rapists' parting words: "If you tell anyone I'll come back and kill you"; "If you report this to the police I'll come back and rape you again"; "If you tell, the next time it will be your daughter." In some cases, the wife or mother of the rapist, one of his friends, or the rapist himself will go to the survivor's home or call her repeatedly and threaten her so she won't press charges. However, it is important to know that rapists rarely carry out these threats or retaliate physically against survivors who report to the police.

Women who are threatened by a rapist but report the crime anyway may be even safer against retaliation because the police know. There have been reports of a rapist returning several times and raping the same woman—someone he did not otherwise know. However, when the woman finally decided to report to the police despite his threats, the rapist did not return. If he sees police cars outside your home, he will know that the police have a description of him and, even more important, that you are not as easily intimidated and controlled as he had counted on. Even if the assailant is not apprehended right away, he knows the police have a record of the assault and a description of him. He will be caught more easily if he tries to do further harm to you or your family.

The Sexual Assault Resource Service in Minneapolis sees more than five hundred rape survivors each year. While over 75 percent of them are threatened if they report, all but a few decide to report anyway. While SARS has been seeing victims for seventeen years, only on two occasions has an assailant returned to try to rape again. On one of these occasions the victim fought so hard, a neighbor heard the noise, called the police, and an otherwise unidentified rapist went to jail. SARS has no other reports of rapists carrying out their threats.

No matter how frightening the rapist's words were, his presence was even worse. In deciding whether to call the police or not, you have the choice of doing what is best for the rapist or what is best for you. Most likely your silence will hurt you, benefit him, and allow him to rape other women. You are probably not the first woman he has raped.

YOU FEARED BLAME OR INSENSITIVITY FROM THE POLICE. In addition to a fear of retaliation by the rapist, you may have decided not to call the police because you are afraid of being blamed for the rape or of the police being insensitive to your fears and concerns.

Maybe you have even had a bad experience with the police in the past. Just as there are still hospitals that don't know how to care for rape victims, there are some police who are insensitive to the issue of rape. Police officers, mostly men, are simply a cross section of the general population, many of whom still believe myths about rape. However, once you have made your initial report, the officers who will do the investigation have had special training in dealing with sexual assault investigation and in dealing with sexual assault survivors.

If you don't report the crime, you may avoid unpleasant reactions to what happened to you; however, this denies you your rights under the law. It precludes any possibility of catching the rapist, and it may place more women in danger.

A police officer's accusatory or insensitive comments say more about him than they do about you and your situation. This is his problem, not yours. The report of your case will list his name and badge number. If you must deal with an insensitive officer, one option that might be helpful to him and other survivors he may encounter is to write him a letter (with a copy to his chief of police) describing how the things he said and did felt to you and affected you.

Fortunately, training programs are changing the attitudes of police toward survivors. While more training is certainly essential, today you are much less likely to encounter insensitive police than you may have been even five years ago. More police today will be supportive, understanding, and knowledgeable about where you need to go for help.

YOU JUST WANT TO FORGET ABOUT IT. Some survivors try to go on with life as if the rape never happened, but at some point every survivor needs to deal to some degree with the emotional impact of the rape. You may not be ready to do that now. That's okay, and it's up to you to decide when you are ready.

Telling the police does mean that you must describe the whole event verbally in detail, which will be hard to do. However, research repeatedly has shown and survivors have found that talking about the rape is the best way to take back control by desensitizing yourself to the horrors. While it was bad, perhaps the worst thing you have ever been through, it's not so bad that another person can't hear the details, and it doesn't make you an "untouchable" or "unclean" person whom no one will accept or respect. Some women report feeling much better after telling someone all the details and still being accepted by that person as a worthwhile human being. The fact that you have been raped need not become part of your personal identity forever.

YOU DON'T WANT OTHER PEOPLE TO FIND OUT. You may not have reported to the police because you were afraid the police cars in front of your house or a possible newspaper article would identify you. After the March 1991 Palm Beach rape case in which the defendant was William Kennedy Smith and the New York City Central Park gang rape of a jogger who wanted her identity kept from the public, a number of survivors did indeed come forward and the issue of anonymity for rape survivors was raised. For much of 1991, once again, newspaper reporters were saying we "should" be able to use the survivor's name. There "should" not be a stigma attached to rape. The survivor "should" be willing to go public with the rape without fear of shame, blame, or reprisal. *Glamour* magazine surveyed its readers and found that, if they knew their name would likely be reported in the newspaper, 63 percent would not be inclined to report the rape. Seventy-two percent felt that victims whose names were published in the media might be further victimized. A *Newsweek* poll found that 86 percent of those questioned believed reporting the victims' name would discourage reporting. In 1990 the *Des Moines Register* published a story about a rape, with the survivor's consent, and won a Pulitzer Prize for excellence in journalism. This article brought an important subject to the attention of the public. The motive behind the victim allowing her identity to be published is good; rape should not result in shame for the victim. Robbery victims are not ashamed to have been victimized. We shouldn't need a shroud of secrecy. But the fact is that we do.

Unfortunately, many people in the general public still *do* blame the victim of rape. As a result, there is still shame and blame associated with being the victim of a sexual assault. It is also and should remain the survivor's decision whom she tells and when she tells them. In 1991 and 1992 there was indeed compelling debate on both sides of the issue, and for a while survivors were more hesitant to report for fear of their name being made public without their consent.

Fortunately, reason has won out and the media has recognized that in this less-than-perfect world, since rape survivors may still be blamed, they, and only they, must be allowed to make the decision about whom to tell. No one else has the right to make that decision for them. You have the right to maintain your anonymity, and you may choose to tell no one about the assault. However, the vast majority of survivors say they feel much better if they at least talk about the rape with a friend or relative.

YOU DON'T PLAN TO GO TO COURT ANYWAY. You may have decided not to report because you don't plan to prosecute and go through the whole court process. Just remember, reporting and prosecuting are separate procedures and separate decisions. Deciding to make the initial police report keeps your options open. You still don't have to go through with the prosecution, but you can. A few days after the rape, once the shock and initial fear have passed, survivors often change their minds about wanting to prosecute. If you make the initial police report, the evidence will be collected and saved and you will be able to prosecute later if you choose to do so. If you do *not* report right away, valuable, irretrievable evidence will be lost and the chances of your case being charged and successfully prosecuted will be substantially reduced.

You Can Still Report

No matter how long it has been since your rape, if you want to make a police report you still can. The value of immediate reports is that the police are better able to question people in the vicinity of the assault, and more material evidence can be collected at the hospital and at the crime scene. People may have seen something they remember as being unusual, which may provide the police with important information.

After the rapist had gone, I flagged down a cab and the driver radioed the police. I told the police the rapist had dragged me from a jogging path through the woods down near the lake. One of the policemen immediately went back to the lake with me. He found the piece of masking tape the man used to cover my mouth and a footprint of a tennis shoe in the sand. [The rapist's] fingerprints were on the tape. The other policeman questioned an older couple sitting on a nearby bench. They said they had seen a man park his car, go into the woods, and come back with his shirt off. They remembered what the car looked like, its make, approximate year, and the last three numbers of the license plate. One officer spent more than four hours trying to identify the car, but wasn't able to at the time. Then, eight months later, the same couple saw the car again. They got a complete license number this time and called the police. When the police went to the man's home with a warrant, they found a tennis shoe whose print matched the picture of the one taken in the sand at the crime scene and he was arrested.

The circumstantial evidence—the couple's seeing the rapist come and go—would not have been sufficient for his arrest without the crime scene evidence also available. He never would have been caught and prosecuted without all components of the investigation. Had this woman not reported and the police not examined the area immediately, this rapist would be free today instead of in jail.

While immediate reporting is important, if you report within the first thirty-six hours, sufficient evidence probably still will be available. (See "Getting Medical Attention" later in this chapter.) You need to know, however, that the longer you wait, the lower your chances will be of obtaining a successful prosecution. Every hour and certainly every day you delay, valuable evidence is lost and the chances of an arrest and conviction are lower. The police estimate that physical evidence that could be collected is available in 90 percent of felony crimes, such as rape. Unfortunately, only 3 to 10 percent of it is ever collected.

Not only is evidence lost when reports are delayed, but unfortunately, your credibility as a witness is also more likely to be questioned. As a result of undispelled myths, some police officers and more people who end up serving on juries continue to believe that women who say they were raped days or weeks earlier are lying. While these attitudes are changing as police departments institute training programs for their officers, change is always slow.

It wasn't anything the officer said when we talked. He just seemed anxious to take my statement and get rid of me. He must have asked me three times why I had waited a week before coming to the police. I told him again and again that I was afraid of the guy. I knew him. He even called and threatened me the next day. I finally got angry. I knew the cop didn't believe me, and I knew he did not plan to pick up this guy. I told him how awful it felt to have been raped and then, when I finally got the nerve to stand up for myself by reporting it, to have the cop look down his nose at me and not believe me. He actually apologized and said he did believe me now. It made me feel good for the first time since the rape. I had really stood up for myself. Somehow I felt like I had won.

If you feel that the police don't believe that you were raped, ask them why. It is best to do so before you get angry, because you are likely to be more effective, but it is important to confront them whenever you can and to let them know exactly how you feel.

Regardless of the problems inherent in late reports, many women who were raped months or even years ago reach the point where they want to report their rape to the police. One of the most common reasons women give for this is the need to acknowledge that what they experienced was indeed rape, a crime. Additional reasons are the desire for others to know that rape really happens and to be counted as a survivor. If you decide to make a late report, it is important that you make your reasons clear to the police. Months after the rape a full-scale investigation probably will not be helpful. Let the police know you understand this, but that you want them and whoever reads the local and national statistics on rape to know the extent of the problem.

What the Police Will Want to Know

Should you decide to report, the police will ask you some very basic questions, such as your name, age, address, and place of employment, in addition to questions about the assault. It is very important that you give them complete and accurate information. Misrepresenting any information will make your whole account less credible. Be sure to give your current address and phone number. They will need to contact you later. Unless there is a specific reason for the police to contact your employer as a part of the investigation, they will not do so, so don't be afraid to give them the correct name. If you don't want to be called at work, let them know that. If you are unemployed, don't be afraid to tell them that either. This information is not going to be used against you. If you may be spending time at a friend's or relative's home after the rape, be sure to give them that phone number as well. If they try to contact you at home a couple of times and are unsuccessful, they may consider you an unwilling witness and not pursue the investigation on your case.

The police also will ask you specific information about the assault, such as the date, time, exact location, specific type of sexual contact that occurred, and description of the assailant. If you are unsure about any details, say so. This may prevent them from following incorrect leads instead of good ones. For most women, the most difficult part of the report is telling them the details of the assault. They do need to know exactly what happened, the sequence of events, and what everyone involved did, including the most intimate sexual acts, and what the assailant(s) said to you. Be sure to quote the rapist's statements to the police exactly as you remember them. They are his words, not yours. The more exact the statement, the more likely it will hold up in court, and the more helpful it will be in identifying the assailant.

They also will ask you about your activities before and after the assault. It is very important for you to tell them the whole truth. You should not be afraid to report to the police because of the circumstances leading up to the rape, or because you have a number of outstanding parking tickets, for instance. Except in rare instances, the police will not check your record and arrest you. The police are not there to judge you. Their concern will be the rape and getting the information that will allow them to find, arrest, and prosecute the rapist. Some survivors hesitate to admit such things as their own use of drugs or alcohol or particular unpleasant circumstances surrounding the assault. When these facts are omitted, the story as a whole may not fit together properly. The police may sense something is amiss and not believe your story at all. Rape survivors have won rape convictions in court in cases where they went somewhere with the assailant to purchase stolen property or illegal drugs and were then raped. A prostitute won a case against a man with whom she had agreed to have vaginal sex; he raped her anally. If there are circumstances or information that you're afraid may be incriminating, it's best to know their effect on your case from the very beginning by telling the police yourself, instead of taking the chance that the defense attorney will bring it up in court. If the case goes to trial and a jury uncovers one instance in which you or any other witness intentionally lied about any aspect of your testimony, everything else you say can be disregarded. This is referred to in legal terms as *false in uno, falsus in omnibus*: false in one regard, false in everything.

If you like, you have the right to have a friend, relative, or counselor with you while you answer the police officer's questions. You also have the right to refuse to answer any inappropriate questions, such as "Well, what did you expect to happen?" or "Why were you out alone anyway?" Often just the tone of voice in which a question is asked can change your perception of blame entirely. The officer probably does need to know the circumstances that put you out on the street alone at 2:00 A.M. You need not, however, answer any question that feels accusatory or inappropriate. It's the officer's job to get the facts, not suggest that it's your fault or that you should have known better. If the question feels inappropriate or blaming, tell the officer so and ask the purpose of the question. While uncomfortable, the question may indeed be important to the investigation, but you certainly have a right to know that and to be asked respectfully.

At some point, possibly in a day or two, you will need to go to the police station to make a formal statement. The detective you see probably will not be wearing a uniform; he or she will be in street clothes. These days most investigators understand how difficult it is to tell anyone, especially a strange man, the intimate details of a rape. It's normal for you to feel embarrassed, sad, angry, or even nothing at all during the interview. Don't worry if you cry or have a difficult time. Those trained to help you will understand.

If you haven't heard from the police within a day or two of your initial report, call them. Ask which investigator has been assigned your case and when they might want you to come down to make your statement. Ask the current status of your case. You have a right and responsibility to keep in contact with the police and to be aware of the progress of your case. This is especially important if a suspect is in custody. He can be held for only thirty-six hours without your making a formal statement, which, after being typed, you will be asked to review and sign. (See chapter 8.)

Police reports are a matter of public record, and all information they contain is generally available to the public upon request. In some states, your identity will be withheld automatically; in other areas, you may need to request that the police withhold your identity. The police may grant this request where they determine that revealing the victim's name would likely threaten personal safety or property.

While reporting to the police is one way to help stop rape, only you can make the decision to report. You may have good reasons why you decided not to report or why you have not yet made a report. Whatever you do, it is important to make an informed decision, not one based on fear or a lack of information.

Getting Medical Attention

Another important decision is whether you get medical attention, and if so, what type of attention, and from where.

Why You Need Medical Attention

While many survivors do not get medical attention after being raped and suffer no ill effects, others suffer serious problems that could have been avoided. In order to avoid potential problems, even if you were raped weeks ago, you need to go to a hospital, clinic, or doctor's office for a pregnancy test and to see if you contracted a sexually transmitted disease (STD), such as gonorrhea, chlamydia, or syphilis. If you seek medical attention within seventy-two hours, you can be treated with antibiotics to prevent these diseases. You also need to make contact with other community agencies that can provide you with counseling and psychological support.

If it has been less than thirty-six hours since you were raped, you also need to seek medical care so evidence can be collected to help identify and convict the man who raped you. Since treatment to prevent a STD and pregnancy is usually included as a part of the evidentiary exam, and is then paid for by the county or state, by getting medical attention early you can avoid extra expense as well as the loss of evidence. Contact the rape crisis center nearest you for information on the policy in your area for payment for the evidentiary exam.

Where You Can Go for Help

There are a number of options available for medical care after a sexual assault. Some of these will provide you with more complete services than others. The choice depends on how much time has passed since you were raped, your needs at this time, and the services available in your area. (See listings of sexual assault nurse clinician programs and rape crisis centers at the back of the book.)

SEXUAL ASSAULT NURSE CLINICIAN PROGRAMS. You will obtain the most comprehensive care following a rape at a hospital emergency department that utilizes the services of specially trained sexual assault nurse clinicians/examiners. Your local rape crisis center or the police will know which hospitals in your area have this specialty. These well-trained, sensitive, professional nurses will be able to provide you with a wide range of services. In addition, institutions that work with these nurses usually have ancillary personnel who have been trained to be sensitive to the needs of rape survivors. Because these nurses are available, on call, solely to meet your needs, you will be treated much sooner. You will not take a backseat to medical emergencies in a busy trauma center.

These nurses will be able to provide you with comprehensive medical care to include documentation and care of injuries; STD prevention; pregnancy risk evaluation and, if you are at risk of becoming pregnant, pregnancy prevention; proper collection and documentation of evidence; and crisis intervention. They also will have the most up-to-date information on other community resources that may be of help to you when you leave the hospital, and they will know what payment sources are available. In addition, they work closely with the police and courts and can act as an advocate for you, helping you deal more effectively with what sometimes can be a confusing system.

If you don't want to go to a hospital emergency department, there are a number of other options, such as any private physician's office or neighborhood women's clinic. Planned Parenthood is an excellent resource, and their fees are minimal. If nothing else, you need STD and pregnancy tests. You don't have to give any specific reason for requesting these tests. The important thing is to have the testing done. Women often have an STD without any symptoms. Early diagnosis and treatment are essential to reducing risks and complications. Some of the tests can be done as early as five days after the rape; others won't be valid until as long as twenty-four weeks after the assault. Even if more time has passed, you still should be tested.

While you may expect that a private physician or clinic will be able to collect evidence for you, many are not set up to do so. If you called or went to your doctor and she or he suggested another clinic or hospital, don't feel rejected. The doctor may just want to ensure that you get the best care available. Evidence must be handled in a certain way for it to be admissible in court. This is called the "chain of evidence." Without experience and the proper evidence containers, it is unlikely that the specifications will be met. While your first priority may not be the obtaining of evidence, like many survivors, you may change your mind in a few days or weeks, especially if a suspect is apprehended. If the evidence is collected immediately and properly, you have the option of using it or not. If it is not properly collected and stored, *it can never* be retrieved.

The Evidentiary Exam

While the actual procedure for the collection of evidence may vary from facility to facility, it will include the same basic components. There are three primary purposes and uses of the evidence collected. The first is to show that recent sexual intercourse occurred. The second is to document signs of force or coercion, so as to corroborate that the sexual intercourse was not consensual. The third is for use in identifying the assailant.

EVIDENCE OF RECENT SEXUAL INTERCOURSE. The occurrence of recent sexual intercourse is confirmed by the positive identification and collection of seminal fluid, sperm, and elevated acid phosphatase levels in vaginal secretions. Cotton-tipped swabs are usually used to collect samples in the areas involved in the rape—the vagina, mouth, and/or rectum. The nurse needs to know all the areas involved so she can collect the proper specimens. Matted pubic hair may be cut off and sent to the lab for analysis and to look for sperm, seminal fluid, and blood.

While there is some variance, in most cases the level of acid phosphatase, an enzyme found in high concentrations in seminal fluid, will remain elevated in the vagina for approximately twelve hours after a sexual assault in which ejaculation occurred. Sperm and/or acid phosphatase may be found for up to thirty-six hours after sexual intercourse; however, sperm begins deteriorating within one hour. Sperm is recovered most often in exams completed within five hours of the rape. The effectiveness of these tests is thus limited, and that is why they are not performed when thirty-six hours or more have gone by. It is also important to note that the absence of sperm does not mean sexual intercourse did not occur. A 1986 study of couples engaged in consenting sexual intercourse, where ejaculation was known to have occurred, recovered sperm in only 25 percent of the specimens taken within twenty-four hours. In the same way that sperm is not always identified in exams conducted on couples who have had consenting sex, sperm is often not found when an exam is completed after a sexual assault. Studies completed by SARS in Minneapolis show that only in about two-thirds of the cases do laboratory results establish proof of recent sexual contact. This may be due to swabbing the wrong area and missing the sperm, the rapist's failure to ejaculate, or the rapist being sexually dysfunctional.

EVIDENCE OF FORCE. Any trauma, including bruises, cuts, scratches, and areas of soreness, is carefully noted, and pictures of injuries are taken to be used as evidence of force, if the case goes to court. One picture is worth a thousand words when dealing with a jury. Since bruises often don't appear at their worst for a couple of days, if you have already had the exam, you may want to have additional pictures taken at a follow-up appointment. The nurse examiner also will retain any torn or otherwise soiled clothing, with your permission, to be used as evidence. With the exception of your underpants, which should be retained, it is not necessary nor is it a good idea for all of your clothing to be held as evidence if you want it back. While you may get your clothing back, it is not released until after the court hearing is completed or the police have decided there is no chance of finding your assailant. It may take a year or longer for this to happen.

Just as the absence of sperm and seminal fluid may not indicate the absence of intercourse, the lack of physical trauma does not mean that force or coercion was not used or that sexual relations occurred by consent. My research has indicated that only about 30 percent of rape victims sustain even minor physical injuries during the rape. A very small percentage, however, are hurt so badly that they must be hospitalized. Your emotional state and pertinent comments also should be recorded as evidence that you were forced to have sex against your will. You can ask to see what was written on your hospital record.

Blood samples often are taken for drug and alcohol screens. If you were drugged by the assailant, the test will identify the drug. If the assailant tries to claim that you willingly exchanged sex for drugs and no drugs are found, this will be used to demonstrate that you did not. When there is no physical trauma, blood alcohol levels may be used to show that you were unable to give consent because you were legally intoxicated.

IDENTIFICATION OF THE ASSAILANT. When found, seminal fluid also can be used to help determine the identity of the rapist by identifying his blood type. Approximately 80 percent of all men and women are secretors. This means that all of their body fluids, including the seminal fluid, contain a substance (ABO antigen) that identifies their blood group. While this test can positively eliminate a man, or include one as a possibility, it cannot be used as conclusive evidence that a particular man is the rapist, because many men have the same blood type. While blood group identifiers also are found in saliva, they are ten times as potent in semen. A gauze square moistened with your saliva will be collected to identify your secretor status, for later comparative purposes.

The best evidence available to identify the assailant, and the most recently utilized, is DNA. While all cells include DNA markers, the specimens used to identify the assailant's DNA are blood, seminal fluid, and sperm. DNA identification was first used in sex offense cases in 1987, and many states now have DNA banks. In these states, convicted sex offenders are required to give a blood specimen, which is put into a computerized DNA bank. In the winter of 1993 Minneapolis became the first state to identify an assailant based solely on DNA evidence. While such evidence is still somewhat controversial in the courtroom, it is not the accuracy of the DNA markers that is being questioned, it is the handling of the specimens. Defense attorneys are challenging the chain of evidence in an attempt to keep DNA evidence out of court.

During the exam, any other foreign matter on your body or clothing that may have originated from someone or something other than you, such as leaves, fibers, hairs, etcetera, is collected and sent to the lab for examination. This includes a combing of your pubic hair for loose hairs possibly belonging to the assailant. Only if the assailant's hair is found and a suspect later identified should the nurse examiner also collect pulled head and pubic hair from you for comparative purposes. Pulling hairs is painful and most of the time unnecessary. The resulting evidence is always retrievable from you, if needed, anyway. Blood and sperm stains on your clothing remain identifiable for months and thus may be very helpful in identifying the assailant.

In a Minneapolis case, an assailant was positively identified and convicted because one of his pubic hairs was found on a survivor. The police reported that this additional physical evidence, along with other circumstantial evidence, was decisive in obtaining a conviction. Each piece of evidence alone would not have been sufficient.

Pregnancy Testing and Prevention

If you went to a hospital directly after the rape, you were probably asked to give the nursing staff a urine specimen, which was used to determine if you were pregnant at the time of the rape. It is extremely important that you understand that this test will tell only if you were pregnant *before* the rape. It will *not* show if you got pregnant as a result of the rape. You should have been told the result of this test while you were in the emergency department. If you were not told, or do not remember, you should be able to call for the results. If you did not take Ovral to prevent a pregnancy, it is essential that you be retested to determine if you got pregnant as a result of the rape. If the emergency department staff did not make an appointment with you for the OB-GYN (obstetrics and gynecology) clinic, you should call and make one now. The test will be most accurate if you make it for ten days after the rape.

If you saw a sexual assault nurse clinician, call her office and ask the policy for follow-up. In most facilities, the county or state pays for follow-up visits for pregnancy checks at the same facility as a part of the original evidentiary exam.

Today a wide variety of home pregnancy tests is available in your local drugstore for a minimal cost. They are very accurate, especially when they indicate you are pregnant. They have very few false positives; however, they do sometimes indicate that you are not pregnant when you are indeed pregnant.

Note: A missed period after you have been raped does *not* necessarily mean you are pregnant. Many women miss a period when they are under stress. A missed period should be regarded as serious and investigated to rule out pregnancy or other problems. But it is relatively common for rape victims to miss one or more periods after a rape and not be pregnant. And, though it is unlikely, it also is possible for you to have a light period and still be pregnant. If you are at all concerned, be sure to be tested. There is no reason to worry unnecessarily.

DETERMINING YOUR RISK OF PREGNANCY. Determining if you were at a high risk of becoming pregnant at the time of the assault is especially important. If you were not on contraceptive pills or using another form of birth control, you may be at risk. If your menstrual cycle is fairly regular and you know the usual number of days from the beginning of one cycle to the beginning of another, you can determine your risk of pregnancy with some accuracy. If, however, your cycle is irregular, as is quite common, then determining whether you are at risk of becoming pregnant will be more difficult. You ovulate fourteen days before your period begins. If you are on a twenty-eight-day cycle, you determine your risk period by counting fourteen days from the first day of your last period. Because sperm may remain alive in the body for two to three days, you are also at risk of getting pregnant during the two or three days before and after ovulation, or for a seven-day period.

TWENTY-EIGHT-DAY CYCLE

1 2 3 4 5 6 7 8 9 10 11 12 13 14 15 16 17 18 19 20 21 22 23 24 25 26 27 28
              * * * * * * *

Day one is the date your last period began. Asterisks mark the days you run a high risk of getting pregnant. Ask your nurse or physician to help you determine your risk if you are uncertain of your calculations.

PREVENTION OF PREGNANCY. If the rape occurred during that time in which you are at a high risk of becoming pregnant, or if you are irregular or uncertain about exactly when your last period was, you may be at risk. If so, you may want to consider prevention.

Unfortunately, there are some physicians who feel, often because of their own religious beliefs, that they have a right to withhold this information from women. They may even refuse to discuss the issue with you or to inform you that you are at risk of becoming pregnant. From their own moral vantage point it may be immoral even to consider the prevention, let alone the termination, of an unwanted pregnancy, even one that has resulted from a rape. Only you can make this moral judgment for yourself. No one else has the right to decide for you. Fortunately, most medical personnel realize that they have a moral and ethical obligation to tell a woman if she is at risk for pregnancy. Only by being provided with accurate medical information and options can you make a decision about what is right for you and your body. Neither the doctor nor anyone else has the right to make that decision for you.

While there are options for preventing a pregnancy, they must be implemented early. Your two primary options include the use of high doses of natural estrogen, such as Ovral, and menstrual extraction. Both of these need a physician's prescription. Discuss them with your sexual assault nurse clinician or a physician.

Oral estrogen (Ovral) is a female hormone that is produced by our bodies naturally. Ovral is a brand of estrogen. It also is commonly used in low daily doses as a method of routine birth control. Higher doses of estrogen are now being used to prevent a pregnancy. This method requires that you take two tablets of the regular-strength Ovral immediately, then take two more tablets twelve hours later. The first two tablets must be taken within seventy-two hours of the sexual contact to be effective; the sooner the better. About one-third of women report nausea and vomiting, so Compazine or Tigan is often given at the same time to prevent vomiting. If you vomit within one hour of taking the pills, be sure to call your nurse or doctor immediately to determine if you need to repeat the dose. You should have a normal menstrual period within about ten days of taking the Ovral. If you just recently had a period, the Ovral-induced period may be much lighter and shorter than is normal for you.

If started soon enough and taken as directed, this method is almost always effective in preventing a pregnancy. However, if you do *not* have a normal period within four weeks after taking the last tablets, you should contact your physician and be tested for pregnancy. You may want to do this earlier, about ten days after the rape, just to be sure.

A major advantage of taking oral estrogen is that it will not cause you to miscarry if you may have been pregnant before the rape. No medication, however, is totally without potential risk.

Menstrual extraction is a method by which the contents of the uterus, including the lining that builds up prior to menstruation and any egg that may be present, are removed by a suction device. If a fertilized egg is still in the fallopian tube, the lack of a lining in the uterus will prevent its implantation and development. This procedure is usually done in the outpatient department of a hospital or at a clinic, and takes only minutes. Most women report feeling a sensation of cramping or burning in the lower abdomen during the procedure.

It is important that you be tested for pregnancy as early as possible. If it has been six weeks since your last period began (you are about two weeks overdue), get a pregnancy test. While prevention is always preferable, early termination of a pregnancy, if you so choose, is quite safe and easily accomplished.

What If You Become Pregnant

Some survivors are so afraid that they have become pregnant that they don't hear when they are told pregnancy is unlikely. With these women the fear and anxiety may reach phobic proportions.

When the rape counselor went to visit Loretta, all she could talk about was her fear that she was pregnant. She had taken Ovral in the emergency department and had had a period since the assault two weeks earlier, so it was highly improbable that she could be pregnant. She was from a strict religious background and sex outside of marriage was prohibited. While she had been a virgin prior to the rape, she was feeling considerable guilt because she had previously felt sexually attracted to men. She felt the rape was punishment for this unacceptable lust, and becoming pregnant would be the ultimate punishment. Her fear was so strong that she told the counselor she continually had visions of going to work pregnant. If that happened, she would be forced to tell people about the rape. Everyone would then know she was no longer a virgin, and the punishment would be complete.

While Loretta was certainly dealing with many difficult sexual issues, the possibility of her being pregnant—however unlikely—had become the focus of her concern.

As studies reported by the National Center for the Prevention and Control of Rape indicate, women rarely become pregnant as a result of rape, but it does happen. Those who do become pregnant have an especially difficult time recovering from the rape, whether they choose to terminate the pregnancy or not.

At the age of twelve, Nora became pregnant as the result of a gang rape. When she was thirteen, she was charged with child neglect and her eight-month-old baby was placed in a foster home. Nora had not wanted to have the baby, but her mother did not believe in abortion.

Upon confirmation of a pregnancy, one option the survivor has is abortion. An abortion should be performed before the twelfth week of the pregnancy, when the medical risk is minimal. While abortions can be performed even after sixteen weeks, the process then involves inducing labor at a point when the fetus will not be able to sustain life outside the womb. Between twelve and sixteen weeks, there is a much greater chance of perforating the uterus and more bleeding is likely.

The type of advice you receive regarding abortion depends on the philosophy of the medical staff at the hospital or clinic you choose. If they are not open with you about their biases, ask them how they feel about recommending abortion and then decide, based on your needs and desires, if you want to get care at that facility or elsewhere. Most areas have clinics that will do an abortion free of charge, or for a very low cost, if the pregnancy is the result of a rape.

Some women who become pregnant from rape do have babies they choose to keep. Others have babies they give up for adoption. Elizabeth, now thirty-six, has a twenty-five-year-old son, the child of a rape. While she loves him, she admits, "I am reminded, even now, every day of the rape. He is my constant reminder. I still have night-mares. I have not been able to put the rape aside."

Since you are the one who will have to carry the baby nine months and then take care of it for the next twenty-plus years, you are the only one who can decide what is really best for you. Abortion is legal in the United States. You must make the moral decision for yourself. Should you need to make a decision of this nature, do find someone with whom you can talk, who can rationally discuss both sides of the issue, and who will allow you to decide for yourself, without pressure. It's an important decision, and it's your decision. Don't let anyone else make it for you.

The Fear of Sexually Transmitted Diseases

After a sexual assault, many women are afraid they may have con-tracted a sexually transmitted disease (STD). This fear, which may be more debilitating than the disease itself, has been magnified with the epidemic spread of AIDS (acquired immunodeficiency syndrome) and before that herpes, for which there is no cure. While more rape sur-vivors do contract a sexually transmitted disease than become preg-nant, the numbers are still small, typically less than fifteen survivors out of one hundred. The numbers are so small because most sexual assault nurse clinician programs, as well as many other emergency departments, have learned to give antibiotics that will prevent an STD from developing to the survivor. While not all STDs can be prevented, the most common ones—gonorrhea, chlamydia, and syphilis—re-spond to this treatment.

You may contract an STD but develop no symptoms at all, or the symptoms may not become apparent for weeks. If you did not choose to take the preventive antibiotics, or if you are still concerned about having contracted an STD, you may want to abstain from sex or have only protected sex for a period of time after the assault. The longest waiting period until you can be tested is twenty-four weeks, and unfortunately it is for the most serious and only life-threatening STD, HIV (human immunodeficiency virus), the virus which results in the disease AIDS.

In addition to gonorrhea, syphilis, chlamydia, and HIV, which are commonly discussed these days, other STDs that a survivor may contract include venereal warts, herpes, and trichomoniasis. Crabs (pubic lice) also may be contracted as a result of the sexual assault. In addition, if the assailant has nonspecific urethritis (NSU) caused by the organism chlamydia, this infection can lead to a very serious, sometimes life-threatening pelvic inflammatory disease (PID). Although chlamydia is now the most widespread sexually transmitted disease, unfortunately, women develop few if any early symptoms other than an unusual discharge, so the disease may easily go undetected until later stages, when severe abdominal pain occurs. Sterility may then result.

Annoying but easily treated yeast infections often also result from the preventive antibiotics you received in the emergency department. These medications destroy the natural flora, or bacteria, in the vagina that prevent yeast from growing rapidly.

While it is always best to consult your clinic or physician if you have any concerns, the following chart will tell you what symptoms to look for.

STD Treatment

If you seek medical help within seventy-two hours of the rape, you can be treated prophylactically for gonorrhea, syphilis, and chlamydia. If it is beyond that time, you will need to look for symptoms. However, you can have an STD without having any symptoms. If you do have any symptoms, see your physician immediately. There are cures for most STDs. For others, such as herpes and HIV, there is treatment but no cure. Even genital warts may reappear after treatment. When vaginal infections are not treated, they can become more serious—in rare cases, even life-threatening. Don't take the chance. You can purchase over-the-counter treatment for yeast infections and trichomoniasis at a minimal cost. A soaplike substance that will kill lice is available in most drugstores. When used as directed before a shower or bath, it is effective in killing crabs.

ACQUIRED IMMUNODEFICIENCY SYNDROME (AIDS). AIDS is spread by a virus, HIV (human immunodeficiency virus). HIV destroys

DISEASE	SYMPTOMS IN WOMEN
Acquired Immuno-deficiency Syndrome (AIDS)	Often no symptoms of AIDS present for years. Will seroconvert and test positive on HIV blood screen in twelve to twenty-four weeks. Fever lasting at least one month; unexplained weight loss; chronic diarrhea; night sweats; swollen glands in neck, armpit, or pelvic area; white patches in mouth (caused by a fungal infection).
Chlamydia	Unusual vaginal discharge, if any symptoms present at all. May lead to pelvic inflammatory disease (PID). PID is a serious infection of the reproductive tract that may result in sterility, and even death in the most severe cases, if untreated.
Crabs (pubic lice)	Symptoms present in four to five weeks. Small bugs about the size of a freckle. Lay eggs that also may be seen. Itching in pubic area. Crusty rash may develop.
Gonorrhea	Symptoms may not be present. If present, symptoms may include vaginal odor or discharge, vaginal or rectal itching or soreness, mucus in stools, sore throat, or swollen glands.
Herpes	Symptoms may not appear immediately. Painful blister usually present at the site of contact, whether in vaginal, rectal, or oral area.

Syphilis   Symptoms may not be present. If present, symptoms may include crusted or open sores (chancres); rash on palms, soles of feet, or general body rash; loss of hair; flulike symptoms; internal organ involvement.

Trichomoniasis   Symptoms present in one to four weeks. Smelly green, yellow, or white discharge. Itching in the vagina. Burning during urination.

Venereal Warts   Symptoms are usually not present until one to three months or more after contact. Appear as bumps or growths in the genital areas, may be pinkish red, soft, and look like a cauliflower. May be itchy.

Yeast Infection   Onset varies. Vaginal discharge that looks like cottage cheese. Itching and redness of vaginal area. Painful intercourse.

cells in the blood that help fight infection and prevent disease. When this virus weakens the immune system in this way, people become ill with otherwise rare diseases, often cancers. When these other serious infections or cancers develop, or when the immune cells drop below a very low level, the person is diagnosed as having AIDS.

HIV exposure is an ever-growing concern of sexual assault survivors today. While 1993 data indicate transmission from men to women accounts for only 6 percent of adult HIV infections in the United States, it now accounts for 75 percent of the adult infections worldwide. In response to this growing concern, many sexual assault nurse clinician programs now suggest that rape survivors be tested for HIV. Exposure requires that infected blood or other bodily fluid, such as seminal fluid, enter the body of an uninfected person. HIV is more likely to enter the body when there is a break in the skin. This may be caused by tearing or by a lesion caused by other STDs. HIV initially was passed so readily by the gay population engaging in anal sex because in most anal sexual contacts, the fragile lining of the rectum tears. This allows the virus, which seminal fluid carries in high concentrations, to enter the bloodstream of the person having receptive anal sex. If you were raped rectally, you are at a higher risk of being exposed to the AIDS virus, HIV, and you should be tested. If you live in a part of the country that has high rates of HIV infection in the general population, such as New York, Florida, or California, testing is even more important.

The test for HIV is a blood test that identifies antibodies that your body produces to fight the virus; it does not actually identify the virus. At first experts were uncertain how long someone could have the virus before a blood test would be positive. We now know that in 75 percent of the cases, a person will seroconvert, or develop antibodies in the bloodstream that can be detected by testing, twelve weeks (three months) after exposure. By six months after exposure, if a person has not turned positive, she can be more than 98 percent sure that she is HIV free. Everyone has heard that the virus can lie dormant for up to ten years before a person knows he or she has AIDS. This is true. The person may not develop any symptoms or identifying medical diseases, but if the person had a blood test, he or she *would* test positive for the AIDS virus, HIV.

In a three-year study of rape survivors completed in 1990 in Minneapolis, a relatively low-risk area, no HIV-positive conversions were found in 412 rape survivors tested. As a result, routine testing is not now done in Minneapolis. Instead, the counselor and survivor discuss the problem, the woman's risk is evaluated based on the type of rape and on whatever she might know about her assailant. If he may be an IV drug user, or bisexual, he is at higher risk of being HIV positive. If he did not ejaculate inside her, her risk is minimal. The disease spreads only through direct contact with the blood or semen of an HIV-infected person. Based on this information, the survivor and her sexual partner can use safe sex practices and make educated decisions about HIV testing in three to six months. In 1988 the Center for AIDS Prevention estimated that the risk of contracting HIV from a one-time sexual contact, without using a condom, with a partner of unknown HIV status, was *1 in 5 million*. If the person is known to be positive for the AIDS virus, the risk for a one-time sexual encounter, without using a condom, is 1 in 500.

GONORRHEA. Gonorrhea is not limited to the vaginal area. If rectal or oral sex was a part of the rape, you may have contracted rectal or oral gonorrhea as well. If you were examined within seventy-two hours of the rape, you should have been offered antibiotics to prevent you from getting gonorrhea. If you are uncertain, ask your sexual assault nurse clinician. If you chose not to take the preventive antibiotics, you will need to return to a clinic for testing in five to seven days, however. To test for gonorrhea later, a culture of the involved areas is taken. To do this, a drop of fluid collected with a cotton-tip applicator is put on a culture plate and grown in a warm environment for two days. It is then examined under a microscope to determine if the gonorrhea organism is present. It is important to identify and treat gonorrhea, as untreated gonorrhea can spread to your ovaries and fallopian tubes and cause a serious and painful infection. Scarring from the infection can result in sterility or tubal pregnancy.

In the past, hospital emergency departments used to test for gonorrhea as a part of the evidentiary exam. Some still do. The rationale was that if you were negative in the emergency room, which shows that you did not have gonorrhea prior to the rape, then positive five to seven days later, the assailant could be tested. His being positive for gonorrhea would provide additional evidence that you got the disease from him and that he must therefore be the person who raped you. There were, unfortunately, a number of fallacies with this rationale.

First, unless he consents of his free will, a suspect cannot be tested without a court order. Since men are more likely to have symptoms of gonorrhea, commonly called "the drip," he is likely to have been tested and treated by the time he is apprehended. In many major cities, individuals can be tested and treated for STDs anonymously. In Minneapolis, two otherwise very good cases were jeopardized and one was lost because the rapist had been treated after the rape. One case was won only after a determined police investigator finally located a small, obscure clinic where the rapist had been treated.

Another problem is that some sexual assault survivors do test positive for STDs in the emergency department. When consent is the issue, a smart defense attorney will use that evidence against the survivor to show that she is sexually active, possibly even to show that she is promiscuous and the type of person who would have consenting sex with the accused. There also have been a few cases where the gonorrhea contracted from the assailant is identified in the specimen taken in the emergency department. The nurse just happened to swab the right or the wrong area. Thus, while it first appeared that the rape victim had gonorrhea before the rape, we later decided that the specimen collected in the emergency room actually identified gonorrhea contracted from the assailant. (In fact, one victim was a *nun*, and we believed she was celibate.)

Since initial, "baseline" STD specimens have not been the help that prosecutors once thought they might be, but in fact have been used against victims in some otherwise good cases, it is best *not* to have these initial tests collected.

HERPES. Herpes is more formally referred to as Herpes Simplex Type 1 when it affects the oral area and Type 2 when it affects the genital area. While the symptoms are similar, most experts believe there are two different organisms involved. Type 1 is believed to affect the genitalia also, but Type 2 does not appear to affect the oral area. There is still no cure for this virus, which may remain dormant, without symptoms, for months at a time. Symptoms may reoccur periodically, especially at times of stress, though some people never have a second outbreak. The most serious problems result when a pregnant woman has an active case near the time of delivery. If sores are present during delivery, herpes may be life-threatening to the fetus. A Caesarian birth will be necessary in these cases to prevent exposure of the newborn. Medication that provides symptomatic relief is available from your physician.

SYPHILIS. Like gonorrhea, syphilis can be contracted through vaginal, oral, or anal sexual contact. A blood specimen is taken to determine if you have syphilis. Much like gonorrhea, baseline syphilis testing was done in the past to compare with later results. This too was not useful and was used against the survivor. As a result it, too, is seldom done today. The best course is to take antibiotics immediately to prevent syphilis. If you did not take them in the emergency department, you should go in for testing to be certain you did not contract this very serious disease from the rapist. You can have syphilis and have no symptoms. You also can have it and not have a positive blood test for up to ninety days. It is therefore extremely important that you be checked at the end of three months. If left untreated, syphilis eventually can lead to serious heart disease, blindness, insanity, and death. Syphilis can be treated easily and effectively with antibiotics, and likely the cost will be covered by the state or county if you made an initial police report.

Care of Injuries

If you were physically injured and have not yet seen a physician, you should do so, unless of course your injuries were minimal and they are healing well. Philosophies vary somewhat as to the best method of assessing your physical injuries. Most sexual assault nurse clinician/ examiner programs will ask you specifically about the assault: the areas involved—vaginal, anal, oral—and the type and place of additional trauma. The role of professionals in these programs is *not* to provide routine medical care and examination, it is specifically to do an evidentiary exam and provide comprehensive care after an assault. They will not do routine PAP smears, for instance, just because they "happen" to be doing a pelvic exam. Based on the assault history you provide, an exam limited to the involved areas of trauma is preferred. You will need to tell the nurse examiner what happened in some detail. It is important to tell all of the sexual acts that occurred so that you get proper treatment. It is normal for you to feel uncomfortable, embarrassed, even frightened or scared. Retelling the story may seem like reliving the events. Don't feel bad if you start to cry or get angry. Remember, you are dealing with a professional who understands.

If necessary, X rays may be taken to determine if you have any broken bones. If there was sufficient trauma to the head, you may have to spend a longer time at the hospital, where you can be observed to ensure there is no bleeding within the brain. In cases of severe trauma, hospital admission may be necessary.

During the days after the attack, you may feel general muscle soreness. If you struggled, you may have overtaxed muscles you seldom used. Bruises can become more painful a couple of days after the assault.

If you were choked or strangled, you may develop little red spots around your eyes in the next day or so. These are broken blood vessels and will heal much like a bruise.

Your Safety and Security

Safety probably will be much more important to you now than ever before. You may want to make changes in your environment so that it is more difficult for a rapist or burglar to get into your home. But more important, you'll need to rebuild your internal, personal sense of security so you can feel comfortable once again walking down the street without the fear that someone will come out of nowhere and rape you. Many women find that taking a self-defense course actually helps rebuild their internal sense of security by making them feel less vulnerable and better able to defend themselves against the unexpected.

During the first few days or weeks after the attack, you probably will find that you need to rely more on external signs of safety, such as changing or increasing the locks you use on your door, while you rebuild your internal sense of security. This is quite normal. Making yourself feel physically safe actually may facilitate the restructuring of your sense of personal security, your personal equilibrium, but expect that to take longer.

Your safety concerns now will vary depending on the circumstances of the assault. If you were raped at home, you may not want to stay there for a while. Whatever the circumstances of the rape, related places and situations may be very frightening to you at first and may make you feel quite anxious and worried about your safety. You need to feel safe so that you can relax. You probably will not want to be alone for the first few days or more. Many women find it helpful, and in some cases necessary, to take time off from work or school. Many actually go stay with friends or relatives, away from the environment in which the assault occurred. You may need to go to a place where you'll have few responsibilities and little pressure, where you can feel safe around people you know and trust, someplace where all of your energy can be directed toward dealing with the trauma and in regaining a sense of personal security and control.

If you decide you do not want to leave your home for a while, or if you are unable to do so, you can take other measures to increase your sense of safety. Doing so will be especially important if the assault occurred in your home or in your neighborhood. This is a good time to evaluate realistically the security of your home. Most police departments are willing to help you do this. If you do not have deadbolt locks on your doors—all of them—make the investment. You can purchase them at a local hardware store and install them yourself. Doing so is not difficult, and there are a number of good products on the market. If you don't feel capable, perhaps a friend or handyman could do it for you. Locksmiths do good work, but they are expensive. There are also a number of security systems available, which, if you install them yourself, also provide excellent security at a reasonable cost. Whether you are home or away, a simple measure that probably increases your actual security more than any other single measure besides locking your door is closing and locking your windows at night. No matter how hot it is at night or how poor your air conditioner may be, a window or door screen is no protection from a rapist or burglar. Screens are easily, quietly, and all too frequently cut, allowing entrance to your home while you sleep. In the fifteen plus years that I have been working with rape survivors, however, I have not yet heard of one case in which a rapist gained entrance to a home by breaking a window.

Women who have had a rapist get in their front door often feel better at first by propping a two-by-four board or chair up against the door at a forty-five-degree angle while they are inside. Others feel safer with the window shades down, so no one can see inside, and all the lights on, so there are no dark corners. Certain lights are available that turn on automatically if any noise or movement occurs

near them. You can install these easily outside your doors. Try anything that may lessen your anxiety and tension and allow you to feel
safer and more relaxed. Don't worry that having a board against your
door seems "strange" or "paranoid," for instance. You don't need to
tell your friends. They might not understand, but they weren't just
raped. They don't know the terror. Although nothing guarantees complete invulnerability, practical home-security measures can make you
less vulnerable.

Rape Crisis Centers

If you did not go to the hospital or call the police directly after the
assault, another option is to call your local rape crisis center. After a
rape, often safety is such an important concern that women call the
police first. Many other women who do not want to report to the
police or go to the hospital—those who try to deal with the assault
alone—may finally call a rape crisis center when they realize that they
do need to talk with someone who understands. Some women have
made these calls as late as twenty years after a rape. It is never too
late. No matter how long ago you were raped, if you have not yet
resolved your concerns, it is not too late to talk about them. A list of
rape crisis centers throughout the country is included on pages 259–
73. They are either hospital or community based. While this is certainly not an exhaustive list, it is representative of centers throughout
the U.S. and includes centers in most major cities.

Hospital-based Programs

While rape survivors may call hospital-based programs directly, the
usual method of contact is through hospital emergency departments.
Many years before rape crisis centers began, staffs of hospital emergency departments dealt with and tried to meet the needs of survivors
of rape. In some hospitals psychiatric nurses became involved; in
others, social workers, chaplains, or trained volunteer groups took
over. All worked toward meeting the emotional needs of survivors
while in the hospital and for various lengths of time after the assault,

depending on philosophy and resources available. In many medical centers these efforts resulted in the establishment of sexual assault nurse clinician programs at the hospital.

The Sexual Assault Resource Service (SARS) in Minneapolis is an example of one of the first centers to send staff to hospitals to help assault victims. Trained professional sexual assault nurse clinicians with extensive experience are available, on call, twenty-four hours a day, seven days a week, to seven Minneapolis hospitals. Whenever a survivor of rape arrives at one of these hospitals, the special SARS nurse is called. She goes to the hospital to be with the survivor, her family and friends, and to provide for all aspects of her care in the emergency department. Before the nurse arrives, the emergency department staff will treat serious injuries. Services available at centers such as SARS may vary, but they usually include: completion of the evidentiary exam, with documentation of injuries; STD prevention; pregnancy risk evaluation and prevention; crisis intervention and supportive counseling; and sometimes long-term individual or group counseling and family therapy. Services are often available for family and friends of the survivor as well, to help them deal with their own concerns and thus better help her.

Community-based Programs

More rape crisis centers are community based than hospital based. They primarily offer individual and group counseling and advocacy free of charge or on an ability-to-pay basis. These programs are more likely to be staffed primarily by volunteers, many of whom are rape survivors themselves.

Why Call for Help?

In some medical facilities, you will be asked if you want a rape crisis counselor called. In others, a counselor will come automatically. Don't be afraid to ask for help or to talk to the person available. It may be difficult to ask for help when you don't know what the person who will come will be like. Will she really understand? Asking for help may be especially difficult when your self-esteem is at an all-time low.

You may be blaming yourself, feeling dirty, and it may be two in the morning and minus 20 degrees outside. None of this matters to the advocate or counselor waiting to help you. She went through weeks of training so that when a rape survivor needs her, she could be there and she would understand.

This counselor is available to provide you with sensitive understanding and caring support and to act as your advocate throughout the medical and legal process if you report and prosecute. She knows the procedures and the system and can help you anticipate what will happen and explain to you why it does so. She knows the options you will have and the decisions you will need to make, and will provide you with the information necessary to make informed choices while you learn to regain or maintain control of your body and life. She can help you and your family understand what happened so you can decide what to do next.

Your rape crisis counselor will help you with whatever your immediate crisis needs are, no matter how unusual. She also will help you with your very practical needs, such as deciding whom you want to tell and helping you anticipate their response so you can be better prepared to deal with it. She may be able to help you find a safe place to stay if you don't feel safe at your home and will know where you can get your locks changed. If you live in a rental unit and your keys were stolen, in many areas your landlord will be expected to pay the cost of having new locks installed.

During the first few hours or days after the assault, you may still be in a state of shock, dismay, disbelief, and numbness. Few women recognize the full extent of the impact the assault will have on their lives in the weeks to come or in the long term. You may really believe you can go home, forget about it, and it will go away. It won't. Keep the door open for support from the rape crisis center counselor. Take her card and keep her name and phone number, so that even if you don't need help now, you'll know where to find help if you change your mind later. Even if you refuse help initially, you can ask for help later. If not tonight or tomorrow, at some point you are going to need to deal with your feelings.

Crises such as rape are important points of change and adaptation. During the crisis period, typically the first few days and weeks afterward, you learn new ways to adapt and integrate this experience into your life. Some ways of coping are effective. Others are maladaptive, ineffective, and only lead to further, perhaps more serious, problems in the future. A trained counselor, familiar with the pitfalls that lead to further problems, can help you avoid them. She can help you identify more effective coping strategies so that you can move on.

TO THE SIGNIFICANT OTHER

You too may have felt confused, angry, in shock, and disbelieving when you first heard that someone you cared about was raped. The hours and days immediately following the assault are a time when, in addition to dealing with your own and the survivor's emotional responses, you have a number of important medical, legal, and safety concerns. Unfortunately, some decisions must be made right away— they won't wait until the emotional crisis is resolved. While most are decisions the survivor must make, there are some matters you will need to decide too, and there are things you can do to make her decisions easier for her.

Don't Take the Law into Your Own Hands

When Denise told her fiancé she had been raped, he was livid. Not trusting the police or the legal system, he convinced her not to report. "They won't do anything anyway. I'll take care of him myself. I'll give him a good scare." After calling two friends, he got his shotgun and left. A few hours later Denise got a call from the police. Her fiancé was in jail, charged with attempted murder. The rapist was still free. *He* had called the police for protection. Six weeks later her fiancé was still in jail. The rapist was out on bail and was later cleared of the rape charges.

After a rape, often the first reaction of family and friends is to want to get revenge. Husbands, lovers, parents, brothers, and sisters may feel the need to do something to "make up" for not having protected the survivor and prevented the rape, however unrealistic that may be. Your judgment may be less than optimal at this time. Like the survivor, you are reacting to the rage, confusion, and disorientation common after a serious life crisis.

Stephanie's father's response was to fight back.

> Stephanie had been picked up on her way to school by two men in a blue van. They both raped her before letting her go. Just as Stephanie's family returned home from the hospital, a blue van stopped at a stoplight in front of their house. The two men in the front seat were in their early twenties and white, just like the rapists. Before anyone knew what was happening, Stephanie's father jumped on the van and tried to force the door open and drag the driver out. The men inside had no idea what was happening. Why was this "madman" attacking them? When the light changed, they hit him to break his grip and sped off with the door partially open. Stephanie's father fell off the van, fortunately unhurt.

While Stephanie's descriptions of the rapists were vague and general, her father wanted desperately to catch the men who had raped his daughter. Still in a state of shock, he wasn't thinking clearly, and his usual good judgment was not operating. He didn't realize at the time how illogical and out-of-control his behavior was.

While these initial impulses to strike out at someone are really quite common, when they go unchecked they can end up getting you hurt or in jail, as happened with Denise's fiancé. Should that happen, not only are you unavailable to help the survivor through the original crisis of the rape, but now she has another crisis to worry about.

Contacting the Police

The best way to catch the criminal is to encourage the survivor to contact the police as soon as possible. More than one-third of the time a friend, roommate, or family member first suggests that the police be called. Encouraging the call is a rational way to deal with your need to get even, to catch the rapist, and to see that the survivor gets the protection she needs and deserves. However, you should not call the police without her consent. In being raped, she has just been in a situation where she was controlled by someone else. Don't take more control from her. Encourage her to call the police, or call with her permission. In the confusion that results from a rape, it may be difficult for a survivor to remember her own phone number, let alone how to get in touch with the police.

If the survivor doesn't want the police called because she doesn't think she wants to prosecute, you can assure her that reporting and prosecuting are two separate procedures. Many survivors who initially don't think they want to report change their minds later. However, it is important to remember that *if the survivor doesn't report now, it may be too late later*.

Find the clothes she was wearing during the rape, especially her panties and any torn or soiled clothes that have not been washed. Put these in a paper bag, with her name on it, and set them aside to give to the police. When the police arrive, they will take a brief statement from the survivor. If the rape occurred within the previous thirty-six hours, they then may take her to the hospital for an evidentiary exam. You can go too. If the rape occurred where they meet you, the police also may take pictures of the crime scene and gather other evidence, so don't disturb anything. You may be destroying evidence by just "straightening up a little." They also may want a description of the assailant and some details of the assault. It may be hard for her to give this information in front of you and the police. It may be hard for you to hear. This is not something with which you should expect to feel comfortable.

The survivor may be afraid that you will feel different about her if you know the terrible things the rapist did to her. Unfortunately, some people do react this way. Men who consider women as property may see them as "damaged" after a rape. With other men, an even stronger bond can be created by being with the survivor during this initial period, being able to know what happened to her and still accept and respect her. This bonding during a crisis can occur even with strangers or rape crisis counselors, who become significant others for survivors of rape.

Only you know what you can and cannot handle. If you aren't

ready to hear the details, it may be a good time for you to excuse yourself to see that the house is secure or to attend to another task while the survivor answers the police's questions.

If you think you can handle hearing the details, and she wants you to stay, this is an excellent time to sit beside her and to hold her hand. If you want to cry, do so. It's okay for you, just as it's okay and healthy for her to cry. And don't be afraid to express your feelings to her once the police statement is completed. That will give her permission to express her feelings to you as well.

Usually it is necessary for her to go to the police station in the next day or so, to see a police investigator in order to give a complete statement. This can be a frightening and intimidating experience. She still may be afraid to go out of the house alone. You can help her by offering to go with her or seeing that she has transportation with which she feels comfortable. If you can't go with her, and she would like someone else to be there for support, perhaps you can help her decide who might be available. Don't forget to consider a rape crisis counselor. Counselors usually are willing to accompany survivors during the police statement. They know the system and her rights under the law. They can be excellent advocates for her and for you. In some cases the police will decide not to issue an arrest warrant. This can be devastating to the survivor. Both of you may feel helpless and victimized once again. The rape crisis counselor can help you understand why the police made this decision. The most important thing for you to remember is to believe the victim. (See chapter 8.)

What If She Doesn't Report?

It is extremely important for you to realize that just because she may not have reported the rape to the police, and perhaps still does not want to report, it does not mean that she wasn't really raped. The first portion of this chapter, "To the Survivor," reviews some of the reasons why she may be hesitant to report. It may be helpful for the two of you to consider them together so that her decision will be an informed one, whatever it is. You may not want her to report for some of the same reasons. Talk about them with her and let her know your feelings, but remember, the final decision is hers.

Medical Concerns for You and Her

It is important that rape survivors receive medical care as soon as possible. The evidentiary exam described earlier is helpful only if completed during the first thirty-six hours after the assault. Even if it has been longer, she still should get medical attention, however. Medication to prevent pregnancy and sexually transmitted diseases (STDs) can be given up to seventy-two hours after sexual intercourse, though the sooner the better.

Call your doctor or clinic and ask its policy. If she is not treated prophylactically to prevent STDs, she should be tested at a later date to ensure she is disease free. *This testing is important. She may have an active STD and have no symptoms.* If you are sexually involved with her, you also could be at risk. While some sexually transmitted diseases can have very serious consequences, most are curable or controllable with the proper care and medication.

If She Won't Get Treatment, What Can You Do?

If she refuses to be tested for STDs and you are concerned about your own exposure, you can be tested on your own. The symptoms of STDs for women are in the first section of this chapter. They are quite similar for men. (See pages 78–79.)

What If She Becomes Pregnant?

You too may experience the fear that the survivor will become pregnant. If she does, what rights do you have in influencing her decision to keep the baby or not if you are her husband or her parents? The fetus is not really any part of you, yet it will certainly affect your life. What if she insists on maintaining a pregnancy from the rape and you disagree? What are her rights if she is a minor? What are your rights? What can you do?

DISEASE	SYMPTOMS IN MEN
Acquired Immuno-deficiency Syndrome (AIDS)	Symptoms usually do not appear for years. Blood will test HIV positive three to six months after exposure.
Crabs (pubic lice)	Symptoms present in four to five weeks. Small white bugs that move and are about the size of a freckle. Lay eggs that also may be visible. Itching in pubic area. Crusty rash may develop.
Gonorrhea	Burning on urination, puslike discharge from penis ("the drip"); sore throat or swollen neck glands; mucus in stools, rectal itching or soreness, and discharge from the rectum.
Herpes	Symptoms may not appear immediately. Painful blister on the penis head or shaft or in rectal or oral areas.
Nonspecific urethritis (NSU)	Itching or burning on urination, possible discharge from penis.
Syphilis	Chancre (crusted or open sore) where the germ entered the body, usually the penis. Later symptoms include: rash on palms and soles, inflammation of the joints, flulike symptoms, internal organ involvement.
Trichomoniasis	While it may cause itching in the penis, there are usually *no symptoms* in men.

Venereal Warts	Symptoms usually not present until one to three months after contact. Appears as bump or growth in the genital area, most often on the penis. In moist areas may be pinkish red, soft, and look like cauliflower. May be itchy.
Yeast Infection	Usually *no symptoms* in men.

These concerns are of grave consequence. If there is any doubt or disagreement between you on how to resolve the issue, by all means seek professional counseling. Shop around for a counselor who will be open-minded enough to help you objectively consider both sides of the issue rather than persuade you toward any particular decision.

One couple who had been trying unsuccessfully to have a baby actually came to the joint decision that they hoped a pregnancy would result. It did not, but they saw this as one way they could have the child they wanted regardless of how it was conceived.

It is essential that you communicate your fears and concerns to each other. Even with open, honest communication, these are trying, difficult issues. They can be destructive to even a strong relationship. Your relationship may or may not survive this crisis.

How You Can Help

She's the one who must have the physical exam, so only she can make the decision to do so. You can best help her decide by gathering information for her, finding out where she can be tested for STDs or pregnancy. You can find out the policy for payment in your area by calling your local rape crisis center (a listing of centers in major U.S. cities is provided on pages 259–73).

You can reassure her that she's important to you, that her health is important to you, and that she deserves good care. She deserves to take care of herself. She doesn't need to hide and be ashamed of what happened. She was the victim of a crime; she's not the criminal. Part of surviving is taking care of her body now that she has control of it once again. Honesty and openness with each other will do the most to improve your likelihood of pulling through this crisis together.

Rape Crisis Centers and You

Rape is traumatic for all involved. In many ways you too have been victimized. You are a secondary victim, and you may experience the same crisis response. Most rape centers recognize this and provide services for family, friends, or roommates, who also may need help resolving their concerns. Even if she decides to try and "go it alone," you can call and get help for yourself. By doing so you are setting a good example for her, and you may be in a better position to help her to adapt more effectively.

3

Sorting Out Your
Feelings and Response

*My last salutations are to them who knew me
imperfect and loved me.*

—RABINDRANATH TAGORE

TO THE SURVIVOR

For most people, rape is the most serious life crisis they will have to
face, with few exceptions. It is a time of overwhelming turmoil, confusion, and disorganization. You may be concerned about the way
you are feeling in response to the rape. You've probably never felt the
extreme and conflicting emotions you feel now—the fears, the rage,
the panic attacks, or the worthlessness. You even may be afraid that
you are "going crazy" or that you will never recover and be able to
go on with your life again as you knew it. But you will. What you
are experiencing is normal after a very serious life crisis. Dealing with
the pain is the first step in the process of recovery. The worst is over.

There are four general phases of response after rape. The first phase, shock and disbelief, and the second phase, confusion, fear, depression, and anger, are discussed in this chapter, along with typical emotional reactions to each of these phases. While the periods vary considerably depending on individual circumstances, the first phase typically lasts a few days and the second phase lasts six to twelve weeks. The third phase, resolution and coping, is addressed in chapter 4. The final phase, long-term adjustment, is discussed in chapter 6.

There is really no such thing as a "normal" response to rape. "Normal" only means the way most people react, the average response of a large group of people. A wide range of reactions on both sides of the average occur. However, using the term *normal* can be helpful because it gives us an idea of what to expect. There are many reasons for the way you are feeling right now. You should not judge your response as right or wrong, good or bad. Rather it is important for you to understand *why* you feel as you do.

The things we do—how we act at home, at work, or at school— are all based on how we really feel about ourselves, about other people, and about what we have experienced. Unfortunately, many people have not learned to be in touch with their true feelings. How we respond to others is not based solely on what they say to us, but also on our own inner feelings that color how we interpret what they say. When Betty (chapter 1) blew up at the policeman who told her she was a nice lady, she wasn't reacting to what he said, she was reacting to her feelings of rage at the rapist.

Learning to be more introspective will give you more control over your emotions and your response to people and situations. It will allow you to sort out feelings that may have nothing to do with the rape from those directly related to it. Once you are able to separate the two, you can choose to identify but not act on that part of your response that is based on feelings about things that happened in the past. You will then be reacting more appropriately to current events. Had Betty been more aware of her feelings, she might have identified her anger at the policeman's words as anger at the rapist and might not have exploded at the officer. Remember, getting to this point is a process, like any physical healing process, and it will take time. While survivors' reactions do vary, most people have the following feelings to some degree at some point after being raped.

Shock and Disbelief

During the first few hours or days after being assaulted, almost all survivors will struggle with the question "Why me?" Women who cannot face the fact that rape actually happens or who believe the myths that the assaulted woman really wanted to be raped or did something to provoke the attack and therefore deserved it probably will be the least prepared and the hardest hit if they or a loved one is raped. As Joyce, a fragile housewife of fifty-three and a victim, said, "No one could rape me. I would fight to the death."

Women who know intellectually that rape can happen at any time, even to them, also will feel shock and disbelief and may not be as emotionally prepared as they might have expected.

It was about three o'clock in the morning. There was no moon that night and it was very dark in my room. I couldn't get back to sleep and I was alone. I remember gasping for breath, a man choking me—but it could have been a dream. And I remember a familiar voice, like a friend of my brother's. But it couldn't have been. I looked around. No one was there. The room looked the same. I was home in my bed where I had slept every night for over eighteen years. I had had nightmares before, but never like this. In the morning I heard my mother and brother downstairs. I got up, though I hadn't slept at all. I felt tense, afraid. I kept telling myself it couldn't really have happened. Then as I stepped out of my room, I stared at the sight of my reflection in the mirror at the end of the hallway. There were bruises all over my neck. It was true . . . I'd really been raped.

Were it not for the bruises, Jane did not think she would have mentioned the experience to anyone, not even as a horrible nightmare. She would just have tried to forget about it and hoped she could convince herself it had not happened.

The rapist had come and gone within fifteen minutes. Jane could not see him and, having been awakened, was somewhat disoriented. In addition, the assailant did indeed turn out to be a friend of her brother's, someone she knew and trusted. How could she possibly believe he would assault and rape anyone, let alone her?

The extreme response, more likely in situations where reality is too difficult to face, is to blank out the memory of the assault. Although it is rare, some survivors do indeed blank out the time between when they are first approached by the rapist and when they are finally free of him and at a safe place again. This happens when the events surrounding the assault are so terrifying that the survivor cannot even maintain the memory in her consciousness. A similar blanking out occurs with people in combat and in other very traumatic situations.

During the very early stages of recovery, most of these survivors remember or dream about only small portions of the assault—a room that strikes terror, a face that awakens them to tears and being stiff with fright. As the conscious mind develops the strength and resources necessary to deal with the memories of the event, those memories return. Flashbacks or nightmares are a positive sign that your subconscious is dealing with the events that your conscious mind may not yet be ready to handle. Some people never reach this point. The memories remain buried, affecting their lives, behavior, and relationships in ways they do not understand.

Your Body's Response

For some people this initial crisis can be physiologically invigorating, giving them more energy and drive than they had previously had. When faced with danger, your adrenal glands release adrenaline into your bloodstream. This protective mechanism helps you remain alert, ready to fight or run. Your body is preparing you to deal with danger. Part of this fight-or-flight response involves chemical changes that result in your body retaining more fluids. Seven to ten days after the rape, sometimes even sooner, the body's biochemical balance returns to normal. When this happens, you will find that you need to urinate more frequently, as previously stored body fluid is released. You also may feel physically weak, with little energy, as a result of this fluid loss. This is a normal biochemical response to stress.

Sleep disturbances are particularly common. Some women will have difficulty falling asleep, because they fear unknown danger. Others will be awakened by nightmares and will have trouble returning to sleep. To sleep, one requires a trust in the environment that recent victims do not feel. Some people find they can sleep during daylight hours only for the first few weeks.

In addition to conditions resulting from actual injuries, it is likely that physical symptoms of distress also will be present during this phase. The reaction will depend on the individual. Many people are prone to certain physical symptoms during times of stress, such as headaches, perhaps even as severe as migraines; others experience gastric distress, such as nausea and vomiting. Skin rashes are particularly common following a sexual assault.

It is important to remember that these very real physical symptoms have been brought on as a result of the crisis and that they will pass in time. Measures to lessen the discomfort, such as aspirin for headaches and a special cream for a rash, may be helpful. Expensive diagnostic tests to identify a physical cause are probably not necessary unless symptoms persist.

Denial

During this initial stage you are most likely to come into contact with others who will want to do something to help you. This also is a time when you may not yet realize the full extent of the assault's impact. You may still expect to be able to continue life as usual. Some women try to do this. If raped on the way to work or school, they may simply change their clothes and continue to work or classes, saying nothing to anyone, convinced they can handle it. While they may recognize the reality of the assault, they deny that it will affect them.

Denial is a primary defense mechanism of many survivors, even some with extensive psychological training themselves. Some women are able to deny the effect of the assault for a while, to put it aside and continue with other activities, but not many, and usually not for long. Naomi was raped just before an important final exam during her senior year of college. She somehow managed to put the rape aside until after the final, then the full impact of it hit her. Maxine was raped two days before a scheduled biopsy to determine if she had cancer. She too put the rape aside until she had dealt with a more threatening and more pressing situation. In these instances denial was an effective defense that allowed these women time to deal with more immediate stresses. They could not possibly have dealt with the rape at the same time.

When our conscious minds deny strong emotions, they remain buried within us at the cost of a considerable amount of energy. If not dealt with consciously, these emotions still will affect our lives, but we may not connect the things we are feeling with the rape. Without making the connection, you cannot resolve the problem. Janette tried to deny how her rape had affected her—unsuccessfully.

> I was raped by a student at the school where I worked just before my last vacation to see my family. I was looking forward to the trip and decided nothing was going to spoil it. I drove home, telling no one. I guess I was in a state of shock. During the vacation I decided I couldn't return, but then I never really liked my job as a school social worker, so I blamed the decision on my dislike of my job. I was still denying any effect of the rape. I quit my job and moved home. A month after returning home I realized I had lost interest in everything. I was bored all the time. I blamed that on the move. I had a lot of job interviews but no job offers, even though I was well qualified. Finally a friend who is a psychologist told me I looked terribly depressed and asked what had happened. It wasn't until then that I realized what was going on. I told her about the rape. It was such a relief.

Since we cannot effectively bury just the bad feelings, we usually bury all our feelings, good and bad, happy and sad, and we become emotionless and empty. You may try to hide your feelings after the rape because you may not be ready for help at first, because you have not yet accepted what has happened, let alone what may result and how it will affect your life. Most rape counselors know this. You probably will feel the need for help later as you move through the next three phases of response.

Confusion, Fear, Depression, and Anger

While the initial phase of shock and disbelief probably will last a day or two, some women essentially pass through it during the assault, and immediately afterward they experience the resulting confusion and disorganization. Many survivors bounce back and forth between the two responses, one moment saying "I don't believe this, it couldn't really have happened to me" and the next moment, having accepted the reality, experiencing turmoil.

Some of the problems you must deal with during this time are specific fears, such as the fear of death, the fear of seeing the rapist again, and the fear of situations that bring to mind the rape, as well as depression, anxiety, thoughts of suicide, anger, guilt, and loss of self-esteem.

Redefining Danger

After being sexually assaulted, most women view at least some situations as dangerous that they felt were safe prior to the assault. Some women who are raped change their perceptions of danger in radical ways. Even women who are attacked but avoid being raped make substantial reassessments of danger. Pauline Bart, in a 1983 study published in the *Journal of Social Issues*, found that, for both women who were raped and women who were attacked but not raped, the fears that follow are to a great extent dependent on the sort of situation in which the attack occurred. Bart found that women were less likely to change their perceptions of danger if the attack occurred in a situation that they had previously identified as dangerous. If the attack took place somewhere they felt safe, such as their own home or a crowded street or public bus, a much more extreme reaction was likely to result.

The reason for this more extreme reaction is that if you can't easily identify a specific place or situation as dangerous or not dangerous, then you can't avoid putting yourself at risk in the future. As a result, you feel frightened anywhere and everywhere. If, however, you were raped somewhere you knew there was some degree of danger, then you can continue to trust your judgment. In an effort to protect yourself, you can avoid such places in the future, or at least not go there alone.

If you were raped by someone you trusted, this too will affect your future perception of danger. The rape may teach you that you can't distinguish rapists from men you can trust and distinguish playful, friendly behavior from a serious threat leading to a sexual attack. Your outlook on the world, when you rebuild it, will be very different. To a woman who was raped by someone she trusted, at a location she believed was safe, the world can seem to be a very dangerous place indeed.

The Fear of Death

The most widespread fear that rape survivors experience is the fear of death. Research I conducted in Minneapolis indicated that well over half of all survivors did not expect to live through the rape. Women may experience this feeling whether weapons were used or not and whether the rapist was six feet five inches tall and 210 pounds or five feet six inches tall and 120 pounds. Rape is a crime of violence and aggression, not a crime of passion. For rapists, sex is a weapon used to humiliate, control, and degrade women. We have all heard stories of women who are raped and then murdered. It is this anger and aggression survivors are sensing and responding to when they fear for their life.

This realization that you were suddenly and unexpectedly vulnerable to death—perhaps in a location where you felt the safest, such as your own bed—may have a significant impact on how you view mundane daily events thereafter. The dirty dishes in the sink or the unfinished report for work may seem much less pressing. New priorities may surface, and more basic needs and desires may be realized.

While right after this life-threatening situation you may respond with fear and panic, you also may respond with genuine elation. You may be so happy to have survived—something you didn't believe would happen—that you are just glad to be alive. Nothing else may seem to matter as much as your survival. Don't be upset if other people are confused by this response. They probably don't understand why you are happy. They don't understand how near death you felt. You may want to explain to them what it is that you are feeling. Clarifying your feelings may be important for them, even though it may seem obvious to you that you are not happy about the rape and that you are not blocking out the trauma, but rather that you are happy to be alive.

Fear of Seeing the Rapist Again

Fear is a universal response to rape. All survivors report being afraid at some point. The things you fear, however, may be very different from what other women fear. More than half of rape survivors express the fear of accidentally seeing the rapist again. He appeared from nowhere once, so he could well do so again, and if he does, what will you do this time? Some survivors have actually seen the rapist again, when least expected, but the second time they were better prepared and it was more of a surprise to him than to her.

I walked into a neighborhood restaurant for a late dinner. It was busy, so my girlfriend and I were asked to wait in the bar. As I turned to walk into the bar, I froze, unable to move. It was him, there was no doubt in my mind. The man who had raped me was sitting at the bar. He looked so relaxed. I felt so tense. I was afraid he had seen me. I didn't know what to do— yell, run? I turned around after what seemed like an eternity and went to the lobby phone. I called the police. When they arrived he was still there drinking. They arrested him. I felt an intense sense of pleasure as the officers put handcuffs on him and everybody watched them take him from the room. He didn't look so relaxed anymore.

Fear of Similar Sounds, Smells, Places

You are most likely to fear those situations that remind you of the rape or the rapist. You have learned to associate any number of places, sounds, or smells with danger. You may react with fear when you smell the same aftershave the rapist wore. If you were raped in a parking lot, you may be afraid to walk to your car alone day or night. If you were raped by a man of another race, you may develop a phobic fear of men of that race. Or your fears may be more general. You may be afraid to go out of the house alone or not feel safe even when at home. As mentioned earlier, these fears result from feelings of vulnerability because you have lost your inner sense of security. This sense of vulnerability is especially common if you were raped in a place you thought was safe and the rapist seemed to appear from nowhere. You are now more fearful because you know such events are not impossible.

It's normal to feel fearful for a few days or weeks. This may be a good time to stay with family or friends. Do whatever you need to feel safer. These feelings will pass eventually, but you may decide you need to seek the help of an experienced rape counselor to resolve them.

Depression

During the first few days after the shock has passed, you may experience the most severe and the greatest number of symptoms of depression. Research on sexual assault survivors over the years has consistently indicated that about one-third to one-half of the women who are raped will experience moderate to severe depression, while only 10 percent of women in the general population will do so. More survivors experience at least some major symptoms of depression. You may feel discouraged about the future, as if you have nothing to look forward to. You may feel as if you will never get over your troubles, as if things are hopeless and will never improve.

You may exaggerate your faults and feel as if you have failed as a parent, wife, or even as a person. A common symptom of depression, and one of the ways it perpetuates itself, is that when you are depressed, you don't remember the periods in the day when things were going well and you felt good. You may misinterpret what people say to you as negative when it is not. Your perception of the world is altered in a self-destructive fashion.

The things you once enjoyed may no longer provide you with any sense of satisfaction, leaving you bored most of the time. Feelings of guilt and worthlessness, self-disgust or self-disappointment, may result in the belief that you are being punished, though you are not sure for what. You even may feel as if you deserve to feel bad and want to be punished.

You may cry all the time or not be able to cry even though you want to. Some women fear that if they allow the tears to come, they will never be able to stop crying, so they fight the tears even more. Small incidents may irritate you more easily than they once did, and decisions about even small matters may seem impossible for you to make. This may affect your work and motivation, making it difficult to get started or continue a task once begun. You may be so completely absorbed in thoughts about the assault that you can't think of anything else. You may feel tired all the time, have difficulty sleeping, or wake up earlier than usual, still tired, but find it hard to return to sleep. Nightmares are also common.

Your appetite may be poor or you may have none at all. Some women lose weight; others gain fifty to sixty pounds within the year, having used food to comfort themselves. You may feel as if you look older or less attractive. You may even try to look less attractive to keep others away, making it easier to withdraw socially.

If these symptoms are severe, you may want to see a counselor to help you resolve them. They can be extremely painful, incapacitating, and disruptive, affecting all areas of your life. Just when you really need other people the most, symptoms of depression and the accompanying low self-esteem may result in your pushing away those who want to help. You may feel unworthy of their help and concern or just not have the energy or motivation to interact with them.

With proper help, the milder forms of depression will be resolved within six to twelve weeks. Without help the depression may take much longer to get through. Even six weeks, however, may seem like an eternity and may result in other significant losses, such as damaged relationships, drops in school grades, or even the loss of a job you no longer feel able to perform. The effects may then continue long after the depression lifts.

The amount of depression you are feeling may vary greatly from one day to the next. You may have a number of good days and then for no apparent reason have a very bad day again. If you have too

many bad days, you might want to consider counseling. Having someone to help you sort out your feelings can make a significant difference.

Anxiety

Anxiety, much like depression and often associated with mild depression, is one of the predominant responses to rape, both initially and
during the first few months. To a great extent it is the result of not
directly expressing the negative feelings and fears that result from the
rape. Symptoms can take many forms, from generalized anxiety to
phobic responses (persistent, irrational fears of a specific situation,
activity, or object) and panic attacks that may occur at unpredictable
times or during specific situations. These are normal responses after
a rape, but when the symptoms persist mental health professionals
consider them to be disorders.

Symptoms of anxiety generally include trembling, shakiness,
restlessness, being easily startled, jitteriness, twitching muscles,
and an inability to relax. You also may experience profuse sweating;
a pounding heart; cold, clammy hands and a dry mouth; light-head-
edness and fatigue; diarrhea; hot or cold flashes; nausea; and a rapid
pulse.

If you are experiencing severe anxiety, you may have the foreboding
feeling that something terrible will happen to you or a loved one. This
may result in considerable worry, apprehension, and difficulty concentrating on other matters.

The symptoms may be less intense but constantly present, only
mildly impairing your normal routine, or you may experience anxiety
attacks that significantly impair your activities. Most often panic attacks are brought on by a specific situation or activity that brings
back memories of the rape. During these usually brief attacks you
may feel intense terror, apprehension, doom, inability to move, shakiness, physical weakness, or fear of losing control. This sense of panic
may go unnoticed by those around you.

To some extent, the fear of the possibility of another panic attack
may be more incapacitating than the panic attack itself. Some women
become extremely dependent and afraid to be alone or to engage in

normal activities for fear of a panic attack. This avoidance of activities or situations may slow your recovery by cutting you off from much-needed support from family and friends. It may also make you more dependent on others—also an unhealthy state if allowed to continue.

When this type of anxiety persists, it is important to evaluate the rationality of your response in relation to the actual danger of the situation. If you experience generalized anxiety or panic attacks when walking alone at night down a dark alley, you may indeed be reacting appropriately, even if the feelings persist for years after the assault. Most people can avoid such a situation easily enough. On the other hand, if you experience the same feelings every time you wait for a bus, even in the daylight with others present, your response is excessive and unreasonable. If the anxiety continues you may want to seek professional counseling to help you resolve your fears. You are no longer reacting to a current danger but rather to unresolved fears resulting from the rape.

The Loss of Self-Esteem

A survivor often experiences a significant, immediate loss of self-esteem that may continue for a long time. Many rape survivors report feeling soiled, dirty, used, useless, and worthless and are afraid they will always feel that way. The events that occurred and the memory of them are so degrading that they feel shame and humiliation and fear rejection by others who know the terrible acts they were forced to perform and endure. The concomitant depression, anxiety, and fears make them feel helpless and unable to regain their feelings of self-worth.

As a result of low self-esteem, you may become very critical of yourself. This may be an indirect attempt to have needs met when you do not feel worthwhile enough to ask. It may be an indirect attempt to get support and reassurance from others. However, self-criticism often does not elicit the desired response, and without realizing it, you may perpetuate your own distress.

You may be self-critical in an attempt to ward off what you feel is an imminent attack by others. You may think that if you're critical of yourself, other people are less likely to be critical of you. Self-criticism also may be a way of keeping others from making additional demands on you that you don't feel able to handle.

Self-criticism also can be very hostile. You may say such things as "I never do anything right," criticizing yourself so that others will feel responsible for and guilty about your pain. Other people will quickly tire of reassuring you that you're not such a terrible person when it becomes a futile "Yes, I am," "No, you're not" exchange. Being hostile to those around you may just drive them away in anger. You need to tell them, "I just feel so terrible about everything," and then deal with the pain, which they did not cause but may be able to help you resolve. However, self-criticism can help you change for the better and grow. Take the time to evaluate what you want to achieve and how you might get your needs met in a better, more direct way.

Guilt

Feelings of guilt often accompany the loss of self-esteem. Guilt results when you turn blame inward instead of focusing it on the rapist, where it belongs. Feelings of guilt may result whenever you feel that something you did—such as hitchhiking, talking with the rapist before the rape, being dressed in something that may be very sexy—made the assault your fault. You may have done something that made you more vulnerable, such as being alone with the assailant, but this does not mean that the rape was your fault. You had no way to know that he would take advantage of your vulnerability and rape you. You did nothing wrong, he is responsible for committing a felony.

Survivors who become sexually aroused during the rape commonly feel quite guilty. Your body may respond physiologically to the sexual contact, but it is still rape. Women—and men—can become physically aroused even when they do not want to have sex. It's a normal re-sponse, just like laughing when someone tickles you. It's not always something you can control or prevent. Although infrequent, physical arousal does happen to some rape victims. Nevertheless, it's still rape.

Withdrawing Socially

Some survivors become very dependent on social contact to feel safe, usually relying on one or two trusted people—a husband, boyfriend, brother, mother, or father. Others withdraw from social contact. You may feel more comfortable alone because you feel as if everyone thinks the rape was your fault. Because of the depression and anxiety, your perceptions change. Many survivors say they feel that everyone is looking at them as if they have the word *raped* written on their forehead.

Some of this withdrawal may be beneficial, in the long run. You may choose to spend time alone, or with just a couple of trusted friends, in order to avoid forcing yourself to smile all the time and lie about how you're feeling. You may want to avoid other people so you won't have to answer questions and talk only about the rape.

You may find yourself withdrawing not because of the loss of interest in other people or fear of blame from them, but simply because your fears make it so much more difficult to get out to your usual places of entertainment and socializing. You might literally be afraid to leave your home, especially after dark.

Many survivors want to attract less attention when out with other people. Often they will begin dressing in a nonsexual fashion, in baggy clothing, in an attempt to blend in with the crowd. Women may do this because they continue to believe the myth that they were at fault because of the way they look or dress. They think that by looking less attractive, they can prevent rape from happening again. A lack of caring about one's appearance might also result from, and be a cause of, depression and a loss of self-esteem.

Withdrawing into yourself, away from others, may be a healthy response for a few days. Time alone to evaluate your feelings, contemplate your current situation, and decide where you want to go from here may be very healthy and helpful. Patricia Frazier, a psychologist and researcher at the University of Minnesota, found in a 1993 study that rape victims who were depressed and withdrew socially for one to three months after the rape were actually doing better six months later than those who had not become more withdrawn. However, if too much time has passed without improvement, or you, or others who care about you, feel that self-imposed isolation is becoming a problem, you may want to seek counseling.

Thoughts of Suicide

You may have thoughts of killing yourself, because you feel that you and your family and friends would be better off if you were dead. Actually making a suicide attempt or gesture is not a common response, however, studies show that 3 to 27 percent of rape survivors do so. Suicidal thoughts are common: A long-term study in 1981 found that nearly half of a group of survivors had at some point considered suicide.

In many instances, suicidal thoughts or attempts may be a way of expressing your most intense feelings of despair when other means of communication have been unsuccessful. If you ever consider suicide, you owe it to yourself and to those who care about you to see a qualified counselor. Even though you may not believe that seeing a counselor will help, in many cases it does. As long as you are alive, you have another chance. Don't punish youself or those who love you even more. You survived the rape. You can survive the crisis that it causes too, but you may need professional help.

Most areas in this country have suicide prevention centers you can call twenty-four hours a day. No matter how badly you feel about yourself, no matter how those around you respond, your life is worth the effort of at least one phone call.

Anger

While rape survivors often feel angry a day or two after the rape, anger usually follows a period of overwhelming depression and anxiety. In many cases depression is anger turned inward; like anxiety, it can be immobilizing. When you fear to release it, anger also can be immobilizing. Often survivors who struggle with depression tell me, "I'm afraid to get angry, because I'm afraid I'll lose control and go crazy." I've seen a lot of people get very angry, some so much so they have even punched holes in walls. One victim released her anger by trashing her apartment, which kept her from hurting herself. She was rageful, not crazy, and had she been able to recognize and deal with her anger sooner, it would not have reached that extreme. But, like many women, her family history did not allow her to express anger. Being angry is different from losing control and "going crazy." I have never seen a survivor become crazy because she admitted to and expressed her rage. But because anger can make other people uncomfortable, it is often discouraged. We are taught when young to hide our anger and deny it, when in fact we should be taught how to recognize it and deal with it effectively, in nondestructive ways.

Anger, when properly focused, is a more functional, less self-destructive response than depression. Nearly all survivors express anger, although the forms of expression and the targets of their anger may vary. Often survivors direct their initial feelings of anger toward all men. This is why many hospitals, rape crisis centers, and police investigative forces have found it helpful to have women work with rape survivors directly after the assault. Survivors direct their anger at individuals with characteristics most like the rapist's. The sex difference is the most obvious distinction to make. The next most obvious and often made distinction is race. If you were raped by a man of a different race, you will likely generalize your fear and anger toward all men of that race. The less experience you have with people of that race, the less able you will likely be to distinguish characteristics and the more likely you will generalize. If he was of your own race, you may focus on his age and be angry, for example, at all males who appear to be nineteen or twenty years old.

This type of generalization and the gradual ability to focus your anger more specifically is a natural process. Prejudices develop when we do not recognize what is happening and allow the anger to remain generalized to a larger group. All nineteen-year-old males are not rapists, even though the one who attacked you was to be feared. It is irrational to blame and distrust all members of this group or to be angry at all of them. The more specifically you focus your anger, the more in control you will be, and the less the assault will affect and change your life.

In the most extreme cases, the survivor expresses anger at everyone and everything. Anger also can be directed inappropriately when you focus it on specific people in your environment who then become scapegoats. You may get angry at your husband or father or at God for letting this happen to you. It is easy to blame other people for your problems, but in doing so you give them a lot of control over your life. You may have the notion that if others are responsible, you cannot be. Perhaps they are just safe targets for your anger, especially if they are people you can trust. You may feel that even if you get angry with them, they won't desert you. However, this misdirected anger is not fair to others, no matter how much they love and care about you. Remember, it is the rapist who deserves to be punished, not you, and not anyone else.

Post-Traumatic Stress Disorder

The diagnosis of post-traumatic stress disorder (PTSD) is now frequently made in reference to those crime victims whose distressing symptoms persist for an extended period of time after a traumatic experience. It is a normal reaction seen in normal people who have been through a terrifying situation in which they could not control what was happening. PTSD first gained widespread recognition after 1980. Prior to that time it was used to describe the combination of symptoms often found in war veterans when they returned home and was known as "combat fatigue." The pattern of symptoms referred to as PTSD includes: the continued reliving of the rape in your mind or feeling as if the rape were occurring once again (flashbacks); attempting to avoid situations or activities that trigger memories of the rape; when unable to avoid the triggering situations, the result is intense anxiety and fear, including a rapid heartbeat and rapid breathing. Other symptoms include: nightmares; trouble sleeping; difficulty concentrating; exaggerated startle response; hypervigilance; inability to recall parts of the rape; loss of interest in activities you once enjoyed; loss of interest in being with other people; inability to experience loving, caring feelings; and feeling as if you no longer have anything to look forward to in the future. You do not need to experience all of these feelings to have PTSD. Once these symptoms were more widely discussed, counselors working with rape victims began to identify the same pattern of symptoms in the women with whom they worked. A 1992 study found that, one week after a rape, 94 percent of the survivors evaluated met the criteria for PTSD and at twelve weeks 47 percent continued to do so. Fifty percent of the women seen at the Sexual Assault Resource Service in Minneapolis in 1993 met the criteria for PTSD one year after rape.

In 1992 the National Victim Center released a report entitled "Rape in America: A Report to the Nation," based on a large national survey. According to the report, 31 percent of all rape survivors developed PTSD at some time and 11 percent still had PTSD at the time of the survey. Some of these women had been raped as recently as a few months prior to the survey; others had been raped as many as three years earlier. The report estimated that 3.8 adult American women have suffered from rape-related PTSD and 1.3 million currently are still suffering the symptoms up to two years after a rape.

Recent research has found that a woman is more likely to develop PTSD if she is more severely distressed initially and improves little during the first four weeks after an assault. This finding is consistent with earlier studies conducted in Minneapolis and elsewhere, which consistently showed that early intervention after rape can prevent many long-term problems, such as those associated with symptoms of PTSD. If you think you might be experiencing PTSD, see a counselor. PTSD can be treated and resolved. The sooner you start counseling, the sooner you will feel relief.

Sexual Dysfunction and Promiscuity

Although most survivors report that the sexual aspects of rape are of far less concern than the fear of being killed, rape often has a significant effect on your feelings about sex. Sex is no longer solely something for pleasure. It has become a weapon that was used against you as a means of intimidation, humiliation, and control—all while you feared for your life. Your response is to a great extent dependent on your past sexual experiences and feelings as well as those of your current or future sexual partners. Survivors' responses range widely from a total loss of interest in sex to the desire to have sex indiscriminately with multiple partners.

At first most women express at least some apprehension and discomfort when faced with the likelihood of any physical closeness, even from someone they love and trust. Physical pain from injuries may occur as well, and sex may be out of the question for a few days or weeks. Many survivors experience less interest in sex, diminished sexual arousal, difficulty relaxing with their sexual partner, a loss of pleasure and enjoyment from sex, fewer orgasms, and a general discomfort with sex. Some even experience "flashbacks" of the rape during sex, suddenly seeing the assailant's face or feeling as if the rape were happening again.

"I feel so cold inside," one survivor said. Many women also experience an intense disgust and repulsion to specific sexual acts that they were forced to perform during the rape. This is especially true of sexual acts in which they did not routinely engage prior to the rape.

My research indicates that approximately one-fourth of rape survivors decide to abstain from sex completely for a period of time after the rape. Others, a much smaller group, may abstain from sex with men only and experiment with homosexual relationships. They may indeed find another woman less threatening and more sexually acceptable. This situation seems to be more likely if they are assaulted when young, before experiencing any satisfactory heterosexual relationships or close friendships with men. Trust of men in general may be very low, and anger at the rapist may, as a result, be directed toward all men. Rape survivors who are incest survivors, or who were raped before, are especially likely to distrust all men and have difficulty regaining trust in the future.

An increase in sexual activity is also sometimes the result of a rape.

Kim, a slender fourteen-year-old virgin, was walking home from her suburban school when two men forced her into a car. They took her some distance to their apartment, where they both raped her. She quickly learned that they were pimps and had no intention of letting her go. Throughout the night and the next morning she was raped orally, anally, and vaginally by many men who came and went. The next evening one of the men put her in his car and left Minneapolis for California. She was beaten regularly and raped repeatedly along the way. Once in California, the pimp hid in the bathroom of the hotel room while she performed sexual acts with johns. One became suspicious as she was clearly underage and unwilling, and reported her to the police. She was arrested as a prostitute, then the whole story was revealed. The pimps confessed to abducting her and Kim was returned home.

Once home, things appeared to be going well at first, though Kim found out she had contracted gonorrhea. Concerned about her safety, her parents insisted on driving her to and from school and did not allow her out alone. She became angry and started sneaking out and going to parties with older boys. Her school grades dropped. By now her mother knew she was sexually active and tried to impose further restrictions. Only more rebellion resulted.

When Kim finally ran away from home, she left her mother a note saying "I'm gone for good. Don't look for me, and don't worry. I'm not selling my body." One month later she was picked up working in a massage parlor.

Teenage girls around age sixteen or seventeen who have been virgins before a rape seem the most likely to became very active sexually after a rape. Sometimes they seem curious to see what "real, normal" sex is like. At other times their sexual activity seems more an attempt to deny the importance of sex or of remaining a virgin until they are married, if that had been an expectation before the rape. They may now engage in sex frequently because they need to lower the value of abstinence and the virginity that had been taken from them. If they continue to value virginity as important before marriage, they can only feel bad about themselves. However, one sixteen-year-old survivor who had highly valued her virginity was able to distinguish between rape and consenting sex and still considered herself a virgin. She said, "Virginity isn't something that can be taken by a rapist any more than by a speculum. It must be freely given."

At other times promiscuity may be the result of feelings of worthlessness and a lack of self-esteem, of no longer valuing yourself or your sexuality, or feeling used and useless. A common practice among pimps is to rape young girls repeatedly, often runaways they pick up off the streets, as a prelude to coercing the girls to work for them. Treatment programs for teenage prostitutes and studies of prostitutes estimate the first sexual experience of more than two-thirds of them is rape or incest as minors—sexual relations forced by an adult.

Most victims of sexual assault find that the frequency of their sexual activity usually returns to normal after three to six months, often in an attempt to please and not alienate their sexual partner. It often takes much longer for women to enjoy sex again.

Factors Affecting Your Response

A number of factors may affect your response to the rape. These include specifics about the rape situation, factors from within your external environment, and variables within yourself.

Circumstances Surrounding the Rape

As we discussed earlier, studies conducted in the early 1990s have found that if you were raped in a place where you thought you were safe, such as your home, walking to school in the daytime, or on a bus, you are more likely to suffer more severe symptoms than if you were raped in a place you considered dangerous, such as walking home from the bus late at night. These same studies have found that you are nearly three times as likely to suffer more symptoms for a longer period of time if threats were made and you feared for your life during the rape. Again, weapons need not have been used for you to fear for your life; however, the fear is more likely when weapons were present.

The greater your loss of control during the assault, the more you may fear a general loss of control in the future. This fear is more likely to result if you were physically injured; there were multiple assailants; you were held captive for an extended period of time; and when there were witnesses who did nothing to help. These situations also may result in more depression, anxiety, symptoms of PTSD, future safety concerns, and especially difficulty in later social adjustment resulting from an understandable generalization of fear and anger.

While physical injury is usually associated with a more stressful rape and a more difficult postrape adjustment, injuries in visible locations, such as your face, actually can help reduce the difficulty of the aftermath. Black eyes, neck bruises, and visible cuts and scratches elicit more sympathy and less blame. Even though the rape was more traumatic, the additional social support will, to a great extent, counteract this and help your emotional recovery.

Sexual dysfunction as well as a loss of self-respect are more likely to result when you were raped by a husband or ex-husband, a lover or date—someone you knew and trusted. For some time it may be difficult to be close to and intimate with another man without wondering when the rules will change and rape will result. You may find trusting any man very difficult. Again, counseling can help.

The Effect of Other Stress

Your recovery is affected by the other things happening in your life at the time of the rape. Some are related directly to the rape, some are not. You also may be dealing with chronic, long-term stresses, difficulties that already have been present over a span of months or years, things that don't go away, but continue to drain your energy reserves. These chronic stresses include such things as ongoing unemployment or underemployment in low-paying, uninteresting jobs with little sense of accomplishment. Both result in economic hardship and strain. Other stresses include chronic substance abuse (drugs and alcohol), long-term personal illness or the illness of a family member, as well as continual conflicts and disruption in close relationships (especially marital relationships). A crowded living situation that does not allow adequate privacy, space, or time to be alone to deal uninterrupted with your own concerns is another difficulty. The other extreme, social isolation with a lack of family and friends for support, is also a chronic stress.

We all have only a certain amount of energy available for dealing with stressful events in our lives. Dealing with rape uses up a lot of that energy, so we don't have much left over. As a result, we are likely to become more upset by other smaller problems that at another time would not seem important at all. For example, Jane had a flat tire one month after she was raped. She became upset, tearful, unable to decide what to do or where to turn for help. The friend who was with her didn't understand Jane's reaction and didn't understand that Jane wasn't really reacting to the flat tire. This same overreaction often occurs in relationships with other people. If you can anticipate feeling easily irritated and annoyed, you may be better able to avoid overreacting to minor irritants in your life. Excusing yourself and removing yourself from the situation before it gets out of hand is an effective technique.

The experience of having your case go to court is another stress for you and for your friends and family, who may also be called to testify. This is true no matter how much you want to see your attacker in jail. Even more stress results if the jury finds him not guilty.

How Who You Are Affects Your Response

You, your background, past life experiences, and current sense of who you are and what you want out of life are the most important variables in determining your response to the rape. Your willingness to face and deal with the reality of what happened and to recognize when you need help and to ask for it will be important factors.

Your past experiences with stressful events are also significant. Typically, rape has the most traumatic effect on those who have had little trauma in their lives in the past or have not addressed directly whatever trauma they have experienced. If you were raped in the past, or if you are the victim of incest and you have not yet sought help and resolved the distress, this rape may seem overwhelming and you will likely decide that you now *must* deal with both issues.

Past experience in effectively dealing with difficult situations prepares you to recognize your strengths and to draw on your resources. You feel more able to deal with any bad things that may occur and more generally in control of your life and surroundings. You likely already know on whom you can rely, with whom you can talk when you need to, and where to turn for help. You also may know which of the strategies that other people use to cope do not work for you. You are already on your way toward resolution of the crisis.

If you have not identified your resources in the past, you will need to do so for the first time now. You will need to learn that you can take back control and that you have the resilience to do so.

The Effect of Those in Your Environment

Numerous reports, books, and articles resulting from years of study and research in all types of crises, including rape, show that next to your own resilience, the key factor in your recovery is support from family and friends. Their support and understanding are important in helping you better deal with the emotional trauma and resolve the fear, anxiety, and depression. It's much easier to take risks and face what you see as potentially dangerous, uncomfortable, frightening situations with someone beside you. Although social support cannot make up for feeling that you lack control over your life and surroundings, it certainly can give you the extra confidence necessary to take calculated risks, face your fears, and overcome the immobilizing effects of anxiety and depression.

This is a time of turmoil. You may be afraid that you'll never recover, but you will. With your own determination and the help of others, you can speed this process and even reach new heights of self-fulfillment you did not previously think possible. Be patient with yourself, however, since any change takes time.

TO THE SIGNIFICANT OTHER

Rape is a social crisis. It affects not only the survivor but those people with whom she interacts and their relationships with her. Rape elicits an emotional response from you too. Your feelings will not be based solely on the rape but also on many other factors and biases. These biases may be so ingrained that you are not even aware of them, but you must deal with them in order to be most helpful to the rape survivor. You must sort out your feelings and decide which are a result of this situation—the rape—and which are based on other factors.

This process involves introspection, looking into yourself with a willingness to be honest with yourself and understand.

Understanding Your Initial Response

Much as the survivor may respond with shock and disbelief, you too may need some time to accept the reality of the rape. This is especially true when she looks the same, when there are no visible cuts or bruises, signs that she was violently attacked. If she has calmed down and is not emotionally distraught, acceptance may be more difficult.

Many studies of people's responses to rape survivors have found that there is less disruption in social relationships when the rape was more threatening to the survivor, such as when weapons were used, when there was physical injury, when she struggled and tried to get away, when there was more than one assailant, and when the rape was a sudden attack by a stranger. Less social disruption occurs because in situations of this nature, the survivor is less open to criticism and blame. It is clear to you and others that it was a rape, against her will, that she did nothing to cause it, and that there was nothing she could have done to escape. She was clearly a victim.

When someone you care about is raped, it is as if the crime happened to you also. Once the shock has worn off, you may respond with many of the same feelings she experienced, such as depression, anger, and fear. Many people close to survivors react in much the same way as survivors. Review the material in the earlier part of this chapter on the phase of confusion, fear, depression, and anger. Becoming familiar with the survivor's feelings may help you sort out your own feelings.

How You Can Help

To lessen the severity of the initial impact, you can do a number of things to help the survivor right now.

Believe Her

If you really want to help her, the first thing you must do is believe her—even if no weapons were used, she knew the single assailant, she didn't make a report to the police, and/or there is no physical injury. It's not necessary for you to decide if she was "really raped," or if there is enough evidence to prove she was really raped in a court of law, or "beyond a reasonable doubt." She says she was raped and that's enough. She feels raped and she needs your support.

When Tammy's mother first got the call from the police station, she was frightened. What could have happened? When she got there, the police officer told her, "I don't want to upset you, but there's something very wrong with your daughter. I think she needs psychiatric help. We found her confused and despondent, wandering in the street. She had only one shoe on. She wouldn't talk with us at first and then she told us this incredible story about a man jumping out of the bushes with a Halloween mask on, dragging her into the bushes, and raping her. But it couldn't have really happened, because *that type of thing doesn't happen in Greensburg*. I hope you can find help for her.

Tammy's mother believed the officer, whom she thought would certainly know what does and does not happen in their town. Tammy was still somewhat dazed and confused, and she did have only one shoe on, but her mother knew she had been fine when she left for school that morning. Her mother was confused, but on the policeman's advice, she called the county hospital's crisis center frantic to get help for her daughter. Since there was a sexual assault nurse clinician program at the hospital, they had the mother bring Tammy in for a sexual assault exam. She was hesitant but agreed. Much to the mother's surprise and relief, they found sperm during the exam. Her daughter was not "crazy."

This story may have ended even more tragically if the rapist had been one of the many who are sexually dysfunctional—unable to

ejaculate—thus providing no proof, or had the mother taken Tammy
to a therapist in Greensburg who also believed that type of thing
didn't happen here.

Your acceptance and support of her in these next few days and
weeks is the one thing that will make the most difference in how the
survivor recovers from this very traumatic experience. You are part
of her social support network, and right now she needs acceptance
and reassurance that you still care. You may be a central source of
her support or a tangential source, someone to whom she hasn't
turned for help often in the past. Depending on the response of the
other people around her, your response could be crucial this time,
more significant than you will ever realize.

Reassure Her

This is not a time to question a survivor. ("Why didn't you run away?"
"Why didn't you yell for help?" "Why didn't you kick him?") What
she did or didn't do is not important now. She lived through it, so
whatever she did was right. She needs reassurance that her survival
is all that really matters. She acted on her instinct at the time, and
that is the best anyone can do. Agonizing over the things she could
have done is really a futile exercise and one that likely comes from
your own feelings of helplessness and inability to "undo" it.

She also will need reassurance that to you she is the same worthwhile person she was before the rape. She needs to know that you
still value and care about her.

Accept Her Feelings

She probably is scared and angry not only because of the rape, but
also because of the emotions she is experiencing—the fears, anxiety,
and depression. These extreme feelings may make her afraid that she's
"going crazy." She knows it's not "normal" to be afraid to go out of
the house or to panic whenever she sees a man with a beard (because
the man who raped her had a beard). However, after a rape this fear
is very normal. It's something that many survivors experience, and it
does not mean she's "going crazy" or that she will always feel this way.

If she can tell someone else, perhaps you, about the things she's feeling, and you accept her feelings without thinking she's going crazy, then she'll find them easier to accept herself.

Be There to Listen

Don't be afraid to talk with her about the rape. If it's painful for you to listen, imagine how painful it must have been for her to experience and how upsetting it is for her to talk about. If you pretend that it didn't happen, you will only increase her isolation. She's going to need someone she can trust, someone who will listen without judging her and how she's feeling, someone on whom she can count when new smaller crises occur. She'll especially need someone who can hear how she's feeling, not just what she's saying. She may need help sorting her emotions out. If she's feeling pain but unable to say so, she'll need someone who can listen beyond her words. Statements such as "I can't do anything right" or continual self-blame and criticism about both the rape and current problems may in fact mean "I feel terrible about myself, I feel confused and upset." Instead of responding to what she is saying, respond to the feeling. You might say, "You must be feeling really bad again," or "You're being awfully hard on yourself. It wasn't your fault. You were not to blame." Let her know that it's safe for her to express her feelings, that you understand and can hear them without being repulsed or judgmental or rejecting her. Just being willing to listen to the whole awful story over and over again can be extremely helpful. Don't tell her to "just forget about it." That's impossible.

Let Her Know How You Feel

If you are honest about your feelings, she'll find it easier to be honest as well. If you feel angry at the rapist or upset that she's in so much pain because of what she had to go through, let her know. If it hurts you when she takes her anger at the rapist out on you, let her know that. She may not realize what she's doing. Again, you need to hear beyond her words. Don't respond to the anger that is misdirected at you. Respond to the real source of her anger. You might want to remind her "Hey, I'm on your side. I'm angry that it happened to you too, but it hurts me when you say those things to me."

Provide Support Without Taking Over

Wanting to rescue a rape survivor, to become overprotective, is a normal response. You weren't there to protect her and prevent the rape, but you are there now and you want to be there in the future. You don't want to let anyone hurt her again. Some parents set more strict limits on their daughter's activities after a rape, feeling it's their responsibility to protect her. While the intent is to keep the survivor safe, the result often seems more like punishment to her. In some cases the restrictions are unreasonable and to some extent *are* punishment. If your daughter was raped walking to or from school or while participating in some activity in which she and her peers normally engage, restricting her from these activities or insisting that you take her and pick her up all the time is unreasonable and only limits her freedom and her own control of her life. On the other hand, if she was at a girlfriend's house until four o'clock in the morning and was raped when she walked home alone, then perhaps more limits are in order.

If your daughter was raped in a situation where you or any reasonable adult would have thought she was safe, such as while working at a fast-food restaurant, while out with a family friend, or while visiting one of her friends, then you are more likely to become overprotective and unreasonable in your limits on her activity. You truly don't know where she is safe or with whom anymore. You might even blame yourself and feel you made a "mistake," misjudging the situation and putting her in danger. There is no way that you could have predicted what would happen, and it's unreasonable to believe that you will be able to in the future. Unfortunately, you can't always prevent her from being hurt, as much as you want to. Restricting her activity unreasonably may be meeting your need to know that she is safe more than it actually keeps her safer.

When unreasonable restrictions are imposed after a rape, even though the intentions are good, it is understandable if the survivor becomes angry and upset. In fact, she may even direct much of her anger at the rapist toward the restrictions and the person imposing them. She may react by rebelling against the restrictions and actually placing herself in even greater danger. While it is certainly important to communicate your concern to her, restricting her freedom is unnecessary and is only counterproductive. This is true whether she complies and becomes dependent or rebels in order to maintain her independence. She must be allowed to continue to make her own choices and to live her own life as she sees fit. The best you can do for her is to tell her how you feel, then let her make her own decisions, even though you may want desperately to keep her close to you, where you "know" she is safe.

The desire to rescue and protect the "helpless victim" is a pitfall of many trained counselors as well as family members, friends, and loved ones. We all need to be aware of this very well-meaning desire within us to protect those we see as helpless, weak, and suffering. It feels good to be needed. It feels good to help people who are in need of help.

The survivor may look weak and helpless and want to be protected and taken care of. We all feel that way sometimes in our life, and at such times it is appropriate to provide support, comfort, and understanding. This can be done without taking over, without taking control away from her. She is not really weak and helpless. She can take care of herself. If you take over for her, she may become weak, helpless, and dependent on you. While it may feel good to be needed for a few days or weeks, as the dependence continues and grows, it won't feel so good any more. It will become a burden. You will become her victim and she yours.

It had been a full year since Jeanette had been raped. She was a social worker at a local high school. She was raped by a student one night as she left work a little late. Being a strong woman, she had managed to wrestle with him, and she got the attention of a passerby. Together they held him outside in the school parking lot where he had attacked her, with his pants still down, until the police arrived.

After a year had passed without resolution of her feelings, Jeanette had decided to seek help. She told a counselor, "I think

I might retire this year. It's much earlier than I had planned, but transportation is too difficult now that I've quit driving. I don't know what I'll do in the house all day while my husband is at work, though. I'm okay at the school after he drops me off, because all the other people are around, but I'll never go out of the building for lunch, and I'd never leave the house alone. He'd be angry if I did, anyway. I guess it's hard for him too. He had to miss a meeting tonight to bring me here. I don't know what we're going to do."

Jeanette's husband was sitting outside the door during the interview. He felt he had to be there to protect her. He was a teacher at a nearby school. While they usually rode together, the night she was raped he had left early and she had stayed late for a meeting. He felt guilty, as if it were his fault that she had been raped. She felt deserted. In the first few days after the rape, he "needed" to protect her to overcome his own guilt and self-blame. She liked being protected and taken care of because she was still afraid and felt vulnerable. They reinforced each other's maladaptive coping needs, which then became exaggerated and imbedded. Things had gradually gotten worse until, a year later, she *never* went anywhere without him. Because of his guilty feelings and need to know she was safe, he had encouraged and held up under her complete dependence on him much longer than most people would.

It is normal for a survivor to need support right after a rape. During the first week or two, many survivors experience severe anxiety and fear. A survivor may even have a panic attack when she is out alone. This is normal and to be expected. It does not mean she is "crazy" or helpless. It means that she is still acutely aware of her vulnerability and is reacting accordingly. She has lost her internal sense of safety and security and for the moment is relying on you to be an external source of safety. One woman who had been picked up off the street and raped hid in her house for three days. She was a chain smoker, and finally on the third day emerged with her rape crisis counselor only because she had to get more cigarettes. They went to the store together.

One of the most important things you can do for the survivor is to help her rebuild her internal sense of security. It is unrealistic for you or anyone else to be there with her all the time. Even if you could, like Jeanette's husband thought he could, it is not good for either of you. She must learn to be independent again, and you must learn to let her be. She *can* rely on herself. She *can* regain an inner sense of security that will allow her to function alone in the world and feel in control and safe again. But it will take time.

4

Your Recovery: Taking Back Control

> *If one advances confidently, in the direction of [her]*
> *own dreams, and endeavors to lead the life [she] has*
> *imagined, [she] will meet with a success unexpected in*
> *common hours.*
>
> —HENRY DAVID THOREAU

TO THE SURVIVOR

As horrible and as physically and emotionally traumatic as it is, rape gives the survivor an opportunity to make changes in her life. You may find that you are no longer willing to continue living with situations that you previously had been tolerating. The turmoil of the rape changes your perspective of what is and ought to be important and has probably disturbed old patterns of behavior. This firsthand knowledge of your vulnerability can serve as an impetus for change. You may have faced the possibility of your own death. Your values are not likely to remain unexamined or unaltered.

By now you may have accepted that the rape happened. The crime cannot be undone. You have experienced the pain and emotional turmoil. Now is the time to begin putting your life back in order, an order not limited by the past or by what other people expect, but instead one that fits your newly recognized goals and aspirations. You need to draw upon your resources to resolve your negative feelings and prevent long-term social and psychological maladjustments. You now have the opportunity to emerge from chaos and turmoil better able to handle other crises you may face.

You do not have to remain helpless and immobilized by your fear, anger, and grief. When you are ready, you can take back control over your life. You'll need to evaluate your resources, choose the coping strategies with which you feel the most comfortable, and begin the process of resolution. You may want the help of a rape crisis counselor or a professional therapist, or you may want to go it alone. The process may be a smooth, relatively easy one, or it may be a very difficult one that takes you years to complete. The amount of progress you make and the speed with which you do so will depend on your situation and the resources available to facilitate your problem solving. Be sure that the coping strategies you use are really helpful. For example, having a drink or taking a sleeping pill the first few days after the assault may offer an escape from uncomfortable or frightening thoughts and feelings; however, keep in mind that if you begin to depend on alcohol or drugs, your recovery will be hindered.

You may be reluctant to begin trying to make positive changes in your life because you are not sure that things can ever really be better for you again. Following routines and knowing what to expect offers a certain amount of security—even when doing so means that you may continue being unhappy. That is why we so often remain in situations and relationships long after they stop being pleasurable or positive forces in our lives. We are afraid that something new and unfamiliar may be even worse.

Just because you start to make positive changes and start on the recovery process does not mean you always will see progress. Often recovery means recognizing we have problems and really feeling their pain. When this happens, you or others may believe that you are getting worse. However, you are not. Recovery involves a lot of ups and downs.

Change always involves risk. If one method of solving your prob-

lems doesn't work, don't waste time worrying that it means you are
a failure as a person or that you will never be able to manage. You
simply need to try a new approach. Even if one method doesn't help
you feel better after you've given it a reasonable chance, at least you
are taking action and are no longer helplessly immobilized. That is
progress. Whatever your experience, with continued effort eventually
you will feel much better than you do now.

Avoid pressure from other people in making decisions about your
life. Your goals and what you do to reach them must be based first
and foremost on your own needs. For instance, if you have always
wanted to take a year off from school, move to Colorado, and work
at a ski area, you may decide that this is the time to do so. Your
friends and family may have a multitude of reasons for wanting you
to stay home—so they can protect you and keep you safe, because
students are supposed to complete a course of education without any
interruptions, because they are afraid you are just running away. You
may want to change jobs; perhaps you never really liked your old job
anyway, there was no challenge. Your boss, however, may not want
you to leave—you are a good worker and training someone new takes
a long time and is expensive. While you certainly need to be responsible to other people, you are under no obligation to meet their needs
at the expense of your own.

Evaluating Your Resources

Everyone has resources that are seldom considered because they are
seldom needed. Now is the time to make a list of your emotional and
physical assets, the resources upon which you now can draw to help
you move from turmoil and disorganization back to control of your
life.

Resources Within Yourself

The fact that you are reading this book is an indication of your
willingness to look at your response and attempt change. This openness to change and willingness to seek information is essential. To

some extent, the tension you are feeling as a result of the assault can be a motivating force and a source of strength. Do not overlook your health and your body's adaptive capacities. If you were physically injured during the assault, the fact that your body is healing itself is an example of its own power.

Your past experiences, your educational background, and your experience dealing with stress can be assets. If you've dealt with serious stress in the past, regardless of how hard it was for you, you're stronger today for having gone through the process. You know more about what to expect. If you have survived something worse, you know you can survive this.

Get in touch with your feelings. Be honest with yourself. It's easy to focus on your faults, but a positive view of yourself is much more helpful. Think about all the things you've done well and feel good about your successes.

Resources in Your Environment

Aside from yourself, your family and friends are your most important resources. Often they are supportive by just being there to care and listen. They may provide more tangible support, suggesting a counselor they like or helping you find a safer place to live. Even more important, they can provide a sense of emotional security. Although some women have no one with whom they feel close enough to share important feelings, most have at least a few close friends. It is important to be as clear as possible in letting these people know how much you need them and what it is you need from them. Don't assume they "should" know. They can know only if you tell them. Don't assume they don't want to help if you haven't asked them for help. They may feel they are protecting you by not mentioning the rape, because they don't want to upset you. Give them a chance to help. Then, if their help isn't enough, look elsewhere.

This may be a time to reexamine those people to whom you go for support. If your current friends are not supportive, you may need to develop new friendships with people you can turn to in times of crisis. Finding out that people you thought were close friends can't be counted on may feel like a huge loss on top of the rape. You may

find you need to look beyond your usual friends, perhaps to a professional counselor.

In addition to your informal support network, you may rely on
the more formal community social support system. Most communities
have a number of public and private agencies available to provide
assistance with particular problems, such as rape crisis centers; victim
witness programs that assist survivors who go to court; victim assistance programs that may provide financial assistance; employment
programs for help in finding a new job or making a career change;
sexuality programs; counseling services; or self-help groups. Your
local rape center may have a list of resources other survivors have
found helpful.

If you're not aware of an agency in your community that is set up
to provide information and referrals, call directory assistance and ask
for the telephone number of a referral agency; some are called First
Call for Help. If there is no such service in your community, your
local United Way or American Red Cross or a member of the clergy
may be able to help. Don't give up on getting the help you need and
deserve. But remember, help won't just come to you unsolicited. You
will need to seek it out.

Coping with Fear, Anger, and Depression

Coping with a problem usually involves dealing with internal and
external conflicts and reducing tension to a manageable level. Some
tension is motivating and facilitates change. Too much is overwhelming and incapacitating.

Take Back Control

While you could not prevent the rape, you can learn to control
thoughts about it and your emotional response to it. Many survivors
report feeling that the rapist controlled their thoughts for weeks afterward, because the assault was all they thought about. It may be
that for a few days or weeks you feel the need to go over the rape in
your mind again and again. This flooding of thoughts with memories
of the assault, while you are somewhere you know is safe, actually

has been found to be one of the most effective ways to take back control. By desensitizing yourself to the events in this way, you make them less threatening to your psychological sense of well-being. You may find it even more helpful to write down or tape-record your memories of the assault in great detail, them reread or play back the tape over and over, until it no longer brings tears.

Many survivors have found the following visualization experience helpful. Just make sure to do it in a safe place where you can take a few minutes to deal with thoughts of the attack. Do so as often as possible, remembering that it's important to maintain control of the situation. First, sit comfortably and concentrate on your breathing, taking deep, slow breaths. Let the actual events of the assault replay themselves in your mind, and use all of your senses to "see" them. Pay attention to the things you see and smell and the sounds you hear. After you have done that a couple of times, change the scenario and you take control, once again using all of your senses. When you first see the assailant in your home, for instance, see yourself become rageful at his intrusion. Stand up and see yourself appear three times his size. See him shrink in fear in front of you, dwarfed by your obvious power. See the fear on *his* face. Then see yourself hit him, knocking him out of your house, clear across the street, and see him run from you in terror. Try different scenarios each time you rewrite the script. The important thing is for you to take all the power and give him all the fear.

If you are not somewhere where you are able to deal with the thoughts at the time, you can try a different approach. Each time you have an intrusive thought of the assault, stop and say to yourself, "I'm not being raped now. It's over and I survived. He's gone. I'm safe, comfortable, warm, and in control of my body. Right now I'm on the way to the grocery store to pick up . . ." and remind yourself of your shopping list.

Combat Negative Thoughts and Feelings

Instead of telling yourself how weak, useless, or helpless you are, learn to focus on how well you are doing and how far you have come since the turmoil immediately following the assault. Each day that you feel less overwhelmed by negative thoughts and feelings, tell yourself, "I'm learning to take back control." Focus on your successes, not on the things you still need to overcome. You can deal with them one at a time, as you are ready to do so.

Make sure you are not misinterpreting other people's reactions to you. For example, maybe you asked a friend to go to lunch with you and she said, "I'd love to, but I have to take my cat to the vet." Your response might have been to feel as if she were rejecting you, didn't like you, were upset with you, or were embarrassed to be seen with you because you were raped. Ask yourself what evidence there is that any of these possibilities could be accurate. Were there nonverbal clues? If so, what were they? Does she even know about the rape?

You may find it helpful to write down the negative thoughts you have about yourself, what you are doing when you start to feel bad, and what people say that you believe is critical of you. You can then review these comments with someone whose opinion you trust and with whom you feel comfortable talking.

Count yourself lucky. Many survivors find it helpful to minimize their experience in an effort to feel better about what happened. They say things like "It could have been so much worse." If they are young they will say, "I couldn't have handled it if I were old." If they are old they may say, "It would be so much harder for a young person without the life experiences I have had." These are self-protective mechanisms to help us feel better about painful situations.

Examine Your Fear

When you are out alone, you may find yourself feeling so afraid that you think you'll never again be able to walk down the street without feeling tense and vulnerable. But you can teach youself to control your emotional responses. Don't pretend that you are not afraid to be out alone if you are afraid. Once you acknowledge your feelings, you can determine what is causing them. Is it being out at night? Did your fear begin when you passed someone, perhaps a man with a beard like the rapist's? Did you hear or smell something that reminded you of the rape or the rapist? It is important to identify as specifically as possible the cues in your environment that elicit these uncomfortable emotional responses. Then ask yourself what the likelihood really is of anything bad happening where you are *now*. Is this current fear a *realistic* fear, based on a real danger in your present situation, or is it an *unrealistic* fear that is based not on a present danger but on memories of the rape? Be as honest in your assessment as you can possibly be.

Sometimes taking a deep breath when you first begin to feel tense helps. Let it out slowly. Anxiety can trigger rapid, shallow breathing. Controlling your breathing will help you control your physiological response to anxiety while it helps you collect your thoughts and increase your awareness. Take time to look around you and see what's happening while you do this.

Another effective relaxation technique is referred to as systematic desensitization. Make a list of those things you are afraid of doing. Put the things you are least afraid of at the top of the list. Next imagine yourself doing the activity at the top of the list while keeping your body relaxed and maintaining slow, deep breaths. Imagine yourself doing each activity in turn. You should not proceed to a more fearful situation until you feel relaxed in the least fearful situation. Because this method is best accomplished with the help of another person, it is described in greater detail in the second part of this chapter, "To the Significant Other," beginning on page 135.

The next step in overcoming your fear is to actually engage in the activities that make you afraid, using the technique just described. You may want to have someone with you first, then go alone. First you should assess the real danger of each situation you fear. If you were raped walking through a dark alley late at night, for example, you may not want to do this again. The fear is realistic and not appropriate for desensitization. If you have trouble separating the real from the unrealistic, rape-related fears, talk things over with a trusted friend or counselor. If you do not confront these situations, you will be victimizing yourself and allowing the rapist to control you long after he has left by placing unnecessary constraints and limitations on your activities.

Express Your Anger in Positive Ways

Expressing anger is one of the ways we can direct blame toward others, such as the rapist, rather than turning it inward against ourselves. There is no reason to fear anger. In fact, acknowledging your anger is crucial to your recovery. Anger need not be destructive if it's constructively channeled. Many survivors are concerned that if they ever allow themselves really to get angry, they will "lose control," possibly forever, or "go crazy with rage." In more than fifteen years of working with survivors' rage, I have never seen this occur, although it is not an uncommon fear. Survivors' anger following rape takes many forms; some are appropriate ways that facilitate recovery, and some are inappropriate ways that hamper or prevent return to normal activities. The effective resolution of feelings such as anger can have a positive and pervasive impact on your ability to function in all areas of your life.

Anger is an emotion many people have great difficulty expressing constructively. They either explode or keep their feelings buried inside. The way you initially express your anger after a rape will tend to be the same as or similar to the way you express anger in other situations. Now is an important time to evaluate your usual way of dealing with anger and perhaps to learn a more effective method.

Telling people who are willing to listen how angry you are, telling your dog or cat, or yelling at the rapist while driving in your car can be very effective releases. Another positive method of dealing with your anger is becoming involved in the legal process. Report the crime to the police, complete the investigative report, and provide information to be used as evidence in prosecuting the rapist. Especially if other assaults have occurred in a particular area, talk with your neighbors or distribute fliers so that others are aware of the danger. To feel less helpless, Tanya and her mother, Selena, used fantasy to deal with their anger.

Tanya, eleven years old, was raped by a neighbor's fiancé. At the time, no one knew he was out on bail and had served time for rape in another state. Tanya was too frightened and intimidated to put up much resistance. Her mother walked into the bedroom as he was zipping up his pants.

Later her mother told Tanya's counselor, "I know what it's like to be raped. I was raped when I was thirteen years old. I still wake up with nightmares, in a cold sweat. I got pregnant, but I didn't tell anyone until the pregnancy began to show, and then they thought I was lying. Tanya and I spent the night after her rape talking about how we'd post her rapist's bail ourselves, then how we'd kill him. We'd never really do it, of course, but the fantasy was a helpful outlet for both of us.

You also can use fantasy to rewrite your nightmares. After you wake yourself fully and reassure yourself that you are really safe, do some deep breathing and relax as fully as you can. Next imagine the rapist approaching you as he did in your nightmare, but then visualize yourself overpowering him and preventing the rape. Use all your senses and allow yourself to be superpowerful.

Keeping a journal is another way to sort out the things you are feeling, to discharge emotions, and to see the progress you make over time. You need not write in your journal every day, but rather when you feel in a more contemplative mood or when something important has happened to you. Be sure to document your feelings about these important events, not just what happened. In your journal you also may want to include your goals and aspirations and strategies to attain them. You may choose to write down your dreams. They can give you important insights into your subconscious fears and concerns. Be sure to include your feelings during the dreams and how you felt when you woke up.

Channel your angry, aggressive impulses into socially acceptable behavior, such as sports. Tennis, racquetball, and golf are excellent choices because you strike a ball and exert considerable energy. Walking, jogging, swimming, and bike riding also are effective. Exercise as an expression of anger has an added benefit. Whenever you exercise to the point of increasing your heartbeat and sustain the exercise for twenty minutes or more, your body releases endorphins into your bloodstream. These endorphins have analgesic properties that help to lower your level of depression. Joggers who experience "jogger's euphoria" are enjoying the benefits of increased endorphin production. Many counseling programs now recommend jogging or other forms of exercise specifically for their positive impact on mood.

Humor is another effective method of expressing anger. Humor allows you to express unpleasant feelings, to focus on realities that may otherwise be too difficult to bear without making yourself or other people uncomfortable. One survivor quipped, "The best way to prevent rape is to castrate all men. Of course, then we would have a number of other problems to deal with." Another survivor, a pacifist who joined antiwar demonstrations during the Gulf War, suggested a just punishment for her rapist would be to "Just blind him, tattoo RAPIST on his forehead, and turn him loose to beg for the mercy of other people."

Still other survivors, even those who have never painted, find that art helps them express their strong emotions. Watercolors, chalk drawings, oils, pottery, and especially finger paintings allow a certain form of freedom of expression that is difficult to duplicate. Colors often have special meanings and associations for people and can bring out deep emotions both for the artist and for the observer. Many communities now offer art shows that include, or even exclusively show, the work of rape survivors.

Anger does not always have to be expressed to be dealt with. Recognizing that you are angry but choosing not to take any action is also legitimate and effective. Or you may at times decide to postpone a highly emotional reaction. However, whether you choose to express your feelings or not, it is important to recognize that you have them so that you don't let them control you.

Identifying the true source of your anger is also important. Very often people become angry because they have been hurt. In the case of rape, you feel angry because you felt hurt and humiliated by the things that were done to you or that you were forced to do. Or you may have been more hurt by the reactions of loved ones than by the events of the rape. You may feel as if every shred of your humanity was stripped away. During the rape you were not in a position to get angry, but now the hurt you feel may be expressed as anger.

Focus your anger *at* the rapist for the rape, *on* the rapist. While initially you may have generalized your anger to all men, or to all men with certain characteristics similar to the rapist's, maintaining that generalization of feelings is not healthy. An important part of healing is directing your anger solely at the rapist, where it belongs. *It is okay to stay angry at the rapist.* You never need to forgive him, forget that it happened, or feel sorry for him. What he did to you will always be a hateful crime. Taking back control from him and appropriately focusing your anger are important steps in the healing process.

Talk with a Friend

Talking about the rape will help you accept it for what it was—a past experience that you should not allow to control your present and future life. Retelling the incident in detail, which usually occurs in the hospital or with the police, is an important part of this acceptance. If you have not told anyone all of what happened, you may find it helpful to do so now. You may have omitted the most upsetting or embarrassing parts of the assault. Verbalizing a painful experience— getting it out of your system—is often a very good way to put it behind you.

Be selective in deciding with whom you share these most intimate details. (See chapter 5.) You may choose to talk with a counselor instead of a friend or relative. A counselor may be better equipped to help you than someone with an emotional investment in you. If there is no one whom you feel you can tell, at the very least write down all of what happened.

Spend Time Alone

If your rape was recent, you may need to learn to be alone again. You may still want others around to provide an external sense of safety. Many survivors, especially during the first few days or weeks, avoid being alone. It is important, however, to have some time set aside to spend alone, to try to relax and sort out your feelings, to remove yourself from the demands and expectations of everyone else for a while. Hard as it may be, go for a walk alone, sit and listen to music, or daydream about things you enjoy doing. You also may want to use some of this time to reflect on the progress you have made. With a concerted effort, soon you will learn to be comfortable being by yourself again.

Have a "Black" Day

If you can't shake the depression, give yourself a day to indulge it instead of fighting it. If you have a trusted friend, ask her to indulge in your black day with you. Give yourself twenty-four hours, if you can last that long, to be as depressed as you can possibly be. Wear all black or the clothes you hate the most, clothes that are uncomfortable and unflattering. Get yourself a black rose, preferably plastic, and wear cheap, raunchy-smelling perfume.

Eat only foods you don't like at restaurants you dislike and try to be seated at the table of a grouchy or slow waitress. See a bad movie or visit with a self-indulging friend. Force yourself not to smile all day, frown if you can, and by all means, do not laugh.

Be Selfish

Do the opposite of your black day, only more often. Treat yourself the way you would treat someone important, because you are. Be patient with yourself and forgiving. Do the things you really want to do, don't wait until it's the "right time" or you have the "extra money." Eat the foods you like the most, buy yourself fresh flowers or a new, flattering outfit. Take a bubble bath. Ride a bicycle. Get up early to allow time for coffee on the sun porch and time to pet your cat. Work out or indulge in a sport you love. Sing to yourself or go to an uplifting movie.

Get Involved Socially

Increasing your activities and social contact also may help. The general increase in social activity will provide you with outlets that can help block the intrusive thoughts of the assault. It is good to have a few people with whom you can talk. Knowing that you are still a worthwhile, acceptable human being with whom other people want to spend time can be reassuring. Research completed in 1981 at the University of Washington, in Seattle, found a direct relationship between emotional health and the presence of understanding others, and even social contact, regardless of the level of intimacy. While it is certainly true that more intimate relationships are the most important social resource, contact with nonintimate friends plays an important role in helping you resolve conflicts and deal with depression and anxiety, even when you do not discuss the rape with them.

A number of clubs, organizations, or classes may be available in your community. This may be a good time to utilize them; perhaps take an art or pottery class, or join a community softball league. Your local university, community center, or church may be able to help you find activities that interest you. This may be the time to join the church choir you had considered joining in the past. Being with a supportive group of people, whether you choose to tell them about the assault or not, may be helpful.

Offer to baby-sit for a friend or relative. Not only do children require your full focus and attention, which makes daydreaming about your fears and the things that make you sad difficult, but they usually offer unconditional acceptance and affection. Take them to a funny children's movie or play.

Change Your School Routine

Some survivors who are students decide to take a quarter off from school. They find that the fears, anxiety, intrusive thoughts, and other symptoms of post-traumatic stress disorder (PTSD) interfere with their ability to study. Others find that studying more is an effective way to keep their mind off the rape. If they were attacked on the university campus, some women decide to transfer to another campus to relieve them of the added pressure of seeing the assailant again or from the social pressure that results from mutual friends taking sides about the rape.

Change Your Work Routine

Some survivors decide to change jobs within a year after being sexually assaulted. In many cases their jobs were uninteresting and dissatisfying, and they had considered a change prior to the rape. In these circumstances the turmoil of the assault provides the impetus to make a needed change.

In other cases the rape was related to their job. For example, women who work evenings and were raped while going to or from work are often uncomfortable with the high vulnerability and look for day work. Sometimes high levels of customer contact become uncomfortable and the survivor chooses to find another job, perhaps in the same company, where she does not have the same level of public exposure.

Other women are just uncomfortable working where so many people know about their rape, feeling they are now being treated differently. This may happen regardless of whether the coworkers' response was helpful or not. They just want to begin anew elsewhere.

Many survivors change jobs not because they want to but rather because the fears and anxieties resulting from the rape are so incapacitating that they can no longer perform their jobs. It may be that you can no longer deal with job-related stress that was manageable before the rape. While the first few weeks are the most difficult, if the case goes to court, the demands on your time and energy may continue for months. A change to a less demanding job may be an effective short-term coping strategy, especially if you were considering making a job change prior to the assault. Some time off between positions also may be helpful, if this is financially feasible.

Should you want to maintain your current job, however, you'll need to talk with your employer about the attack. Obviously you don't need to go into detail about it, but you should be up-front about how seriously it has affected you and about your need for a certain amount of time off. This is necessary to your physical and emotional well-being, and you should be given the same consideration as someone dealing with the stress of illness or childbirth. This may include time off, possibly sick time, or a vacation or a leave of absence without pay. Negotiate these options with your employer. You will better represent yourself if you decide what arrangements you would like to make before speaking with him or her, then present your ideal. You may not be able to afford leave without pay, or you may not have accrued much sick leave. Decide what will be best for you, then present the reasons for your proposal. Even if it has been three months and you're just now going to trial, you may need more time off to deal with and recover from the courtroom experience.

Be sure to check the reimbursement policy of your local crime victim reparations board. This organization may have money to reimburse you for wages lost as a result of the initial stress of the rape as well as the time you need to take off to participate in the court process. If available, it is a wonderful resource.

Change Your Place of Residence

If the assault occurred in or near your home, the location may become a constant reminder. You may continue to feel vulnerable and afraid. Those women raped in their home who do not, or for financial reasons cannot, move seem to have the most difficult time during the first few months. Women who move usually do so soon after the attack because the fear and anxiety are so overwhelming. While some women do continue to feel afraid even after moving, the great majority feel relieved. Yet, although moving often helps, it is no magic cure. Other fears may remain. Emotional recovery takes time.

Rebuilding Your Self-Esteem

Eventually the anger will dissipate, the depression will lift, the anxiety will pass, and you'll be able to resume your normal activities. You'll find that while you are not "over it," you do feel better about yourself in general. Positive feedback from other people is directly related to how we view ourselves. The things we value about ourselves are often the things other people value about us. The more isolated you are, the less chance you have to hear good things about yourself or to do things you feel good about doing.

Unfortunately, women more often than men assume personal responsibility for failure and bad things happening to them and attribute success and positive happenings to chance or other circumstances beyond their control. Men do just the opposite. They take credit for their successes and attribute failure to chance or outside influences. Recognizing that we are responsible for our successes is an important component in feeling good about ourselves and building our self-esteem. It is important that you learn to accept credit for your success as you resolve this crisis. You alone are responsible, you alone are in control, and you alone deserve the credit for success.

You need not feel guilty about the assault. Don't judge your response to it as right or wrong based on hindsight. There is no right or wrong response, whether you were aroused or whether you wanted to hurt or kill the rapist. If you have strong religious affiliations, you may want to discuss your guilty feelings with someone from your church or synagogue. Remember, however, that person may not understand rape and may have some biases that will be hurtful to you.

Learning to Enjoy Sex Again

Six to twelve weeks after the assault, most survivors resume the same frequency of sexual activity as prior to it. This is especially true when women are involved in an ongoing sexual relationship. On the surface, sexual activity may appear to have returned to normal, or their sexual partner may feel it has. A large number of these women, however, report that they are not as satisfied with sex. It is no longer as enjoyable to them. Often women report that this lack of interest, enjoyment, and satisfaction continues through the first year and, in some cases, much longer.

Women in general report that physical closeness, being held, being cuddled, and feelings of warmth and caring are a very important part of sexual relations. To many women this closeness is as important or more important than the physical act of intercourse or having an orgasm. Sexuality is much more than simply having intercourse. It's feeling comfortable, close, and intimate with another person. It involves feeling attractive and likable and being able to feel good about yourself. Don't try to maintain the relationship by satisfying only your partner's sexual needs. Make sure to ask for the closeness you need. If you give up the positive aspects of sexual intimacy, usually you also give up much of the related emotional intimacy. It may reflect a loss of satisfaction in other areas of your life.

In order to be comfortable with sex, you need to be comfortable with being physically close to another person. This may involve learning to trust men or a particular man again and not feeling forced or coerced into being closer than you want to be. It also involves learning to feel good about yourself and your body. While you now know how sex can be used as a weapon, you must remember that it also can bring pleasure, and it can be a way of sharing yourself with the partner of your choice.

If you are having sex but not enjoying it, or if you are feeling pressure from your sexual partner to be more intimate, you need to talk with him. First it is crucial that he understand that it is not him you are rejecting but memories from the rape. Many survivors actually have flashbacks of the rape when they first become sexual again. You may need to be more assertive and draw limits on the level of physical closeness you want during these first weeks and months. It is also best if you just hug and cuddle first, with you both understanding that you will not have intercourse at that time.

It is essential that your partner agree not to pressure you to have sex. You need to be in control and be the one to initiate intimacy. If he pushes you, it will feel like the rape again and slow your recovery. When you do feel ready to be intimate, the sexual activity should be as different from the rape as it possibly can be. Engage in different sexual behaviors, different positions. If you were raped in the dark, keep the lights on. Focus on his face and constantly remind yourself whom you are with. As difficult as it may be, talk with him beforehand and let him know where not to touch you, what not to do. Also get assurance from him beforehand that he will stop when you ask, should you feel threatened—that he will allow you to be in control of what you do and do not do sexually. If you feel uncomfortable, say so. A caring partner will respect your wishes.

Getting Help or Going It Alone

You also must decide if you need extra help from someone skilled and experienced in dealing with issues you now face, so you need to know what asking for help means.

What Does Asking for Help Mean?

Some people find asking for help much easier than others do, because asking has a different meaning for each of us. Some people see asking for help as a sign of personal failure. To them, asking for help is a sign of weakness or brings dishonor to their family. These people ask for help only as a last resort, when all else fails.

To other people, asking for help is a sign of intelligence and resourcefulness. To them, asking for help is a sign of wanting to do things better than they could by themselves. These people don't feel the need to be an expert at everything, and they understand that they don't need to be able to handle everything on their own. They feel good about being able to find and use available resources.

Don't forget, you get help with the less important things in your life without feeling that it's a sign of failure. When your television breaks, you don't expect to fix it yourself; you probably took lessons to learn to swim or play the piano, because you wanted to do it well. By getting help from someone who is trained to deal with a crisis such as rape, you can speed your progress toward recovery. You can accomplish much more than simply keeping your head above water.

Getting Help and Maintaining Control

Getting help does not mean that you are turning yourself or your problems completely over to someone else to solve. They are still your problems, your responsibility, and you are the one who must solve them. Each of us sees our life and our problems a little differently from the way someone else will. The fact that someone else is a trained professional does not necessarily mean he or she is better able to sort out the problems or determine a better solution than you can. Only you can decide what is a problem for you and what will be the best solution for you.

However, the professionals from whom you seek support can play an important role in helping you sort through your feelings. Since they are not emotionally involved with you, they are in a better position to help you understand the source of your feelings and behavior. They can help you evaluate coping strategies you have used in the past, suggest new strategies for you to try, and help you recognize options that may not be readily apparent.

Therapists, counselors, and advocates are there to facilitate your recovery. They can provide you with support and encouragement while you try new approaches to life and new ways of interacting with the world around you. They can help you see the world and yourself from a different perspective, allowing you to achieve insights that will help you change. Remember, though, that the therapist is not there to make you better but to help you to better help yourself recover.

How to Choose a Therapist

Before you look for a therapist, you may want to check your health insurance policy, if you have one, to see what restrictions are imposed on payment. Many policies will pay only if a medical doctor or licensed psychologist is involved. Some policies will not pay for any counseling. Most limit the number of visits. You should know this before deciding whom to see.

Psychiatrists have medical degrees and are the only counselors at this time who can legally prescribe medication. Some, though not all, rely heavily on medication. While short-term use may be helpful for you, overdependence on medication is something you want to avoid. It is easy to develop unrecognized dependencies on even prescribed drugs if they are used over an extended period of time. Psychiatrists also usually charge the highest fees.

Psychologists usually have a Ph.D. Those with only a master's degree may be more limited in their experience or practice. A person with a Ph.D. in counseling or clinical psychology will likely have in-depth theoretical training and may have considerable experience in a specialized area, such as biofeedback or hypnosis. Their fees will be somewhat lower than those of a psychiatrist. You also may see a psychiatric nurse, social worker, counselor, or paraprofessional, each of whom will be less expensive than psychiatrists and psychol-ogists.

You may begin your search for a counselor by calling a rape center or a friend and getting a recommendation. Before making an ap-pointment to see a counselor decide if you want to see a man or a woman. You probably will want to see someone who has experience working with rape survivors. Ask if the counselor has any specific background or experience in this area. When you call, also be sure to ask about his or her fees. Ask if there is a sliding fee scale, and if he or she meets the criteria of your insurance carrier. If your insurance carrier requires you to pay 20 percent of the fee, for instance, ask if the counselor will waive your copayment; many will do this. If the counselor meets your payment criteria, ask for an appointment.

When you go to see the counselor who has been assigned to you, it does not mean that you have made any long-term commitment to see her weekly for six months, ten times, or even for a second visit. You can decide to continue only after you find out more about how compatible the two of you are. Whether her services are free or very expensive, the time spent should be productive and worthwhile.

When you first see the counselor, ask about her training and back-ground. Ask her how many rape survivors she has worked with in the past and why she feels women get raped. Unfortunately, some counselors still believe many of the myths about rape that the general population believes; because of this they are less effective in helping rape survivors. One male therapist even asked an eighteen-year-old survivor, "You've had sex before, right?" The client replied, "Yes." The male therapist then said, "Well, sex is sex, so what's the big deal? You weren't hurt."

Size up the counselor during the initial interview. If she tells you things you simply cannot accept as true for you, ignore them. Don't judge yourself on the basis of other people's truths and values. Recognize and trust the value of your own uniqueness.

In deciding if you will return, ask yourself these questions: Did she ask me how I feel and what I see as the problem? Did she ask me what I want to accomplish by seeing her? Do I feel stronger, more in control, rather than more helpless, as if she is trying to bring me in line with her expectations? If the answers are positive, then you may have found a good therapist. If not, try someone else. Don't be afraid to tell the therapist that you will not be returning or that you will decide later and call if you want another appointment, and don't be discouraged and give up if the first person you see is not right for you.

Do keep in mind, however, that a good therapist may make you feel uncomfortable. Recovery is hard work and requires facing difficult issues. She may ask you questions to which you do not know the answers or bring up topics that upset you. Trust your instincts but make sure you evaluate carefully how you feel at the end of the session. Choosing a good therapist is an important process. Her opinions and values will have an impact on your recovery process.

TO THE SIGNIFICANT OTHER

Just as recovering from rape can be a growth experience for the survivor, you too can learn about yourself through the way you respond to her and her pain and the way you deal with your own feelings. Expressing feelings and concerns is especially important during times of stress, for both of you. By being available and open, you can give the survivor permission to talk with you and utilize you as a source of support. If you are a woman, sharing your innermost feelings may be easier than if you are a man. Most women are used to talking freely with at least one female friend. Men, on the other hand, tend to share activities more than feelings with lovers, friends, and relatives. If you are a man, providing the kind of emotional support the survivor needs may take a conscious effort.

Should She Be Over It By Now?

The physical wounds of rape—the cuts and bruises—will heal first. The psychological wounds are much deeper and take much longer to heal. One of the most unfortunate yet frequently faced dilemmas of rape survivors is the expectation from others that they should "be over it" in two weeks to a month, by the time the cuts and bruises heal. Once the outward signs of the trauma are gone, it is more difficult for others to see the inner turmoil. It may be hard for you. You may be tired of hearing about the assault and the fears that have resulted from it. And you may be tired of telling the survivor it's okay. You may be "over it," but then you didn't actually experience the trauma firsthand.

You may begin to feel drained by her continued need to talk about the rape, and you may want to withdraw, not be there any more for her. You may think she's feeling sorry for herself or change the subject when she brings up the rape. These are normal responses on your part. It is a difficult time for you as well. Understand that her repeated reference to the rape and her need to talk about it are her ways of attempting to integrate the event into her life experience. Unfortunately, this integration may take some time, but she needs the time, and your patience, so she can see it through successfully. As she integrates the event, references will become more tangential—less direct—and will diminish in frequency. Once this integration occurs, she'll need to spend less time talking about the rape. Your willingness, or that of someone else, to listen will be a key factor in her recovery.

If she is unable or unwilling to talk with you, she may have someone else with whom she does feel comfortable talking about the assault. Teenagers, for example, often have trouble talking to parents. While you may feel rejected or hurt, just try to be glad that she does feel comfortable talking with her girlfriends, for instance. No matter how much she trusts and respects you, she may feel more comfortable talking about sexual issues with her friends.

Some survivors are unable to talk about the assault for weeks or months. Others have told no one even years later. They continue to deny the reality of the rape, the extent of the trauma, and the impact it is having on their lives. Unfortunately, well-meaning but uninformed people around them often encourage this denial by telling them how "strong" they are and how "well" they are doing. In reality, they are too frightened to face the rape. By now they may be trying very hard simply to please other people.

Those people around them who are relieved by the denial also may be too uncomfortable or too afraid to face the terror of the rape themselves. For the moment, denial is easier for everyone—everyone except the survivor.

If you know a survivor who seems unable to talk about the assault, you may want to try some of the approaches suggested in chapter 5. Give her permission to talk about the rape without pushing her to do so. Be patient with her, and allow her to address issues when she is ready. With some counseling or crisis intervention, it will probably take her six to twelve weeks to begin to feel "over it" and able to function in the day-to-day activities she did before the rape. However, some women take much longer to reach this stage.

What You Can Do to Help

During the first few days, perhaps a week, you and she just may want to relax. You both probably will be exhausted from all the activity and stress. After this initial period of recuperation, however, you may want to begin looking at specific problems. Let her set the pace. She needs to be in control.

Safety is often an important issue to both of you. Your concerns will vary depending on the circumstances of the assault.

John feels a cold chill when he enters his apartment. He had been out of town when Sandy was raped in their home. He has felt unsafe there ever since. He doesn't want to come home from work at night because he knows this terrible foreboding feeling will return. The noises in the building sound so foreign now, so threatening. He can't relax. He knows he can't continue to live there. They will have to move soon.

Usually the survivor feels uncomfortable and unsafe, but husbands, family members, and male or female roommates sometimes experience this same terror as well. If the assault occurred in your home, you too may decide it's easier to move, to start fresh somewhere else, somewhere without the haunting memories. You and the survivor can take precautions to increase your sense of safety. The important thing is to avoid taking over for her and making her dependent on you or anyone else in the process.

Helping Her with the Blues

It is important for you to be aware that while she is feeling sad or depressed, she will be more likely to misinterpret comments and events and see only the negative side of her current experiences. Unfortunately, this tendency also makes the depression worse. You can help her evaluate her perceptions. She may feel as if everyone knows she was raped and as a result is treating her differently or looking at her "funny." She may hear only bad in whatever is said to her. Help her more realistically evaluate the things that she is interpreting negatively. Is it really happening, or is it her altered perception?

Physical and social activities are good ways to lessen her feelings of depression. By providing her with motivation, helping her plan activities, encouraging her to participate, you'll be able to give her the support she needs to get started again.

Because her perceptions of herself are altered, just like her perceptions of other people, she may not see what she does well. Point out her successes to her. Remind her of the progress she's made. Help her see more of the positive side of events.

Helping Her Deal with Her Fears and Anxieties

Because fears and anxieties are so disabling, they may need to be dealt with before she is able to participate more actively in outside events. One of the most effective ways you can support her is by guiding her through a process of slow and systematic desensitization to specific fears and situations. The first step is to have her write down the things she is afraid of doing and to arrange them in order, writing the things she is the least afraid to do at the top of the list and the things she is the most afraid to do at the bottom. For instance, Ann made the following list:

- going out of the house with someone during the day
- going out of the house alone during the day
- going out of the house alone after dark
- walking the dog alone during the day
- taking out the garbage alone at night
- walking the dog alone at night

Next evaluate the list and determine which of the feared activities are unrealistic fears, things that in reality are probably safe for her to do, and which are realistic fears, things that are dangerous enough that she should avoid doing them in the future. In addition, you will need to consider the necessity of the activity in your life. Ann and her husband decided that her walking the dog at night was probably a real danger and there was no need for her to do so. He would take the dog out at night in the future.

The next step is to help her learn to reduce tension. You can do this by utilizing the following exercises. You will want to choose a quiet, private place where you will not be interrupted and where you both feel comfortable. This may or may not be your home. You will act as her coach.

RELAXATION EXERCISE. Have the survivor sit comfortably and close her eyes. Ask her to tense and then relax her muscles, beginning with those in her forehead and around her eyes. As she tightens her muscles, she should take a deep breath and hold it, then slowly breathe out as she relaxes. Work from the head to the neck, shoulders, arms, hands, chest, abdomen, thighs, knees, calves, feet, and toes. Ask her to concentrate on feeling the tension flow away as she relaxes her muscles. With practice, the survivor will be able to feel completely relaxed in just a few minutes.

VISUALIZATION EXERCISE. While the survivor is sitting comfortably in a relaxed state with her eyes closed, ask her to picture herself doing each of the fearful activities that remain on the list, beginning with the least frightening ones. Slowly talk her through each activity. In Ann's case, since the first entry is "going out of the house with someone during the day," you would begin by asking her to picture herself putting on her coat, walking slowly to the doorway with you, standing in the open doorway, looking right then left, and stepping outside with you beside her. Remind her frequently to take slow, deep breaths. If she becomes frightened, have her raise a finger so you can ask her what she is seeing that is frightening her. The whole process for each activity should take from twenty minutes to one hour, depending on her level of comfort. You both should find the process relaxing and invigorating.

If she feels comfortable with the imaginary walk, the next day you may want to take a real walk. Do the same thing, except now with your eyes open and for real. Each time she feels anxious or afraid, stop. Have her identify what is frightening her. Help her evaluate if there is any realistic danger. If not, have her concentrate on taking slow, deep breaths and relax her body from head to toe. Then continue. If she can't relax again, slowly turn around and go home. Just as with your imaginary walk, each time she should be able to go farther and do more and still be relaxed, comfortable, and feel safe.

Do the same with the next item on her list. In Ann's case, this would be going out of the house alone during the daytime. Practice each step until it loses its ability to frighten, then move on to the next level.

Dealing with Her Anger

Don't be afraid of her anger. Angry, even rageful outbursts are a common symptom of post-traumatic stress disorder. While it is a sign that she has a lot of repressed anger still inside, blowing up at small things is certainly better than turning the anger inward or hurting herself. If she becomes furious because you overcooked her eggs, for instance, let her yell or scream until she is finished. Don't try to stop her and don't become defensive or argue with her. Most important, don't take it personally. Remind yourself that her anger has nothing to do with you or how you cooked her eggs. She is misdirecting repressed anger at the rapist toward you. Once she has got it off her chest, tell her, "I know you are under a tremendous amount of stress and I know you must be very angry about what happened. I'm really sorry you have to go through this."

Once she has calmed down, help her identify constructive ways of expressing her anger more directly. This might include things such as putting a picture or drawing of the rapist on a dart board and throwing darts at it; getting a punching bag and pretending it's the rapist; engaging in active sports; or whatever she has found helpful in the past to resolve her anger. Let her know that while you understand she's not really angry at you, and you are willing to work with her, it's not okay for her to continue to take her anger out on you indefinitely either.

Avoiding Burnout

While initially you may like the feeling of having her depend solely on you, this may become overwhelming. You can and should do certain things to avoid being worn out while she is still in need of your support. Don't wait until you just can't help any more and then try to set some limits.

Probably other people on whom she can rely to meet some of her needs are available. Don't discourage her from doing so. You don't need to be her sole support. You may even want to help her explore who else in her group of friends may be a good source of support, such as a friend who was raped herself and with whom she has felt comfortable in the past. While you may remain a central source of support, it's best for both of you if you are not her only one.

After the first few days or weeks, it also may be important to set some limits on how long you're available to be with her or on how long you spend talking about the rape when you're together. Thirty minutes a day or an hour three times a week may be plenty. Set that time aside to talk about her concerns, when you don't expect to be interrupted.

Remember that you can provide support without spending all your time discussing the assault. Plan some leisure activities, things you both enjoy, that you can do together. Biking, hiking, going to the movies, or visiting with friends will allow you time together that's not focused on the rape. It's important to try to maintain your relationship without basing it solely on the rape.

You will need some time apart as well. Wanting time alone is normal under any circumstances, but it is especially important when you are both under additional stress. Daily time alone may work best for you, or you may decide a full day or two is necessary. You must give yourself permission to recognize this need. Wanting time for yourself does not mean you don't care or that you are deserting each other.

Remember that it's normal for you to have many of the same feelings she does as a result of the assault. However, you will be able to help her better if you maintain some emotional distance. She needs you to help her sort out her feelings of anger and anxiety, rather than experiencing them for her; to do this, you must first deal with your own reactions.

If you can't resolve your feelings, you may decide together that it would be helpful for her to see a professional counselor, someone not emotionally involved. You may both want to become involved in counseling. This is something important to consider and discuss. Through counseling, you may both change and grow in response to this crisis.

Being There When the Others Have Gone

Perhaps at first she didn't turn to you as a source of support. She may have relied more on others in her network of friends. Two weeks, two months, or even longer after the assault, when the others have "burned out" and no longer feel able to support her, may be when she needs your support the most. Being available to talk with her at this later point may be more important than it would have been earlier. Usually many people are willing to provide support during the first few weeks. It's likely that she now has fewer sources upon which to draw.

Safeguarding your emotions is still important. You may still need to guard against overdependence—especially if her previous support system tried to take over and rescue her. That relationship may have ended because the others could no longer deal with her dependence. If so, it is especially important for you to set limits from the very beginning, to avoid her transferring those dependencies to you. Your support of those dependencies will do her no good. The initial crisis is over. She needs to begin functioning more on her own.

What If You Can't Talk About It?

The rape may have had such an impact on you that it has become unmentionable. You may be afraid you'll say the wrong thing and make it worse. You may not want to talk about the rape because you don't want to admit it really happened. Even words make it too real. You may not understand how it could have happened, or you blame her, or you may even feel differently toward her now, knowing she had sex with another man, even if it was against her will.

If she needs to talk about the rape but you want to change the subject each time she brings it up, the first thing you should do is explain your feelings to her. Be as honest as you can. It's better to explain your true feelings than for you to keep changing the subject or for her to keep trying in vain to talk with you about the rape. Both of you will become anxious, frustrated, and perhaps even angry with each other if the problem is not dealt with openly. She needs to know that at this particular time it is difficult or impossible for you to talk about the rape, but that you are not rejecting her and you still want to be with her and talk about other things. Let her know that you understand she's ready to talk and needs to talk, but that she has to find someone else better able to deal with her concerns. You do not feel able to do that just now. Being direct also will give her permission to find someone else with whom she can express her concerns, someone who will understand and provide her with the support she needs.

Other people have had all the feelings you are experiencing. They all can be resolved. Try to identify your concerns and the source of your inability to discuss the rape. Remember, you are a secondary victim. You too may need help understanding your reactions to this very serious life crisis. You may want to look for a counselor who has worked with friends and families of rape survivors.

5

Telling Other People

Whatever my secrets are, remember when I entrust them to you, they are part of me.

—JOHN POWELL, Argus Communications, 1982

TO THE SURVIVOR

He had gone. Afraid to move, Carol was still gripping the sheets tightly up around her neck. Her first thought was that she had to hide what had happened. "If no one knows, it will be less real. It's over, so I'll just forget about it and go on like nothing happened." But she couldn't block it from her mind. And she discovered that she didn't need to tell her family that something has happened. The bruises on her face made that apparent. Her teenage brother was angry. He wanted to kill the rapist. Her parents felt guilty and responsible. They had been right there in the house with their daughter but had done nothing to stop the assault. She had screamed and they had not heard her. They didn't want to call the police. Then everyone would know. Even the neighbors would know about the terrible thing that had happened—know it was her parents' fault—know they hadn't stopped this man and protected their daughter. They knew Carol needed help. They needed help too. They decided to call their minister. Carol showered, changed clothes, and cleaned up while they waited for him to arrive. She felt detached as she watched herself go through the motions. The reality and the unreality of the moment seemed to converge.

Deciding if you will tell anyone about the rape, and, if so, whom you will tell, when, and how, are certainly important decisions that will affect your recovery. Many survivors are afraid to tell anyone. Sometimes these fears are unfounded and sometimes they are quite reasonable. The crisis is likely to facilitate an evaluation of your life in general as well as an evaluation of your friendships. You will find both good and bad surprises as it becomes clear to whom you can and cannot turn for support. You will learn to know your friends better—their strengths and weaknesses—as a result. Don't judge them too harshly. Likely there will be some individuals in your circle of friends who are well meaning and would like to help, but don't have the necessary resources or skills. Perhaps they have serious problems of their own to resolve.

Even without any physical signs, it is not easy to hide the emotional trauma that results from rape. People who know you well will probably notice that you seem different, especially right after the assault. You may need to offer some explanation. While there are risks involved in telling other people, these risks are outweighed by the benefits. Telling other people certainly does not guarantee a positive, helpful response. However, not telling denies you the support or assistance that is available. It is important to find at least one person whom you can tell about the rape. You'll be surprised at what you can endure if there is someone to whom you can turn and on whom you can rely. People who care about you can help you overcome the low self-esteem that often results from rape, and much more. They can help you rebuild your self-confidence and assist in problem solving.

The Fears of Telling

Take some time to consider the most likely response of others to the news that you were raped. If you anticipate a lack of understanding from someone you feel the need to tell, you can be better prepared for the response and better able to keep it in perspective. It may be that people you expect to be supportive will not be. You need to be prepared for these unfortunate surprises as well.

Remember that we all interpret events according to our own dispositions. Others' responses say more about their personalities and their view of the world than they do about you or the rape. While it is unpleasant to deal with blame or rejection, it is important to keep these reactions separate from the way you feel about yourself.

Fear of Blame

Depending on the circumstances of your assault, you may want to be selective about the people you tell. If people ask you what you were wearing, for instance, ask them, "Why do you want to know that? What I was wearing makes no difference. No matter what a woman has on, no one has the right to rape her." Confront them directly and make them deal with their biases and belief in rape myths before you provide them with any more information. Try to avoid sounding too defensive when responding to their questions. This is a chance to educate them and help yourself and other survivors.

You may want to respond in a similar way to other questions, such as "Did he have a knife?" "Did he threaten to hurt you?" "Did you know him?" "Did you fight back or resist?" "Was there more than one?" "Are you divorced, married, or single?" In many instances, these questions are attempts on the part of others to determine how much consolation they think you "deserve" and how much you are to blame.

Fear of Being Looked Down On

To some women, rape is a great disgrace. They want to keep it secret because they are afraid people will see them differently or be too curious about the details. While these feelings are certainly uncomfortable and at first may result in a lower self-esteem, they are usually short-lived. Your feelings of self-worth must come from your own inner strength and competence. Don't elevate the opinions of others above your own. Often there are as many different opinions about a single issue as there are different people considering it. You are still a worthwhile human being. The assault did not change *who* you are. You must learn to reject any blame or negative labels from other people, even those people who are important to you. You must keep clear in your mind what you know to be true: You are not to blame, you were not at fault, you were the victim of a crime, and now you are a survivor.

If the people in your community or religious organization do not understand rape and you believe that their knowing about your assault will stigmatize you, don't tell them. This is probably not the time to try to educate them about the realities of rape. Get confidential emotional support from someone outside your community.

Fear of Being Overprotected

You may be afraid that if you tell people who care about you, they'll become overprotective and take away your freedom and independence in the process. While the intention can be good, overprotectiveness can be destructive. If those close to you respond in this way and you are unable to talk effectively with them about it, an uninvolved third party—a friend, rape counselor, minister, or anyone else whose opinion you value—may be able to help. Whoever is being overprotective needs to see that instead of helping you, his or her behavior is hampering your adjustment and recovery. That person is the only one who, in the short term, is benefiting from this behavior: He or she doesn't need to worry as much about your safety if you are being overprotected. But in the long run, it will hurt them too. You may end up becoming overly dependent on them, as we discussed in "To the Significant Other" in chapter 4.

Whom to Tell

You will tell some people because you want to tell them. You believe, based on past experience, that they will understand and be supportive. Others you will tell because they need to know. You may choose not to tell others because you are being protective of them and you do not want an aging or ill parent, for instance, to become overly worried about your safety.

If people are helpful, supportive, and make you feel better about yourself, spend more time with them. If being with them makes you feel worse about yourself, avoid them. There is no reason to subject yourself to these bad feelings. Set your own boundaries. Make new friends if necessary. Join new organizations. Choose to be with people and engage in activities that encourage a positive outlook, growth, and feelings of self-worth. You deserve and need to feel good about yourself.

You need to remember that some people, even close friends, may withdraw because of their own fears. Don't judge them in terms of your own experience and values. They may not be as informed, or strong, or understanding, as you expected. And don't assume they are withdrawing because they don't care about you. A negative response does not necessarily indicate a lack of concern about you. You may want to try being with them again later, when you feel stronger.

It also is important not to expect whomever you tell to fix everything. Telling someone else is not a magic cure, no matter how understanding and supportive that person may be. Such unrealistic expectations will result only in disappointment and frustration. Although the rape cannot be undone, you will recover from it. You may move far beyond the point where you were before the rape, but that will take time, effort, and the desire to change on your part. Giving someone else the sole power to make you feel better will only delay your recovery. For you to change, you must be responsible, and you must be in control.

When you're deciding whom to tell, be realistic about whom they might tell. Everyone has a best friend, or spouse, whom they tell all their secrets, and yours. You can ask them not to tell anyone, but to them that may mean anyone except that one special person. If you don't mind their talking it over with other people, let them know that too. You may even want your mother to tell your grandparents, for instance.

People Who Need to Know

You may decide to tell only those people who need to know. These may include the police, hospital personnel, your parents, your husband, your children, or your roommate. Your relationship to them and the response you anticipate from them will influence this decision. The circumstances of the rape may be such that you need not tell them. Even if you have cuts and bruises, you may tell some people you were attacked without mentioning the sexual assault. Often parents decide to tell small children this. Usually it is unrealistic to think you can avoid telling them anything happened. They are too close to you not to feel the difference in your behavior, and their imagination can be vivid. They, much like a few other people in your life, will need some reasonable explanation for any behavior change. But they, like other people, do not need to know the whole truth, and you should not feel guilty not telling the whole story. You have the right to tell whom you want what you want. But do make that decision carefully.

Cheryl decided not to tell her employer anything after she was raped. She chose to continue her job as a waitress, trying to pretend nothing happened. However, her attitude and behavior toward the customers changed. She was no longer friendly and became irritated easily. Her boss didn't understand why she was acting so differently and was on the verge of firing her.

Cheryl's boss may have been more accommodating and understanding if she had known about the rape. She might have moved Cheryl to a position without direct public contact. Cheryl didn't even take any time off work after the rape. She worked the next evening, though her adjustment may have been easier had she not done so. It may be helpful to take some time off, perhaps to take sick leave. However, you will need to provide some explanation in order to do so. Survivors in school who have told their instructors about the rape have been able to delay exams for which they were not prepared or able to study. Some even decided to take incompletes and finish up much later rather than chance a lower grade that could affect them for years to come.

Some survivors who live at home will report to the police but then ask them not to tell their parents. They may fear anger, blame, or new restrictions on their activities. Unfortunately, this is seldom a realistic expectation. In order to investigate the crime, at some point the police will need to speak with the parents. If you are in this situation, you may want to consider your parents in the need-to-know group and get help to deal with any negative response.

People You Want to Know

There are also people you will decide to tell, because these are the people on whom you rely for support and understanding during good times and bad. They are the sounding boards for your anger and the people who help you make order out of chaos. You trust them to accept you and be there for you.

Members of the clergy are often the first people to whom families will turn for help. They are familiar people and can be trusted to maintain confidentiality. They usually don't judge you. Fortunately, usually they also do not attempt to deal in isolation with all the issues brought to their attention. Rather they act as an entry point into the larger community support network. This was the case with Carol and her family. Their minister recognized the need for immediate medical, legal, and emotional support for the family, and with his reassurance, the decision was made to call the police and a rape crisis center.

It may be that with this crisis you will rely on people in addition to or other than your usual support system. Your best friend, your mother, your husband—the people who usually provide support for you during crises—may be so upset by the rape that they are unable

to help you. Some survivors even find themselves with the extra difficulty of needing to allay the anger, fear, and anxiety of those closest
to them. They must become caretakers of their "support system."

A coworker, with less emotional attachment to you than a friend
or relative, may be in a better position to provide objective support
without experiencing all the terror herself. She may be better able to
maintain the emotional distance necessary to help you through the
crisis.

The need to talk with someone who can maintain the objectivity
offered by this emotional distance is one reason survivors decide to
talk with counselors. You may find a support group helpful too. Many
rape crisis centers offer these on an ongoing basis. You need to tell
someone who can care, without becoming part of your pain.

When to Tell

Unlike the police and medical personnel, other people will not necessarily need to know immediately. When to tell may be a function
of external factors. You may decide to tell some people before your
case goes to court, because you want them to hear it from you, rather
than finding out from someone else first. If a big family event is
scheduled, you may decide not to tell anyone until after the event, to
avoid curiosity. On the other hand, you may want people to know
so they can understand if you act differently, or so they can be supportive. These are decisions only you can make. They should be based
on your own needs and desires.

Nancy knew her parents would become overprotective and want
her to move back home. She wanted to stay in her apartment.
This was her first time living alone. She knew she was still on
shaky ground and it would be too easy to become dependent
on her parents once again. She decided she would need to resolve
some of her fears before telling them. She knew it would be
hard for her mother not being the first to know, but she decided
to wait anyway.

How to Tell

Charlene called her parents in another state. She knew they would be worried, so she prefaced the statement with "Mom, I want you to know I'm all right now. I'm home, I wasn't badly hurt, and there are people here with me to help me. But I also want you to know my apartment was broken into. I was assaulted. I was raped."

Charlene knew it would be easier for her mother if she gave her some reassurance that she had survived without serious physical injury. The reassurance that she was safe now and had help made it easier for her mother to deal with the fact that she had been raped.

It is important to give those people you tell as much information as you can about what is going well. People often automatically anticipate the worst. If they are not with you, as Charlene's parents were not, it is more difficult for them. Charlene was wise to tell them she was okay before she told them she had been raped, because they didn't really "hear" what she told them afterward. They called her the next day, when the shock had subsided, and asked her to repeat much of the conversation.

You may pick a "good time" to tell, or there may never be a "good time." You may be glad you told some people, or you may wonder why you even considered telling them. The process may go smoothly, or it may be awkward and uncomfortable, not at all as you planned or anticipated. You cannot know these results ahead of time, but you can be prepared for various possibilities. Most important, you need to feel comfortable with having done what you felt was right. If they don't understand, it's their problem. Don't let it become yours.

TO THE SIGNIFICANT OTHER

Not every rape survivor feels comfortable telling other people about the assault and seeking help. You too may be uncomfortable about her telling other people. The largest single reason women give for not reporting incidents of sexual assault is pressure from other family members not to tell anyone. However, comfort, acceptance, and understanding from the people with whom she interacts are the heart of her social support.

In a 1981 study conducted in San Francisco, California, Renee Binder found that the primary reason adult women gave for not reporting rapes as children was social pressure from friends and family. More than one-third of the women said they did not report because "my parents did not want me to report." Since 89 percent of women sexually assaulted as children did not report the incident when it happened, family pressure not to tell is indeed significant. Sometimes the survivors wanted to tell, and at times they too were uncomfortable, or uncertain about telling. The incident then became a family secret, a secret with tremendous power, to be covered up and hidden. It's also possible she hasn't told you. If so, what do you do? What can you say?

What If She Didn't Tell You?

You may have heard about the rape from someone other than the survivor. Perhaps she doesn't want you to know, or she just hasn't been able to tell you yet. But now you know, so now what do you do?

If the rape is general information, she knows that. In this case, it is probably best to acknowledge that it is general information. If everyone is talking about the rape, it's best to talk with her rather than about her. She probably can use the support. Don't be afraid to bring it up. If she doesn't want to talk about it, she need not do so. However, if she would like to talk about the rape but doesn't know how to bring it up, this gives her the opportunity. A good opener is a simple statement like "I heard you were raped. I feel really bad, and I was wondering how you are doing now." She's free to say nothing more than "Fine, thanks," or to go into greater detail.

If someone close to her told you and made you promise not to tell, then you have a special problem. While it's best to avoid making such promises, of course, you may need to weigh the importance of breaking the confidence against the importance of talking with the survivor about the incident. Your decision to talk with her about the rape will depend on other factors in your relationship and her circumstances. If she has had the opportunity to tell you but has not done so, and if she has an adequate support system, you may want to forget about the incident unless she decides to bring it up.

You may make it easier for her to mention by being more sensitive to her moods and openly recognizing any change. Statements like "You seem nervous. Is there something bothering you?" may make it easier for her to tell you what is on her mind. Be careful not to push. It's important that she choose when and with whom she wants to talk.

You may be angry and hurt that she didn't tell you. Recognize, however, that her not telling you doesn't mean that she doesn't like you or trust you or need and want your support. She may be trying to protect you from the terrors she went through, which now seem too horrible even to talk about. It may be that your acceptance of her is so important, so crucial to her, that she is unwilling to risk the possibility of your rejecting her or blaming her. Perhaps she does not want you to be worried or to fear for her or yourself. It is also possible that she just can't ask for what she needs yet, especially if she is depressed. Just keep letting her know that you are and still will be there when she is ready to talk.

You don't know why she didn't tell you or hasn't told you yet. You can only guess. Perhaps she assumes you know and you don't want to talk about it. I have had many survivors tell me, "I know he knows, because my best friend told me she told him. I don't understand why he doesn't bring it up." She has enough stress to deal with now. Your anger at her or withdrawal from her will only add to that stress. If the secret she is keeping is affecting your relationship—and it may well be—then by all means bring it up. Talk about what is going on. Both of you probably will feel much better.

What Will Other People Think?

People May Treat Her Differently

One of the reasons you also may not want anyone to know is a fear that if others know, they will treat her differently. You may fear others will see her in all the stereotypic ways as devalued, tainted, or used. You may want to protect her from exposure to any or all of the myths and biases associated with rape.

It also sometimes can be hard to deal with other people who are always around wanting to help when you want to relax and be alone. Your privacy is important, and you have a right to protect and insist on it. Their need to do something could take power from her and make it more difficult for her to regain her independence and sense of control. This oversolicitousness can make you feel indebted. If you have insufficient opportunity or resources to reciprocate, you may feel uncomfortable and reject help that is offered even when you too could use additional support.

Although not wanting others involved is certainly a personal decision, it is important to evaluate your reasons for your attitude. If it is due to a fear of indebtedness that you won't be able to reciprocate, evaluate your concern. Perhaps you don't have to refuse the help offered, although you may want to share your concerns with these people. Being able to help someone in a crisis is rewarding in and of itself. Friends may benefit as much from giving help and support as you do in receiving it. At times it is best to accept help graciously without feeling any obligation in return.

Neighbors May Be Afraid

In many neighborhoods, especially the quiet suburbs or university campuses, people attempt to project an image of safety and security onto the neighborhood. Many people choose to live in these areas specifically because of that image. They may not want to know that rape occurs in their safe, secure quiet refuge, and you may not want to upset or frighten them.

But by keeping quiet, are you really doing them a favor? Perhaps not. If they are willing to hear and accept the reality, they may be more careful and less likely to become victims themselves. If multiple assaults have occurred in your area, it is even more important that people know so they can be more cautious.

People May Blame You

If you are hesitant for others to know because you are afraid they will blame you for not having protected her and prevented the rape, you are feeling unrealistic guilt. In some way you feel responsible because you weren't with her, were out of town, didn't lock the door when you left that morning, et cetera. You need to resolve these feelings, not cover up the rape.

Other people may blame you for the same reasons they may blame the survivor: They believe the myths and they want to maintain their illusion of invulnerability. They want to believe their wife or child will be safe because, unlike you, they will be there to protect them. No matter how unreasonable such blame may be, it can hurt. If you have come to terms with any guilt you might feel, you will deal with these insinuations much better. Don't place other opinions above what you know to be true.

Remember, rape is, unfortunately, different from many other crises. Robbery victims don't fear they will be blamed. Car accident victims don't worry about having their character questioned. It is harder to tell other people about something as devastating as rape. There are, however, circumstances that make openness safer, although no one can guarantee what people's responses will be.

Conditions That Encourage Openness

By revealing your feelings and fears to another person, you become much more vulnerable to disapproval and rejection. Therefore, you must begin by letting the survivor know she can trust you. If you accept what she has told you without judging her, no matter how poor you feel her judgment may have been, she will be more open with you in the future. You may not like what she did, because in some way it may have made her more vulnerable and thus led to the rape. But it is important to tell her that whatever she did or didn't do, you still have the same acceptance of her and high regard for her.

Maintain a reciprocal relationship. If there are things she can do for you, she may feel more comfortable asking you to do things for her. Another important dimension of any relationship is the balance maintained by each person between dependence and independence. When one person becomes overly dependent on another, losing the sense of independence, an insecure attachment develops. This is a result of the dependent person's feelings of anxiety and apprehension that should the relationship end, he or she would be unable to cope. The natural desire for closeness with the other person is thus accompanied by an intense insecurity and fear of losing that person. This dependence and exaggerated need may threaten the relationship.

When one person experiences anxiety resulting from insecurity, the other person is likely to withdraw from the relationship. The dependent person may then hold on even tighter, becoming more dependent. As the dependency grows, it becomes more and more of a burden. Disaster—the termination of the relationship—often results when the dependency reaches that point. To maintain a healthy relationship, we must each maintain our own sense of separateness, our own sense of responsibility for solutions to our problems and of control over our lives.

6

The First Anniversary and Beyond

Only those who dare truly live.
—Ruth P. Freedman, *Each Day a New Beginning*

TO THE SURVIVOR

Anniversary dates are extremely important in our culture. While we all recognize and celebrate birthdays and wedding anniversaries, we often attempt to discount the importance of the anniversary date of traumatic events. However, these anniversary dates have been found to have a significant impact on people's behavior and emotional well-being, often reawakening concerns they thought they had put to rest.

As the Anniversary Approaches

Many survivors, even those who have resolved effectively most of the trauma from the rape, will reexperience symptoms as the anniversary approaches. Often your symptoms may be so vague or mild that while they are uncomfortable, you may not recognize them as related to the rape. They are easier to ignore and try to live with. For instance, if you were raped in the wintertime, when the first snow falls you may find that you become sad or even depressed, but simply attribute it to the ending of summer, even though you never experienced a similar mood change when summer was over. If you were raped near Easter, not only the coming of spring weather but holiday decorations and celebrations may elicit a generalized anxiety and a sense of fear and foreboding you didn't feel in the past. You may even avoid going out alone, or fear for the safety of your loved ones, perhaps become somewhat overprotective of your children, restricting their activities.

Much as you did initially, it is important to recognize that you are responding to the many rape-related cues—the weather, holiday decorations, the approach of the anniversary. These are not new, real dangers but rather unrealistic fears stimulated by things that are reminding you of the rape. This is a normal response and in most cases will pass. Often just recognizing what is causing the renewed fears will give you control over them and reduce them to a manageable level. You may want to utilize once again some of the techniques that helped you resolve your initial trauma. If you saw a counselor but stopped, this is a good time to return for one or two visits.

When You Are Not "Over It"

The way you feel on or around the anniversary of the rape depends on how completely you have recovered from the assault, emotionally and physically. Some survivors may not yet have readjusted by the end of the first year. For instance, they may not be able to enjoy sexual intercourse yet, or they may still be afraid to go out alone at night. They continue to experience considerable pain and anguish, which is magnified by the arrival of the anniversary, making it an especially traumatic time.

Many of these women resort to heavy drug or alcohol use as a means of escape, or try to sleep the anniversary date away. Sometimes thoughts of death surface; survivors may say things like "I wish he had killed me. It would be so much easier." Thoughts of suicide may become intense as the anniversary approaches and especially on the anniversary date. If this happens to you, spend time with a trusted friend and talk about your feelings. Don't stay alone. If you feel you may act on suicidal feelings, seek professional help.

Anger that has been tolerable can turn to rage. While often directed toward men in general, homicidal thoughts toward the rapist may be experienced once again. As long as you don't act on these feelings, they are healthy, but do find an outlet for them, such as golf, racquetball, boxing, or jogging. Write a letter to the rapist telling him how you feel, or to the county attorney or judge, then throw it away. Throw darts at a drawing of the rapist, or go to a firing range and use his picture as a target. Anger turned inward can result in severe depression that lasts several weeks around the anniversary date.

If a year has passed and you are still unable to face the events of the assault, you may want to find a counselor or therapist, if you have not already done so. If you have been working with a therapist ever since the rape but are still having problems readjusting, don't worry. Many women need more than a year to recover emotionally. Just keep working on your areas of concern and eventually they will be resolved.

When You Have Essentially Recovered

Unlike those who have not recovered, if you have essentially resolved the crisis you may spend considerable time thinking about "the day." On the anniversary, instead of avoiding thoughts of the assault, you may go to great lengths to face the events of the rape, reviewing and reliving the day, hour by hour, watching the clock carefully. Many survivors return to the scene of the crime, this time in control. One woman who was raped in her basement spent much of the anniversary day there "putzing around, being in that space." Another woman used a lamp in her home that the rapist had turned on—a lamp she seldom used before or since the rape.

Reviewing the changes you have made and the problems you have overcome makes you more acutely aware of your progress. Sit down and make a list so you really can see what you have done and the progress you have made. Feel good about the inner strength you found and developed—strengths you didn't know you had. It's important to acknowledge and feel good about yourself and your development. Although it was a painful experience, you survived—an entire year has passed. You can turn your back on that chapter of your life.

Do something special in recognition of the anniversary. One woman called and registered for a self-defense course on the anniversary date. Another quit a job that had been unsatisfying. She had survived a whole year and was ready to move onward and face new challenges. Others spend the day with friends engaged in favorite activities.

Survivors Who Don't Remember the Anniversary

Not every survivor will take notice of the anniversary date. You may have spent the whole year trying not to think about the rape, putting it aside. Perhaps you don't remember the exact date.

Even if you do not take particular notice of the exact date the assault occurred, around that time of year you too could feel anxious and not know why. If you were raped in the winter, you are especially likely to not know why you feel the strange anxiety or renewed fear when the first snow falls. If you were raped in the summer, when it's warm again and you are outside without your coat, you might be ill at ease, having no clue as to why. The resulting anxiety is seldom of the intensity you experienced immediately following the rape. It is more likely to be a general sense of discomfort, with the expectation of some unidentified danger lurking around the corner.

You may not relate changes in your behavior on or around the anniversary to the assault. Increased sexual activity, such as one-night stands, in otherwise monogamous or sexually inactive women is not uncommon. One survivor recalled, "It was so unlike me. I started going out to bars and going home with men I met. I don't know why I did it. I slept with six different men in two weeks, more men than I'd slept with in the previous two years." For some women this is an attempt to regain or maintain a sense of control over their sexuality. For other women it is an attempt to discount the importance of any one sexual contact . . . and of the rape. If you find yourself uncharacteristically behaving this way, make sure to evaluate your behavior to ensure you are really meeting your needs and not just rebelling against social convention.

Things That Facilitate or Delay Recovery

Reviewing the preceding year and noting the things that you or others have done that helped or delayed your recovery is beneficial. Doing so may enable you to direct your energy more effectively in the year to come.

The efforts of supportive friends, both male and female, will probably head your list. These people were willing to listen, seemed to understand, and helped you sort out your feelings. However, you may have found that your friends and family seemed so proud of how "strong" you were that it was difficult for you to express the pain you actually were feeling. They may have needed you to be strong because they were unable or unwilling to face your pain. Although being strong—being able to cope with daily life—has its place, to recover fully you need to recognize and deal with the pain. That's not being weak, it's being realistic and smart. Remember, no one can feel "good" all the time, no matter how well she handles the stress of everyday living.

You made the greatest progress when you decided to address your problems directly and took back control of your life. The changes you made in your job—where you live, who your friends are, and the activities you participate in—made you feel safer and removed unpleasant memories. These were steps you took to facilitate your recovery. Keeping busy with friends, hobbies, clubs, or counseling also may have helped.

When you stopped accepting the blame, you took an important step toward recovery. At the very least, you realized that you don't need to waste energy deciding where to place the blame for something that happened in the past. The task now is to put your life back in order, and take control of your feelings about the rape today and of the things you do or do not do today.

Survivors report that the most difficult event they face during the first year is having the assailant go to trial and be found not guilty. It's bad enough when he's not caught or not charged, but having to go through the experience of court only to see him set free can be devastating. While many survivors express some satisfaction in having at least had the chance to tell their side of the story, they still find an acquittal difficult to deal with.

You must remember, no matter what happens to the rapist, you survived the rape, and now you have survived another year. Give yourself credit for your progress even if you have not yet completed your journey.

The Special Fears

Many survivors are still afraid to go out alone a year after the assault, and some for years after that.

There was a beautiful path through the trees down to the lake, but since the rape, each time Edith had gotten to the edge of the path her overwhelming fears had stopped her. She changed her route to a much less pleasant, longer, busier road. One evening she and her boyfriend decided to take the more scenic path again. As they approached the dark wooded area, Edith felt the fear and anxiety begin to rise as usual. Her muscles tensed, she started looking around her, and her breathing be- came more shallow and rapid. She noticed that her boyfriend, six feet four inches tall and muscular, continued walking, ob- livious to what she was experiencing. Fear of a dark quiet area was not even part of his world. It did not need to be. Her fear turned to anger at the inequity. He, by virtue of his size and strength, was in control of his world. She was not in control of hers.

Special fears that remain for years are most often associated with the circumstances surrounding the rape. Many survivors express panic when someone walks up behind them. Others continue to be afraid when home alone, especially at night. One survivor who was raped by a man she invited into her apartment became tense and afraid more than a year later whenever her roommate brought a man home.

Many women are embarrassed to admit their fears to family or friends, feeling that "It's been so long. I should be over it by now." Unfortunately, fear has no time limit. That does not mean, however, that you must continue to live in fear. If you have not yet tried the techniques in chapter 4, you may want to do so now. If you've tried to deal with the fears yourself and they have remained, you may want to seek professional help.

Safety

Concerns about safety continue for years after an assault or attempted assault. Many women report that they are just more careful now, because it makes sense to be more careful. They now keep their house and car doors locked, even when inside, and are more aware of what is going on around them. Some carry Mace or whistles, and some take self-defense classes. They no longer trust strangers or accept rides from acquaintances they have met recently, nor do they offer rides to people they do not know well. As Rita said, "I'm more careful when I'm out, and more selective about who my friends are now. I don't trust just anyone. I guess I'm less naive." She had learned to be careful, because rape can happen to anyone, anytime.

Rather than decide to distrust everyone, however, it is important to be more selective about whom you trust. Otherwise you may close yourself off unnecessarily from interesting, sincere people whom you really can trust and with whom you would enjoy spending time. Learn to be less vulnerable without building a wide wall around yourself. Don't become afraid to trust again. That's not recovery.

Talk to your children about your concerns and about the risks they may or may not want to take, but let them maintain control and make their own choices based on the information you have provided. The best you can do for your children is to help them learn to think for themselves and be responsible for their own choices.

Years to Come

While the first anniversary is the most difficult, it is normal to experience anniversary concerns for many years to come. Each will be less severe, and with each year you will have more successes on which to focus. Use each anniversary as a time once again to evaluate your present situation, recognize your successes, and plan your strategies for the future.

Changes for the Better

While rape itself is never a positive encounter, nearly half of all survivors report experiencing some beneficial results from what happened after the incident. This does not mean that the impact was not initially disruptive, traumatic, and painful. It means, rather, that they were able to mobilize their resources, overcome the turmoil, and constructively rebuild their lives.

At the end of the first year following her rape, one survivor described the assault as "a door open to set me free." She has made many positive changes in her life since the assault, including deciding she no longer needed to conform to the expectations of others but rather had the right to decide for herself what was right for her. She terminated an abusive relationship, quit a job she had never liked, and started an eighteen-month course at a trade school. She and many other survivors report feeling stronger and more self-reliant, serious, introspective, and thoughtful than ever before. They have learned to trust and rely upon themselves, often for the first time.

Some women deal with past sexual or physical abuse issues that were unresolved and had been affecting their lives for years. This rape was the impetus to change. Other survivors who had been denying the extent of personal drug or alcohol problems for years were able to stop as a result of the changes in their lives that followed the assaults. In most of these cases professional assistance was necessary.

The assaults were the catalysts they needed to recognize the toll drugs, alcohol, or past psychic trauma were having on their lives and that they needed help resolving.

By recognizing each individual step toward recovery that they had taken successfully, these survivors gained the strength and confidence to risk more, try more, and take the next step toward attaining success they had not believed possible. They had, one step at a time, put the rape in the past and taken control back from the rapist. They had learned to live in the present and make constructive plans for the future.

TO THE SIGNIFICANT OTHER

Your Anniversary Concerns

You may or may not be aware of the change in the rape survivor's behavior as the anniversary of the rape approaches. If you do note any change, don't be afraid to mention it to her, but avoid sounding critical or judgmental when you do so. Instead, tell her what you observe to be different. You may simply say, "You seem to be staying home more and you look sadder to me lately. Is something bothering you? Could it be that it's almost a year since you were attacked?" She may be concerned but feel uncomfortable bringing it up again. This gives her an opening to talk about any anniversary concerns that exist. Perhaps she noted a difference in her behavior but did not connect it with the assault.

It is important not to assume that your evaluation is accurate. Ask, don't tell. Although she may act differently, something other than the assault may be the cause. If so, talk to her about these other concerns at this time.

If she still has not resolved the trauma but continues to be very angry and upset, she probably will avoid your attempts to discuss the rape. Her energy will be directed at avoiding the issue and escaping her memories of the assault. If she becomes more angry and depressed as the day approaches, don't take her anger personally. You may become the target, but remember that the rapist is the cause of her anger. Remind her that you're on her side. "You seem angry. I don't want to make things more difficult for you. I'd like to help. Do you want to talk about what's bothering you, maybe the rape?" If she doesn't, she'll let you know. Respect her decision.

If she still isn't ready to review the rape, don't try to force her. Let her know that you care about her and would like to see her get the help she deserves, that she does not need to continue living with the pain. Tell her that, if she would like, you will help her contact a counselor who knows about rape.

Even though she may not have completely resolved all her fears and anxieties, you should recognize the progress she has made in the past year. This is a good time to tell her the things you think she has done well and how good you feel about her having found the strength to do them. Some survivors, usually those who have completed a large part of the resolution process, want to take some time on the anniversary to review the experience and the progress they have made. Your friend may want to do this alone, or she may find it helpful to do this with you and get your input on the changes she had made as well. She may want to keep busy and distracted, or she may prefer not to recognize the day in a special way. Ask her what she would like to do on the anniversary day. Once again, it's important to respect her wishes. Only she knows what will make the passage of the day easiest or most beneficial for her.

This is also a good time for you to evaluate the changes that have occurred in the past year. Consider the ways your relationship has grown, the ways it is stronger. Are there things you know about yourself or about her now that you did not know before? Do you feel different about yourself or about her now from the way you felt last year? What have you learned?

This is also a good time to consider your goals for the year to come, both together and individually. If she is not ready to review the past year and you are, by all means do so on your own. What else would you like to change? How would you like to do things differently? How would you go about making these changes?

You too have survived the rape and the year that followed. You too have discovered strengths in yourself and in her of which you were not previously aware. Share these discoveries with her. You have come a long way, even if the crisis has not been resolved entirely. You are continually changing and growing. It's important to take the time to recognize, evaluate, and appreciate your progress, whatever its magnitude.

Is She Really "Over It?"

Surviving rape is a long-term process. While a few women will continue to be dysfunctional years after the assault, and a few will recover "completely" without emotional scars remaining from the trauma, by far the majority will return once again to their daily routines, and for the most part they will successfully integrate the experience into their lives. They will adjust. However, one or two problems are likely to remain—fears, concerns, or instances of maladaptive coping, unnoticed by most people with whom they come into contact.

You may or may not be aware of these fears and anxieties. You too may continue to have fears and concerns that have not been resolved after the first year. As the years pass, the maladaptive patterns of coping will become more deeply imbedded and more difficult to resolve. How can you know if the survivor has really recovered? If she hasn't, what can you do to help? How can you tell if *you* are "over it"?

Sit down together and write out the things in your life and her life that are different, then evaluate each as positive or negative. You may want to consider desired future changes now as well. For instance, if you've been spending all your time together, you may decide now is the time to set some limits on this, diversify your interests, and both of you develop new friends. If she quit working or took a job with less responsibility and stress, perhaps she is ready to look for something more challenging again. If she stopped any or all extra activities because of her fears, perhaps it's time to consider resuming them. Maybe you want to do this together. If you don't miss the old activities, there is no reason to resume the same type of participation, but it may be time to choose new activities.

Some special fears, anxieties, and concerns may bother you more than they do her. As long as she feels comfortable with the situation, she will have no motivation to change. It is important to let her know how you feel. Maybe she isn't aware of the danger you see or of how she directly affects you. If you can talk about it, you may be able to reach a decision on how better to deal with these issues. Before she develops a more appropriate long-term solution, you may need to stop meeting her needs. You may decide to seek a counselor's help in resolving the more difficult issues or areas about which you cannot agree.

She still may be constantly sad, having lost interest in life and not seeming to enjoy the things she does or the things you do together. This lack of interest and enjoyment in life is most likely the result of a chronic low level of depression. It may get much worse at times. Depression is infectious. Being around someone who is depressed can make you feel blue too, as well as helpless to do anything for her. After a while a common reaction is to avoid being with her. Before it gets to that point, preferably as soon as you recognize what is happening, talk with her about the situation. Try to figure out how you both can feel better.

Remember that while she may look fine on the outside and may have returned to her usual routine, if she still harbors fears and concerns, she is not functioning at her optimum level of ability. Before deciding on your course of action, be sure to evaluate the reality of your concerns in relation to your newfound sense of vulnerability. If either of you is in doubt about how adequately you have resolved your feelings, talk with a competent counselor. Get an unbiased opinion.

What If She Won't Get Help?

What are your options if she is still having difficulty coping with her life but refuses to seek help? If you are sexually involved, but she is there "in body only," what can you do? What can you do if you are roommates and she won't allow you to bring home men whom she does not know, or gets angry and upset when you do? If you're her parent and she's moved back home, afraid to live on her own, what can you do?

Being aware of your own feelings is the first step. It's easy to blame your feelings of discomfort on the survivor or, conversely, to accept her bad feelings as your own. So be certain of the origin of any conflict between the two of you. The next step is letting her know how her behavior or feelings affect you. It is important to have your own boundaries and to communicate these boundaries clearly and respectfully, without sounding judgmental or rejecting. You have a right to be concerned. You have a right to set a specific time limit on how long she can live with you, for instance. Tell her what behaviors you find infringe on your freedom and comfort, and discuss how you would like to see the situation change. She is probably dissatisfied as well, but does not see or believe that change is possible.

Encourage her to seek help. Give her a list of resources, with names and phone numbers. Offer to go with her to see a counselor. If she's hesitant to get help, explore the reasons with her one by one. Did she have a bad experience with a counselor in the past? Perhaps you know someone who had a good experience she can talk to, or perhaps she just needs to give herself another chance. Is she afraid or unwilling to face the problem?

If she won't get help and the problem is interfering with your life, consider doing things differently yourself. See a counselor to help you deal with your feelings. If you cannot change the situation, you may need to remove yourself from the relationship. Let her know that you are considering doing this, and let her know why. It could serve as an impetus for her to get help, since she will now see how serious you are about her need for help.

If you are a parent and believe it inappropriate for her to continue living with you, ask her to find her own place. You have a right to live your life as you wish, and she has the responsibility for hers. Asking her to move may be the best thing you could possibly do to help her recover. Her continued dependence beyond the crisis, and especially beyond the first year, is indicative of other problems. Family counseling would probably benefit you all.

While it's important to honor our commitments and help other people, especially those we love, it also is important to evaluate the assistance we offer and keep the commitment at a level that we can handle. You must decide when you are no longer willing to forgo your own needs and desires by adapting your life to her unresolved fears. Decide at what point doing so is no longer really helping her anyway, but rather allowing her to avoid facing her problems and making real change. When the situation reaches this point, by not taking action you are contributing to the problem. Remember, enabling destructive behavior to continue is not helpful in the long run. Doing so makes change more difficult later on; it may even destroy your relationship.

7

Overcoming the Trauma of a Childhood Sexual Assault

*. . . There is nothing in man or nature which would
prevent us from taking some control of our destiny
and making the world a saner place for our children.*

—ERNEST BECKER, *Escape from Evil*

TO THE SURVIVOR

If you were sexually abused as a child, this experience probably has
affected the way you view men, sex, and your own sexuality, especially
if you have never discussed the assault with anyone. It is never too
late to talk about it and to get professional help in dealing with
whatever unresolved feelings may remain. For instance, it is not uncommon to resent your parents for not protecting you and preventing
the unbearable pain and torment. It is not uncommon to believe that
it was at least in part your fault, because that's what the offender told
you, and he was an adult authority figure, so it must be true. It is
not uncommon to feel too much shame to tell anyone.

Sexual abuse of children includes all sexual contact or stimulation inappropriate for the child's age and level of psychological development. It is sexual abuse if the contact occurs through the use of intimidation, misrepresentation, or force by an adult or older child. Sexual abuse also occurs if the offender offered the child gifts, such as candy or money, in exchange for sexual contact, and the child complies. The National Center for Child Abuse and Neglect estimates that more than 100,000 children are sexually abused each year. Estimates from other sources run as high as 500,000 per year. Since the mid-1970s, when we first began to talk more openly about child abuse, we have seen more than a 500 percent increase in reported cases. A 1990 national survey reported that 27 percent of all women were sexually abused as children, although other rates reported vary from 5.9 percent in a 1990 Durham, North Carolina, survey to 53 percent in a 1987 South Carolina survey. Unfortunately, due to the social taboo that surrounds incest and other sexual abuse of children and the continued secretive nature of the encounters, only a fraction of cases are reported even today.

Most children are *not* sexually abused by strangers enticing them with candy. They are abused by people they know and trust: family members, close family friends, baby-sitters, school-bus drivers, leaders of boys' and girls' group activities, and neighbors. While the majority of young girls report being molested by men, some are molested by adult women. More than half of the young boys who are sexually assaulted are victimized by women or older girls. Very often older children or teenagers, many of whom were sexual assault victims themselves, become child abusers.

Kim, two and a half years old, was brought to the hospital by her mother because the area around her clitoris was red and swollen, and itching. When questioned by the nurse, Kim initially said she couldn't tell what had happened. When pressured and assured that it was okay to tell, she told the nurse that Terry, an eleven-year-old neighbor, "puts his potty thing in my potty thing" when he baby-sits.

Jamie, five years old, told the nurse that a seven-year-old neighbor boy told her, "I'll beat you up if you don't make sex with me." He then proceeded to make her suck his penis.

Carl, five years old, told his mother that his sixteen-year-old baby-sitter "made me touch between her legs and put my pee pee there too." The baby-sitter had been sexually assaulted by a neighbor when she was five years old.

Children are sexually abused in all kinds of neighborhoods. The problem is not limited to certain ethnic or socioeconomic groups. Research indicates that approximately one-third of American women admit to having been sexually assaulted as children by adult men.

A 1983 study done in San Francisco found that 31 percent of almost 1,000 adult women had been sexually abused by a nonfamily adult male before they were eighteen years old (20 percent of these before their fourteenth birthday). When incest is included with sexual abuse by a nonfamily member, the figure jumps higher. And when encounters with exhibitionists also are included, well over half of the women reported being victimized as children, many of them more than once.

If as a young child you were the victim of a single incident of brief sexual contact, such as fondling, with no threats, no rewards, and no penetration, you may have experienced little or no significant trauma. If you were allowed to talk about the incident with a trusted adult who did not blame you, you may have put it aside quickly and resumed normal activity. The more hysterical your parents' or other adults' response was upon finding out, the more traumatic the experience probably was for you.

Incest or sexual assault by a trusted friend often is more devastating than sexual assault by a stranger. Not only is it more likely to involve an ongoing relationship in which the child must deal with feelings of being a helpless captive of the abuser, but additionally she must deal with the violation of her trust and love. If you were the victim of incest, while feeling helpless and vulnerable, you also may have liked the extra attention from the loved one who forced or coerced you into sexual relations, then swore you to secrecy. The result was probably confusion, ambivalence, and emotional turmoil. Long-term sexual abuse also is more traumatic because of the fear of doom or disaster should anyone find out what you were told to keep secret. That was a heavy responsibility to carry, perhaps for years.

It's difficult to feel good about yourself when you must carry such a terrible secret. Your self-esteem may have remained low as an adult, and your coping skills few. As a result you may have become easy prey for other men later in life who also chose to abuse you. You even may have found that you are attracted only to abusive men. This self-destructive behavior, the result of your low self-esteem or continued feelings of guilt, may make you feel deserving of continued punishment.

In more traumatic cases, the child's general psychosocial development stops at the age and developmental level at which she was abused. Even though these children continue to mature physically and intellectually, socially and sexually they may act and feel like little children. Long-term therapy may be necessary to overcome these effects.

Sexual dysfunction in later life is a frequent sequel to childhood sexual abuse. You may pick unaffectionate men in one unconscious attempt to limit your sexual involvement. Or you may gain excessive amounts of weight to make yourself unattractive. Sexual unresponsiveness is the most common result, feeling "sexually dead" and participating in sex but not having orgasms. In the most extreme cases, women avoid sex completely as a result of their fear of or abhorrence toward the act. Still other women, especially those who learned early on to accept rewards in exchange for sex, engage in prostitution. These women remain victims. They have learned to cope in a very self-destructive manner. As many as 80 percent of the hundreds of thousands of male and female prostitutes have reported they were sexually abused as children.

While anorexia nervosa has many causes, it too has been associated with previous ongoing sexual abuse. While a 1993 study disputes the link between eating disorders and sexual abuse, previous reports have found as many as 50 percent of anorexic or bulimic patients had a history of sexual abuse. This figure is indeed higher than all but the very highest general population estimates, as well as higher than the 28 percent in the study control group, indicating that there is indeed a relationship between sexual abuse and anorexia nervosa, even if we can't prove a causal link. Studies of the eating disorder population also have found that sexual abuse is associated with greater psychological disturbance. While it may not be the sole cause of their eating disorders, it is clear that sexual abuse is indeed a significant issue with this population.

At sixteen Jan was admitted to a hospital because of a significant weight loss due to anorexia nervosa. Her older sister, eighteen, was involved in prostitution. In the course of therapy it was discovered that both Jan and her sister were repeatedly abused by a hired hand on the family farm. Jan's anorexia began six months after the first incident of sexual abuse.

What If You Just Remembered?

As the years passed you may have effectively blocked all memories of the incident, not associating your chronic depression, anger, resentment, or continued vulnerability to victimization with the assault. Love, once used against you in a destructive fashion by a parent or trusted guardian, is confusing in the memories of a young child. Now, although you are uncertain why, you may mistrust or even fear any man who claims to love you.

It is quite common that a sexual assault as an adult will reawaken childhood memories of horror. You may first remember bits and pieces in your dreams, hoping against hope that they are just nightmares. However, remembering what happened is the first step in taking back control over the results of the abuse. It is the first step in recovering and not allowing the abuse you suffered as a child to continue to affect your life in ways you don't understand. If you believe you might be recalling past incidents of abuse, see a counselor experienced in dealing with sexual abuse. Don't continue to be afraid to face the memories. With the help of a counselor, you *can* overcome them.

What If You've Been Labeled "Crazy"?

Lindsey was raped by a family friend whom her father had asked to drive her home from a wedding. At thirteen, she was too young to stay late and enjoy the whole party. The trusted friend raped her on the way home. Two months later, when she discovered she was pregnant from the rape, she told her father. (Her mother had died the year before.) He swore her to secrecy about both the rape and the pregnancy. Not even her brothers or sister were to know. She was sent away before the pregnancy became apparent. Everyone was told she had had a mental breakdown as a result of her mother's death. Three days after her daughter's birth, she returned to her small town alone. Her classmates teased her mercilessly about being "psycho" and about her tremendous weight gain. She had become "different" and forever after would remain different. She could tell no one what had really happened, how she really felt.

The trauma didn't end with the birth of her child; Lindsey became an outcast at school and severely depressed as a result of everything that had happened. But she could tell no one. Her father finally sent her to the town doctor when she cut her wrist to avoid going to school. Once again she was sworn to secrecy by her father about the rape and the child, "or you'll really be an outcast."

She eventually married a man she didn't love, a man selected by her father. Although she harbored intense anger, she was not allowed to express it. Whenever she became angry, her husband called her psychiatrist and got her medication increased. When her anger became severe, she was hospitalized and drugged into sleep and submission. This pattern continued for over forty years, until she was raped as an adult.

When Lindsey began to talk about the most recent rape, the floodgates opened and the story of her abuse as a child poured forth. By now she too had come to believe that she was "crazy." While she had certainly been extremely angry and depressed, and had good reason to be so, a review of her records for all those years showed she had never been "crazy." This news relieved her greatly, and she felt new power and strength. She was in control of her life for the first time in over forty years. While she grieved the loss of all those years, she knew she had been a victim long enough. Now she was becoming a survivor.

Symptoms of sexual abuse that are no longer associated with the incident still result in women being hospitalized and given inappropriate psychiatric diagnosis much too often. In the past the preferred term was hysteria; today it is more often personality disorder. Often the therapist never asks about past sexual abuse; at other times the woman has blocked the memories. I am always amazed when women tell me about the years of therapy they received, when they clearly remembered being abused, but it was never discussed as a therapeutic issue. Some women brought the abuse up, only to have the therapist change the subject, due to his discomfort with the issue. As therapists become better trained these days, I hope that this problem of avoidance will diminish. If you are seeing a counselor and have been abused in the past yet have not discussed the abuse with him or her, bring the issue up. If the therapist refuses to discuss the abuse with you, find another one who will.

Clinicians working with dissociative disorders, including multiple personality disorders, have found that over 80 percent of their patients report childhood sexual abuse. In an attempt to escape the ongoing trauma, it seems likely that these children learn to divorce themselves from their own abused body and personality. Developing multiple personalities is an adaptive measure that allows individuals to separate from the part of themselves that is being abused and that they are unable to face. The new personality is amnesic to the abuse, totally unaware that it is occurring or has occurred in the past. Severe emotional distress often precipitates this dissociation. Multiple personality disorder, which is difficult to diagnose due to the subtle nature of many of the symptoms, may go unrecognized. Generally the original personality, amnesic to the abuse, is rather reserved and mild, and a secondary personality, aware of the abuse, will express the anger and pain. Childhood sexual abuse was not widely recognized as a precipitant of multiple personality disorder until the 1973 publication of *Sybil*. In the book, the author, a psychologist, discusses his work with a young woman who had developed multiple personalities after being abused as a child. While rare, it is important that the condition be diagnosed early in order to be treated properly.

It is important that you resolve feelings stemming from sexual abuse as a child. Now, as you cope with a recent sexual assault, is an ideal time to do so. Information in chapter 3 and chapter 6 will be helpful for you to review.

TO THE SIGNIFICANT OTHER

Our children are vulnerable to abuse by adults. There is a wide discrepancy between the power of a small child and that of an adult, often an authority figure, someone the child has been taught to respect and obey. It's not surprising that this power, control, and status can be used so easily to exploit a child. However, it is often hard to imagine why someone would do so. This disbelief, unfortunately, contributes to the safety of the abuser and thus makes the child more vulnerable.

Long-term effects will vary with the child's age at the time of the incident, her relationship to the offender, the number and types of contact, the reaction of a nonabusive parent or other adult to disclosure, and treatment received. The first step in dealing with sexual abuse of children is learning to recognize symptoms and clues.

Clues to the Sexual Abuse of Children

While some children immediately will tell one of their parents or a trusted friend about an incident of abuse, many more are so intimidated by the perpetrator or so confused by the complexity of their feelings that they keep the event a secret. They usually blame themselves and fear discovery and punishment almost as much as they feared the assault. Children who are sexually abused typically will not fully learn the developmental tasks they would otherwise learn during the period when the abuse occurs. Sexual abuse reduces children's feelings of self-worth, often resulting in self-degradation and difficulty in accepting themselves. The children also lose a sense of their own competence, as the assault comes from a powerful force outside herself. They are not in control. This feeling of powerlessness produced by sexual abuse will extend into major areas of development. Abused children likely will avoid challenges with new learning potential. The abuse also slows development by "distracting" children from normal developmental tasks. Cognitive energy is taken away from achievement in normal developmental areas. The children's personal strengths, developed prior to the abuse, will provide defenses to the ravages of the trauma and can result in a wide range of individual differences in their response to abuse.

Infants

Unfortunately, no child is too young to be safe from sexual abuse. Infants less than one month old have been sexually abused by adult caretakers. The sexual abuse of infants is usually limited to manual genital manipulation and in some cases oral sex. Often it is discovered when the child develops a redness in the vaginal area or a vaginal infection, most often gonorrhea. Any vaginal discharge apparent in an infant should be brought to the attention of a physician immediately, and sexually transmitted disease testing should be completed.

Preschool Children

Sudden unexplained changes in behavior are important clues that something is different in a child's life. Don't ignore regression to a previous type of behavior once outgrown, such as clinging to a parent, thumb-sucking, or bed-wetting. Sometimes a child develops a sudden fear of men or of a particular person or avoids a particular place or activity. Any change in behavior should be explored with the child in a nonthreatening manner. It's important for your child to know that you notice these changes and that you want him or her to feel safer and better about whatever is happening. Tell your child that being touched anywhere or in any way that makes him or her feel uncomfortable is not okay. You want your child to tell you when and if these things occur so you can protect the child and ensure it does not happen again.

Other important clues to look for include symptoms of depression such as sleep disturbance, withdrawal, listlessness, loss of appetite, and sadness. Physical symptoms include any vaginal discharge, genital rash, itching or soreness and swelling around the clitoris in girls and a pussy discharge from the penis in boys. An unexplained inability to gain weight also may be indicative of prolonged sexual abuse.

It is important to remember that these physical and behavioral symptoms can have other origins as well. It is appropriate and important to question a child to determine the cause of any unexplained physical symptoms or behavior change.

Preschoolers are most often abused by caretakers, including trusted adults and older children. A child can be easily coerced, manipulated, or intimidated into cooperation with a person in a powerful position. It is unlikely, therefore, that there will be any signs of violence, because physical force is seldom necessary. Most often the sexual assault of preschool children is limited to genital manipulation. However, this is still extremely frightening and threatening to the child and may have a significant emotional impact on her or him.

While vaginal-penile penetration is involved occasionally, it is, fortunately, the exception. If extensive bleeding from vaginal tears results, surgical repair may be required. The presence of blood in urine or stool may indicate vaginal or anal penetration. In one exceptional case involving a five-year-old child, the abuser's accomplice, an older family friend, attempted to sew up a vaginal tear with needle and thread. The incident came to the child's mother's attention only after an abscess resulted, causing the child severe pain.

Preteens

Preteens, too, are most often abused by trusted family members and caretakers. Between the ages of six and twelve, children also are quite vulnerable to coercion, threats, intimidation, and bribes in exchange for sexual favors. As a result, physical force is again seldom necessary, and physical trauma is unlikely. However, vaginal penetration is more likely when the child is over ten years old. Since intercourse will likely cause vaginal tears and bleeding, any spotting of blood on a child's underwear should not be overlooked. The child should be questioned calmly and matter-of-factly.

Any symptoms that resemble those of a sexually transmitted disease, such as a vaginal discharge, should be investigated thoroughly. Other physical symptoms include skin rashes, gastric distress, hysterical convulsions, or seizures. High levels of anxiety can bring these symptoms on. Genito-urinary problems are also common signs of abuse and are the result of infections as well as the psychological distress focused in the genital area.

Regressive behavior and phobias toward people or places frequently occur in cases of abuse and should not be taken lightly as "growing pains." The child may fear men and cling to the mother, or become precociously seductive toward men and reject her mother, whom she now sees as sexual competition for their favors. She may become overly busy, attempting to fill every moment in order to block out thoughts of the assault. Truancy often results, as the child attempts to hide from her peers, whom she feels "know" the atrocities she has endured. These extreme or unusual behaviors, in addition to the child's inability to concentrate, impair schoolwork and may cause grades to drop abruptly.

Teenagers

Sexual exploitation of the teenager is in many cases the most devastating. Teens are most often sexually abused by strangers or trusted adults, such as schoolteachers, members of the clergy, or neighbors who gain their confidence. While they may be abused by a family member, this usually begins earlier, most often at eight years of age. The teenage years, when children's self-image changes, are difficult enough without the added trauma of sexual abuse. The self-doubt, self-blame, guilt, and feelings of worthlessness that often result from sexual abuse can crush an already fragile ego.

An abused teen may go as far as to tell you about a friend who is being sexually abused when it is really herself. Or she may ask you, "What would you do if someone told you her father...?" She also may withdraw suddenly from any form of physical touch, even from you. While this may be a normal developmental striving for more independence, especially in the younger teen, it also could be a clue to abuse.

Severe depression with sleep disturbance, eating problems, and nightmares often develops. Social withdrawal, truancy, and even running away from home are not uncommon. The fewer friends the survivor has, the easier it is to keep the secret and hide her feelings of separateness. Drugs and alcohol, often readily available to teenagers, become a form of escapism.

Since adolescence is a crucial time of psychosexual development, it is likely that the survivor's attitude toward sex will be affected. While she may fear and avoid men, as younger children often do, the teenager also may become more curious about sex and even sexually promiscuous in the months and years to come.

Unfortunately, when the sexual assault is not disclosed, all too often the teenager is labeled a behavior problem, a "bad girl," and further blamed and shamed for her behavior. If she discloses the assault later, often her credibility is questioned and she may not be believed.

What to Do If You Suspect Sexual Abuse

Children are often naive, trusting, and gullible enough to believe the most absurd ploys their assailants use to keep them silent. An eleven-year-old child was afraid to tell about her ongoing sexual abuse by a seventeen-year-old friend of her brother's because he had told her he would be electrocuted if she told anyone. An eight-year-old girl remained silent because an older neighbor told her he would kill his ailing wife, who was confined to a wheelchair, if she told anyone. A twelve-year-old girl allowed a close family friend to give her weekly rubdowns "to release the tension, so you won't get pregnant like your older sister." When he began to rub her crotch more often and to have oral sex with her, she finally became uncomfortable enough to tell her mother.

These children were made to feel responsible for someone else's safety. In cases of incest, many sexually abused children also feel responsible for any family turmoil or breakup that occurs.

The eleven-year-old just described began to get severe headaches and stomachaches, and considerable tension developed between her and her mother. When she finally told what had happened, she expressed anger at her mother, whom she felt should have somehow known and protected her. Anger is a common response and often is the origin of tensions that build up following the assault. It is important that your child know you did not know what was happening, but now that you do you will protect her as best you can.

The child may want to tell but may be too afraid to do so. She may desperately want her mother or father to "know" or to ask, thus absolving her from the guilt and responsibility of telling. A parent may suspect that something is wrong but, hoping desperately that it is not true, be afraid to ask. The parent may try to block the thought of such a horrible atrocity from the mind, pretending not to think about it, making other explanations more plausible, hoping it isn't real.

Finding Out

A child will usually let you know she has been sexually assaulted in one of three ways: spontaneously, accidentally, or intentionally. The small child is most likely to make a spontaneous disclosure when he or she first comes into contact with a trusted adult, whether parent or friend. However, the small child also is easily intimidated by threats and later may deny the incident, making prosecution difficult.

You may find out accidentally by walking in during or just after the assault, or by coming across some evidence, such as the blood-stained underpants of a nonmenstruating child.

> I frequently left my six-year-old daughter with Tom, a seventeen-year-old neighbor, when I went shopping. I would never have believed he could do such a thing if I hadn't seen it with my own eyes. I was almost at the store when I remembered leaving the receipt for an item I wanted to return, so I had to go back for it. When I went into the living room, there he was, kneeling on the floor between my daughter's legs. She was looking scared to death, sitting in a chair without any pants on. It was probably the worst thing . . . the most appalling thing I have ever seen.

Sometimes when a seemingly unrelated problem is brought to the attention of a doctor, school nurse, teacher, or counselor, he or she will discover the sexual abuse upon closer inspection or in the course of taking a routine social history.

While a child may tell you about the assault shortly after the incident, she is more likely to do so months or even years later. Children who are intimidated into silence when young often bury the incident, but they do not forget it. Some women first talk about the assault around the time of a first date, their first consenting sexual encounter, an engagement, a marriage, the birth of a child, or after another assault. These events may cause them to reflect on the incident and its impact on them at the time as well as today.

Your Response

The reaction of the parent, brother, sister, or friend first told about the assault can have a significant impact on the child. It is important not to become hysterical. Hysteria will only frighten the child more or make her feel she has hurt and upset you. Do not suggest that she just try to forget about it or not talk about it. Instead, tell her how glad you are she told you; how pleased you are she was finally able to talk, how important it is to do so. Support how she did the right thing by telling you, even if she promised to keep it a secret. Remind her that those kinds of promises don't count. She was right to tell you. It was not her fault. She's not to blame. She is not in trouble.

Don't be afraid to talk with her about it in the future, even if the abuse happened a long time ago. If you avoid discussing the incident, she is likely to interpret your silence as blame. Remember, regarding sexual abuse of a loved one, everyone is uncomfortable and is afraid of saying "the wrong thing." By your attentive and sympathetic listening she will know you care and you support her, and that's all that really matters.

Whatever happened, you can help her most by letting her know that you believe her. Children, especially young children, *do not* make up stories about being sexually assaulted. They have nothing to gain in doing so. If it didn't happen, it wouldn't even be a part of their world.

Doreen, fourteen years old, first told her older sister about her assault by a neighbor. Her sister encouraged her to tell their mother, which she did. Their father, a friend of the man who had assaulted her, did not believe her. "Tell me the truth. Who really did this? Who are you covering up for? Was it that guy you hang around with? I told you to stay away from him. Don't you realize what a serious matter this is? You shouldn't lie about something this serious." Although Doreen insisted it was the neighbor who had raped her, she could not convince her father that she was telling the truth.

Fortunately for everyone involved, once the case was under investigation, another neighborhood girl testified that this man had assaulted her the summer before. She hadn't told anyone until she heard about Doreen. She had known that it would be her word against his and had felt too ashamed and embarrassed. The man pleaded guilty.

Remember, some children, especially teenagers, may giggle or laugh inappropriately because of their anxiety, not because what they are saying isn't true or is funny to them.

Helping the Child

Your first concern should be ensuring that the child is safe from further sexual abuse. Unlike incest, which may continue for years, the sexual assault of a child by a nonrelative or noncaretaker is more often a one-time or short-term event. If the assault involves someone with whom the child has continuing contact, it may be ongoing, and the child may not have the power to protect herself. The best, safest way to protect the child is to report the incident to the police. It is unrealistic simply to tell the child to stay away from the person who assaulted her. The child has come to you for help and protection. Besides, if you just try to keep the child away from the assailant but make no further report, it is likely that another child will become his victim.

If you know the assailant, contacting the police probably will be difficult for you. You probably don't want to believe it really happened. But remember, it has and he has traumatized a child or children, perhaps seriously impairing their psychosexual functioning for the rest of their lives. He must be stopped. He also needs help himself. "Normal," healthy, well-functioning men do not engage in sex with children.

It is also important to reassure the child that however she was coerced or enticed to engage in sexual behavior, it was not her fault; the assailant is responsible. It is very common for children to fear being blamed, no matter how good their relationship with their parents may be. They have heard the phrase "I told you not to do that" so often in the past. They have seen you and other adults get angry at them when they got dirty playing, tore a new shirt, or even cut themselves when using a knife. They knew they didn't mean to do these things, and they may even have tried to avoid them, but they were scolded nonetheless.

Children who participate in sex with adults because of threats actually experience fewer sexual problems later than children who are rewarded for their participation. The latter children often experience more ambivalence and have more guilt about succumbing to the temptation without threat of physical force. They need more help, support, and reassurance to absolve themselves from guilt. They should not be held responsible for poor judgment or bad decisions.

Just as when an adult is sexually assaulted, it is important for the child to have an evidentiary exam as soon as possible, preferably within thirty-six hours of the sexual contact. If vaginal or anal penetration was involved, it is important to determine if genital trauma occurred. No matter how long has elapsed since the assault, testing for sexually transmitted diseases should be completed, even if the child indicated the assault was limited to oral contact or manual manipulation. Children are sometimes poor historians. While the chances of contracting an STD may be minimal, it's best to be safe. The same is true with pregnancy testing. Any girl eleven or twelve years old, close to the age of menarche, should take a pregnancy test, even if she has not yet menstruated. Girls who never had a period have become pregnant.

Seek supportive counseling for the child and yourself. Crisis intervention, though often consisting of only three or four sessions, may prevent years of torment and turmoil. The best therapist to assess the impact of the assault on your child is one who has worked with other child-assault victims. Your local rape crisis center can help you find a knowledgeable individual. In the long run, it is much easier to deal with difficult issues immediately rather than to allow them to continue to affect you or your child for years to come. But at the same time, be aware that as the child matures, other related problems may develop that you also will have to deal with, even if you did everything possible when the assault occurred.

Remember, It's Not Your Fault

However much you would like to be able to protect your child, in reality you can't be with her all the time. It would be unhealthy for both of you if you tried. Nor can you anticipate all possible problems and prepare your child for all possible dangers ahead of time. The fact that your child was sexually assaulted does not reflect on your parenting skills. While you certainly may find the assault upsetting, you need not feel guilty.

> Marie was visiting with a friend's child in the hospital. The child had been very seriously beaten by a man who attacked and raped her on her way home from the grocery store. They were uncertain if she would live. Suzette, another family friend, happened to come at the same time and left with Marie. She told Marie, "It just makes me so angry that anyone could do that to a child." Marie told her, "It makes me angry too, but it scares me even more. My daughter is the same age. I'm afraid it could happen to her as easily too." Suzette said, "If you were a good mother your daughter wouldn't be out at night alone."
>
> Marie felt absolutely devastated. She felt helpless to counter this irrational remark, and yet she was very angry. Her daughter went to the corner store or walked the short distance home from a friend's house after dark. Was allowing this really unreasonable? She felt empathy for the child's parents. "I can't

imagine what they must be going through. Their daughter has been brutally raped and may die. And friends like Suzette must be blaming them. I wish I could help more."

How Can You Keep Your Child Safe?

The first and probably most important step in keeping your children safe is recognizing that they are vulnerable to sexual abuse by people they know and trust as well as by strangers. The next step is teaching your children, without frightening them, what sexual abuse is, what it may involve, and what to do should a family member, friend, or stranger make them feel uncomfortable.

To do this, of course, means you must discuss sex with your child. Sex is a taboo subject within most families, except perhaps when a mother warns her daughter to be careful not to get pregnant if unmarried. This taboo is exactly what keeps the sexual abuse of children a secret and allows it to continue undiscovered.

The Illusion Theatre in Minneapolis has developed a very effective program directed toward children of all ages. The format focuses on various kinds of touch and teaches children that being touched can make them feel good or bad. Children know that some touches make them feel uncomfortable. What they don't know is what it means when they get uncomfortable and what to do when it happens. Children need to talk about good and bad touches with their parents or in school with their teachers and peers. When you discuss touch with them, use the children's terms to refer to their genitals so they know what you are talking about. Using dolls also may be helpful, especially dolls with anatomical parts. A number of children's books dealing with this subject are now available to help you.

Your children should know that whenever they feel uncomfortable in a situation, or if someone touches them in a way that makes them feel uncomfortable, they are to tell the person to stop and say they must leave immediately. They should do this even if the person is an adult authority figure. They should then go to a place where they feel safe. If they are at school and are unable to reach you, they should tell the teacher, the school nurse, or another trusted adult. Talk with your children about a number of situations in which they might feel uncomfortable and help them problem-solve by considering what they might do in each situation. Discuss who they might feel comfortable telling if you are not immediately available—a neighbor, cousin, or guidance counselor. Let them know that you want to know and will not be angry at them, because whatever happened, it was not their fault. Even if the abuser is someone you both know and trust, and even if he made them promise not to tell in the past, they should tell you, because a promise to hide something so unfair to them should not be kept.

One sure way *not* to protect your children from sexual assault is by not talking about it and pretending that it happens only in other neighborhoods. That attitude might even make them more vulnerable and less prepared to seek help and protection from ongoing abuse. Remember, however, that you need not frighten them or make them afraid to be touched by all men. Be sure to stress that hugs and cuddling feel good and are an important part of growing up feeling safe and secure. Hugs and cuddling feel different from sexual abuse, just as rape feels completely different from making love. Children know the difference, but they need your permission, reassurance, and encouragement to talk about uncomfortable feelings should they arise.

8

Prosecuting and Convicting the Rapist

*The mood and temperament with regard to treatment
of crime and criminals is, in any country, one of the
most unfailing tests of its civilization.*

—WINSTON CHURCHILL

TO THE SURVIVOR

In order to understand better the chance your case may have in court,
you need to be aware of the factors about you, the assailant, and the
circumstances surrounding the rape that are likely to have an effect
on the case. You may find the following information discouraging and
may feel that what happens in court is not fair or right. It can all be
pretty frustrating, but you should know what to expect. While the
process may sometimes seem futile, it is not. Sometimes convictions
do result from cases that were thought unlikely to be won. However,
for a case to get the attention it merits, sometimes the survivor, and
in some cases her family as well, must push and insist on being heard.

All cases do not get the same thorough, unbiased investigation.

You may need to convince the individuals within the system of the merits of your case and your credibility as a witness. You may need to convince them that you will be available to testify should the case go to trial, that you will not back out at the last moment. The police, attorneys, and judges involved in your case may be wonderful and understanding, or they may be terribly biased. If you deal with them one at a time, these people probably will be more willing to reevaluate their biases and more willing to change than will the system as a whole. Your efforts today, combined with the efforts of other survivors and those fighting to change the system, are what will make change possible in the future.

Be sure to dress appropriately for any meeting in which you will discuss your case. Even if it is a hot summer day, don't arrive in shorts or a halter top. Dress conservatively. This applies to any time you are meeting with anyone involved in your case.

The Problems in Prosecuting

There are two primary strategies within the legal system for prosecuting sexual assault. The first is to arrest and charge as many suspected rapists as possible and let the courts decide on their guilt or innocence. To a great extent, this occurred during the mid-1970s with the push to reform rape laws. The result was that it took hours of police time to gather evidence and do a thorough and complete investigation for each case. The prosecuting attorney then expended considerable thought and effort to build a case and go to trial. All this concentrated attention was emotionally trying for the survivor as well. Then despite all this effort, juries found only 2 to 3 percent of these men guilty. In the large majority of cases, the survivor, the police, and the prosecuting attorney expended a great deal of time and effort only to see the assailant go free. A considerable burden was placed on the criminal justice system with minimal payoffs in convictions.

Out of frustration, many prosecuting attorneys and police departments have opted for the alternative strategy of carefully screening cases before making an arrest. Today they are less likely to take a marginal case to court. Current cases are compared with past cases that have been won in court. "Good" cases with "good" witnesses are won more often than "bad" cases with "bad" witnesses. The situation is frustrating, and losing too many cases can hurt prosecutors' careers. The more "good" cases they lose, the more carefully they screen cases and the more selective they become about issuing warrants and taking cases to court.

If the police spend days or weeks investigating a case only to have the now cautious prosecuting attorney refuse to charge the suspect for the assault, they will become more selective about the cases they spend long hours investigating. Frustrations and feelings of futility and helplessness "trickle down" one step further to the survivor.

Most women who have been raped in the past and whose assailants went free don't even bother to report a second rape. The police may even discourage these women from making a report when they don't believe it will result in a guilty plea or conviction. They don't want to see the women subjected needlessly to the extra emotional strain of an unsuccessful trial.

The end result of this caution and frustration is that, for criminals, the system has become safer. A lot of "good" cases are not reported by survivors, investigated by police, or prosecuted by the state. More rapists go free, having learned that rape, although illegal, is socially "sanctioned" by the system.

To a great extent, the progress of your case through the criminal justice system and the response you get from the police and the prosecuting attorney will depend on how similar or dissimilar your case is to other cases they have won. In addition to their past experience, the myths they believe about "real" rape cases and the stereotypes they have about "good" or "bad" witnesses also will determine the outcome of your case.

While progress has been made recently, our criminal justice system still has a multitude of problems that make prosecution of rape difficult. In 1981 only 10 percent of all rapes ever went before a jury. In Minneapolis in 1991, only 3 percent of the rapes reported went to a jury, although 88 percent of those defendants were found guilty. However, another 10 percent were charged and pled guilty, for a total of less than 13 percent of all *reported* rapes resulting in a determination of guilt, and that is considered a good percentage nationwide. The sentences were more severe for those who went to trial and were convicted than for those who pled guilty. Typically only one-third of the convicted rapists are sent to prison, one-third get probation, and one-third get treatment.

It is important that you understand the system and the process involved, along with the problems and roadblocks you may encounter along the way. There are points at which you can express your opinion and have an effect on the outcome of your case. However, you may not be asked to express your opinions and perhaps not even be made aware of the possibility of doing so. You may decide you do not have the energy to fight for your rights within the system. Whatever you decide to do, you have a right to know your possible courses of action. With a better understanding of the system, you can better evaluate the progress of your case and make more informed decisions.

A Successful Case in Review

You are one of the lucky ones. You called the police right after the assault and you had a good description of the assailant, a stranger to you. The police took you to a hospital, a detective came down and took your statement after the sexual assault nurse clinician completed the evidentiary exam, then you went home and waited.

The next day you got a phone call from the police. They had picked up a man who fit the description you gave. Although he, of course, denied he had been involved in the rape, the police asked if you would come down and identify him in a line-up. As you were a little nervous, you called the rape crisis counselor who had been with you at the hospital and asked her to accompany you, which she did. At the station, you positively identified your attacker. You also told the police about an abdominal scar on the assailant, which the police confirmed was present on the man you identified. The man was charged with rape.

The suspect was arraigned in court. You were not required to appear. He pled guilty, so you did not need to go through a jury trial. He was sentenced three weeks later and went to a prison that had a respected treatment program for sex offenders. Most cases are not this simple. Problems occur with police investigations or prosecuting attorneys. At a number of points along the way someone could decide that even though a suspect has been identified, your case should not be prosecuted. While it may seem that there is nothing you can do if this occurs, you can pursue a number of avenues within the legal system. Unless your area has a legal advocate or victim-witness assistance program, you may not be made aware of these options. At first, the system and its language may seem intimidating and overwhelming. However, you soon will see that, taken step by step, the legal system is manageable and recourse is possible.

Survivor Attributes That May Affect Your Case

What has been found to have the greatest impact on the legal outcome of the case is not circumstantial evidence but rather the survivor's background—specifically, alleged past nonconformist behavior or "misconduct" on her part. Misconduct and nonconformist behavior include such things as having a child when unmarried, sleeping with a boyfriend, a past record of criminal behavior, suspicion or allegation of prostitution, working as a topless dancer, involvement with drugs, or being seen drinking excessive amounts of alcohol (especially in a bar alone).

Juries, as well as personnel within the criminal justice system, often have minimal physical evidence to use in evaluating the testimonies of the survivor and the accused. There is seldom a witness to the assault, unless an accomplice was present. Therefore, the jurors' personal thoughts on a case often are based on other factors, primarily their perceptions of you and the accused—your honesty and credibility. Their opinions depend on their own often-stereotypic beliefs about which rape accounts are "real" rapes and which ones are fabricated, what type of person gets raped, and what type of man rapes. While it is not fair, the reality is that you are now being judged, and when someone does not know you, they often judge you by how you look. First impressions are important to you. You don't want to look seductive.

No one says openly that men have a right to rape women. However, individuals on juries, attorneys, police officers, and perhaps even your neighbors have come to tolerate rape when it involves a woman who does not act the way a woman—or "lady"—is expected to act.

Streetwise men are aware of these biases and use them in selecting their victims. Runaways are especially vulnerable. They are usually young; often naive; have no resources, no money for food, often nowhere to spend the night; and thus are dependent upon help from strangers for their subsistence. One rapist told the young girl he raped, "I know you're a runaway, so you won't go to the police."

On the other hand, a 1979 report by Gary LaFree at Indiana University indicates if a woman is living with her parents or husband, instead of alone (especially if divorced or widowed), or is living with another man, a conviction will more likely result. By our social standards, she is more respectable and less likely to lie or consent to having sex with a man other than her husband or significant other. Furthermore, if the assailant is of a different race than the survivor, the jury is also less likely to believe it was consenting intercourse and more likely to convict the accused of rape. This is particularly true if the survivor is white and the defendant black.

Some studies have found that carelessness on the part of the survivor prior to the assault is more likely to result in an acquittal. Carelessness involves such things as leaving a door unlocked, being out walking alone at night, or accepting a ride from a stranger. While these may be important factors in determining which cases go to court, once in court, other factors become more important. The courts have treated hitchhiking very harshly. In 1987 a California judge reversed a rape conviction, explaining that unless there was an emergency, a female hitchhiker is inviting trouble. According to this judge, "It would not be unreasonable for a man in the position of the defendant here to believe that the female would consent to sexual relations."

Another major determining factor is how rapidly the woman reported the crime. The case is more likely to be won if the report was immediate, which jurors interpret as an indication of sincerity and lack of consent. Even a few-hour delay, unfortunately, may negatively affect the credibility of the survivor and raise doubts about her motives. People may assume that she "got angry the next day when the assailant didn't call, so she cried rape to get even with him." In a 1977 study of rape cases won, not one case reported more than twenty-four hours after the assault resulted in a conviction. As discussed earlier (see chapter 2), a delay in reporting severely hinders the investigation because evidence is lost so quickly.

Cases involving adult women under thirty years of age are more likely to result in acquittals, even though most rape survivors fall into this age category. When the woman is older or white, it is more likely that the man will plead guilty, possibly to a lesser crime, and the case will not need to go to trial. The defense pushes a plea bargain either because he or she does not feel there is much chance of winning in court, or as LaFree suggests, because older women are more aware of the stress of court on them and more anxious to avoid it. They or the prosecuting attorney thus may be more willing to accept a guilty plea for a less serious crime, such as second-degree rather than first-degree criminal sexual conduct, or a less harsh sentence in order to avoid the additional stress of court.

While the laws in many states define rape as more traumatic and deserving of more severe punishment if a pregnancy results, juries seem to disagree. Most jurors do not see pregnancy as a factor aggravating the traumatic nature of the assault, but rather as a factor that raises doubt as to the survivor's motives. As a result, attorneys often counsel women not to volunteer information to the defense about a pregnancy that occurred or an abortion that was needed.

If the survivor is black, it is less likely that the accused rapist will plead guilty regardless of his race. And it is also, sadly, less likely that the case will be won in court regardless of his race. LaFree found that our criminal justice system is prejudiced against black women. It is no wonder that so many black women choose not to report to the police, even though they may go to the hospital to have injuries treated and for STD and pregnancy prevention. "My brothers will take care of him. The police won't do anything anyway," one black woman said. One assailant chose to go with the police, whom he had called, instead of facing the survivor's three brothers, who were waiting outside his door with baseball bats.

This prejudice against black women was evident when Desiree

Washington charged boxer Mike Tyson with raping her. Even black college women were quoted as saying "She got what she deserved." Instead of being sympathetic toward her, they were angry that she had charged a prominent black man with rape. Even though he was convicted in a court of law, on a February 20, 1992, ABC *20/20* broadcast, Barbara Walters stated, "Some supporters . . . have said . . . that Mike Tyson was convicted because he was a black man." Washington replied, "That puzzles me, and that hurts me, because our people fought for years for equal rights . . . and to take the side of a black man over a black woman is not equal."

According to a Madison, Wisconsin, judge, just being female is sufficient reason to be blamed for rape and for the accused to be set free. In 1980 he refused to sentence a fifteen-year-old rapist, saying, "Women are sex objects. God did that, I didn't."

Offender Attributes That May Affect Your Case

The attributes and assumed character of the offender also significantly affect the outcome in rape cases. The respectability of the assailant and his physical and social attractiveness have been found to be significant factors in assumptions made about his honesty. Even the most disheveled assailant will turn up in court clean-shaven, with a haircut, and often wearing a suit and tie. He will not appear to be the type of man who could rape. He is likely to have his wife, mother, father, and even older children accompany him and sit behind him—the picture-perfect, middle-class American family unit. The more he can look like the police, the judge, or members of the jury, the more likely they are to empathize with him and the less likely they are to find him guilty.

Married assailants are less likely to be arrested and charged with the assault. They arouse the empathy of the police, who feel that "they have more to lose than the victim if the case is charged." However, single assailants who are younger than twenty-five are more likely to be arrested and convicted. If the suspect has a criminal record of any kind, the police are more likely to arrest and charge him. If the record includes sexual offenses and if this information is allowed in court, he is also more likely to be convicted. However, if the defendant does not take the witness stand, he cannot be asked about his sex offense record and the prosecuting attorney cannot bring it up. The jury would then not know about any past convictions. Sometimes prosecutors can work around this by getting special permission from the judge to call another woman raped by the same man (if she agrees to testify).

Ulana had been held captive for more than thirty hours by a man who had come to look at a car she was selling. He knew a friend of hers. Once in the car, he had driven to a deserted location, where he raped her. He then took her to a friend's house, where he repeatedly raped her. She finally convinced him she would be missed if he did not release her. Once free, she reported the rape to the police. He was arrested and claimed she had consented.

The court case was going badly until Vera, a fifty-five-year-old schoolteacher, took the stand. Tearfully, experiencing the pain and horror once again, she told of her rape five years earlier by the same man. She too had advertised a car for sale, and he had raped her during a test drive. He had been sentenced to prison and was released only four days before raping Ulana. He was found guilty and returned to prison.

The victim's race has been found to be a much more important factor in the outcome than the assailant's race. While black men make up a large percentage of the prison population, a thorough review of court cases found that they were less likely than white men to be convicted of rape—probably because they are more likely to rape black women. As mentioned earlier, cases involving black survivors are less likely to result in convictions. Once the data are controlled to account for the survivor's race, black men are convicted at the same rate as white men. The system is more biased against the black woman than against the black man.

When more than one assailant is involved, once charged, the case is more likely to result in a conviction. In such cases juries are less likely to accept consent as a believable defense. It is also more likely that the people will find discrepancies between the stories of two or more men, especially when they are separated quickly before being interviewed. Sometimes one decides to cooperate and testify against the others in return for a more lenient charge and sentence.

A Senate Judiciary report released in May 1993 found that prosecutors are hesitant to bring charges in cases of acquaintance rape, because they feel such cases are less likely to be won in court. In a 1992 Minneapolis study, Patricia Frazier found that while a suspect is identified in nearly 70 percent of the acquaintance rape situations and only 25 percent of the stranger rape situations, acquaintances are given lighter sentences. Only 14 percent of the acquaintance rapists were convicted; only 40 percent of these were sent to prison, the others got probation or treatment. Of the stranger rapists, while only 9 percent were convicted, more than twice as many, 88 percent, were sent to prison.

Many people feel the lighter sentence for acquaintance rapists is more a result of the fact that acquaintance rapes typically do not involve a weapon or an injury than of the rapist's relationship to the woman. Typically acquaintance rapes are more coercive and less violent. Physical injuries to corroborate that the sexual contact was against the woman's will are also less likely. The woman is more likely to trust the assailant and find herself in a vulnerable situation, such as in his home, before she realizes there is need for concern. Witnesses who saw them drinking together earlier in the evening, leave a bar together, and appear to both be enjoying each other's company are commonly found. The man will likely claim consent, and it will be his word against the survivor's. In such cases the biases of individuals within the legal system then come into play. In July 1993 a police officer in a large metropolitan midwestern city told a nineteen-year-old university student, raped on a date by a coworker, "Dates lead to sex. You have to expect that."

Circumstances of the Assault

Circumstances inconsistent with common consenting sexual encounters are more likely to result in convictions. For instance, if the rape occurred in conjunction with another crime, such as robbery, and especially car theft, the woman probably will be believed. However, since police too are biased about what they think women should and shouldn't do, where they should and shouldn't go, and how they should and shouldn't dress, this is not always the case.

> Dolores returned to her car after a late evening of drinking. She was wearing a tight, short skirt, and she was quite inebriated. Two men she had never seen before jumped her as she opened the door and threw her into the backseat. They each raped her, then dumped her out and drove away in her car. She stumbled into the street to stop a passing police car. A high-speed chase resulted, with the two men running stoplights, signs, and eventually wrecking her car. They told the police she was the girlfriend of one of the men and that she often let him borrow the car. The police let them go and told Dolores, "It's your word against theirs." The assailants, while questioned by the police, were not even issued a traffic violation.

In Minneapolis in 1986, a similar, much-publicized case of a gang rape of a thirty-nine-year-old woman by five men occurred. After three and a half years they were finally punished for damaging her car but not for the rape. They had damaged her car by beating it and jumping on it as they took turns beating and raping her. Both the woman and the car were left for dead on a cold January night. A sixth man, who even testified against his friends, returned to the scene and drove her to a safe location, probably saving her life. While the five men claimed the woman consented, they could not claim the car consented and so were convicted of the car damage. Each had to pay a five-hundred-dollar-fine in five-dollar weekly installments.

Another factor that has considerable impact on the outcome of the case is the relationship of the woman to the assailant. Seven states still have a marital exception to rape laws. As a result, in these states, a husband cannot be charged with rape, ostensibly because a man cannot be charged for taking what is legally his. This problem is discussed in greater detail in the section on rape laws beginning on page 204. In addition to marital exclusion laws, the courts, legal personnel, and juries are suspicious of complaints made against individuals with whom the survivor was previously acquainted. The establishment of a prior relationship with the survivor, especially a sexual relationship, casts doubt on her story and motives, regardless of her behavior just prior to the rape. A Kent State University study published in 1988 by Dr. Mary Koss also found that there was a direct correlation between the extent of the woman's relationship with the assailant and the steps she was likely to take to report. The better she knew him, the less likely she was to report or prosecute. If women are less likely to report rape by an acquaintance, and the system makes it more difficult to prosecute an acquaintance-rape situation, these cases are indeed underrepresented within the court system. If the assailant is a stranger, he is more likely to be charged and convicted and more than twice as likely to go to prison once convicted.

If you were legally intoxicated or even drinking "heavily" at the time of the rape, it is more likely that jurors will blame you for the rape and not convict the assailant. Not only does drinking result in greater blame of the victim by the general population, but it raises the question of credibility: How much do you really remember about what happened? Any lapses in memory will be used to discredit your statement.

If anal sex was involved, it is less likely the jury will believe the survivor consented, and a conviction is more probable. If the woman was injured in any way, if the case gets to court it probably will result in a conviction. Her injuries are proof that she resisted. She is more likely to be believed in an attempted rape case than when she actually is raped. This is because too many people still believe the myth that a woman can be raped only if she wants to be. Unfortunately, many states automatically cut in half prison sentences resulting from attempted rape charges, because the offense is seen as less serious. This rightfully infuriates survivors who know that the rapist would have completed the rape if he had been able to do so.

If the survivor willingly let the assailant into her home, was seen drinking with him, agreed to leave a bar with him, or accepted an invitation to his home, an acquittal is common.

The response you encounter within the legal system will depend to a great extent on how well you and the circumstances of the rape fit the stereotypic "good" or "bad" case. It is important to remember that the decision of the prosecuting attorney not to charge a case does not necessarily mean that the police or the prosecuting attorney do not believe you really were raped. It reflects their knowledge and beliefs about which types of cases will be won in court and thus which cases are worth their effort and your effort in trying to win. While you cannot control most of the factors, there are things you can do to facilitate a positive response to your case and to exert more control over the outcome.

The next section reviews the process and the roadblocks you may encounter and offers suggestions on how you can deal with the roadblocks.

Rape Laws

The average survivor does not realize that the criminal case is *not her case.* It is the state's case, because rape, like other criminal charges, is a crime against the state. While a very important witness, the survivor is only a witness. The prosecuting attorney is thus not her attorney but the state's attorney and is acting in the interest of the state. Should a conflict arise, the needs and desires of the state come before the survivor's. The survivor has no real rights in the decision process, although out of common sense and courtesy, or directive, most prosecuting attorneys will involve the survivor as much as possible.

Rape laws originally came from the Roman law of *raptus. Raptus* was a violent theft that could apply to any kind of property that belonged to a man, including his slaves, children, or wife. It referred to abduction and theft, not to sexual violation. If a sexual assault occurred, it was still the abduciton, *raptus*, that was charged. From the beginning, rape laws have been designed to protect a man's property, not to protect women.

Acceptance of the concept of women as property of fathers or husbands is the real reason why, until recently, a husband who raped his wife was legally protected from prosecution by a spousal exclusion. Lord Hale, a British journalist, asserted that a husband could not be guilty of raping his wife, because, by their mutual matrimonial contract, the wife had given herself to her husband and she therefore had no right to deny her husband sexual access to her body. Her feelings or consent were irrelevant. In some states this exception also includes people living together, legally married but separated, or in common-law marriages.

The National Organization of Women (NOW) National Task Force on Rape has been active in lobbying for rape-law reform. A small victory was won by women in the mid-1970s when legally separated husbands were first removed from the spousal exclusion and could thus be charged with rape. Now in many states the spousal exclusion clause has been removed completely from rape laws. Major victories have been won in rape-law reform, though many problems still remain. Rape laws still vary from state to state. You can obtain a copy of your state's rape laws by calling your local prosecuting attorney's office, by going to any law library, or by calling your state documents registrar. The term used to describe the offense also varies. In some states it is called rape, in others criminal sexual contact or sexual assault. Most states have varying degrees that correspond to what particular types of sexual assault that state considers more serious and deserving of a harsher sentence.

In most states the offense is considered most serious when penetration occurs; when the victim is legally a child; when weapons are involved; when physical injury or pregnancy results; or when another felony, such as kidnapping, is also committed.

Now, in most states, penetration need not occur for the crime to be considered rape or criminal sexual contact. Any nonconsenting contact with the sexual organs, including the breasts or buttocks, is considered rape. Revised laws also make it explicit that "sexual intercourse," in addition to vaginal penetration by the penis, now includes penetration of the vagina or anus by an object (except for medical purposes) and by a person of the same or opposite sex.

The change in the sentencing structure is another important point of reform. In the states where rape conviction could result in death, castration, or life in prison, women were less willing to report, police and attorneys were less willing to charge, and juries were unwilling to convict. With more reasonable sentences corresponding to the severity of the assault and the past offenses of the assailant, conviction is more likely. Minnesota, for instance, in 1992 implemented a "three-time-loser law." Now a rapist convicted of rape for the third time goes to jail for life without parole.

The determination of consent is an especially important issue. Many state laws require the woman to prove she resisted—by screaming, fighting back, kicking, or trying to run away. When weapons are not used and physical resistance is not apparent, some states still do not consider the assault rape. In other states the analysis of consent is based on the woman's character, reputation, or chastity, as discussed earlier. She is on trial instead of the assailant. Sexist stereotypes must be eliminated for true justice to result. The most progressive laws now recognize that lack of the use of force doesn't indicate consent. They recognize the use of force *or coercion* as equal. The assailant should not be acquitted because he believed in his mind that the woman really wanted sexual intercourse even though she told him otherwise. Today's laws must specifically include coerced submission as rape.

The Police Investigation

As we have seen, the police investigation and report is limited by the laws in your state defining what is and is not rape, as well as by the personal biases of those people who enforce the law. The police, like others in the system, have "learned" by experience which cases are "good" or "bad" ones, which cases are deserving of more time and effort than others. Some police will try to investigate every case thoroughly regardless of its initial merits; others feel they do not have the time or resources to do so.

The police investigation can have five possible outcomes. It may be *redlined; unfounded; exceptionally cleared; inactive, not cleared;* or *cleared by arrest.* Use of these categories may vary somewhat from precinct to precinct, so it is important to check with your police department for their definition of terms. Don't be afraid to ask.

Cases are "redlined"—that is, not investigated—infrequently and only in the most unusual circumstances. The women involved in these cases include those who are thought to be psychotic, for example. Though a report may be made, no officer will be assigned to the case, so no investigation will occur.

The most controversial cases are those labeled "unfounded." Cases that are unfounded include those that the police have decided are not "real" rapes, or in which the legal criteria have not been met. In states that still have a spousal exclusion, rape by a husband will be included in this category. This category also includes cases in which the suspect claims the survivor consented and the officer does not believe there is enough evidence to prove that rape occurred. In addition, this category includes cases where the woman has recanted, that is, she came back later and told the police no rape occurred. In some cases there actually was no rape; in others, she may have recanted because she was threatened by the assailant or his family and has changed her story to avoid an attack on her life or on the lives of her loved ones, or simply to avoid continual harassment.

Police have considerable discretion in determining which cases are included in this "unfounded" category, as no clearly written criteria exist. As a result, the myths and stereotypes subscribed to by the police become major factors in deciding which rapes are "real." Usually the police assigned to investigate in special sex crimes units have had special training and have resolved most of their own biases. However, no matter how fair they may try to be, some officers are more biased than others. Some make no attempt at hiding their prejudices.

The third category involves cases that are "exceptionally cleared." For the most part, these are cases the survivor wants dropped. She may simply miss her appointments with the police or won't return their calls. She really may want the case dropped, or she may just not have the energy to see it through. In a few unfortunate instances, a misunderstanding disrupts the process. Cases have occurred where the victim expected the police to contact her again, while they thought she did not want to prosecute and were waiting for her to call them if she changed her mind. Perhaps they only have her home phone number and she is staying with family or friends for a few days as a result of her fear for her safety. The police may "exceptionally clear" her case because they made three phone calls and were unable to reach her.

The fourth category includes inactive cases—cases pending, not closed, but not actively being investigated. The length of time a case can remain inactive depends on a state's statutes of limitations. For adult sex offenses it is usually three to five years, and for cases involving children, seven years. This category includes cases in which there is a good description of the assailant but he cannot be found and those in which the county attorney would not issue a warrant due to lack of sufficient evidence. The police keep the cases open in hopes of obtaining additional evidence so they can be resubmitted in the future or of apprehending a suspect before the time limit runs out.

While a case is inactive, another similar assault may occur. If a suspect is apprehended for the other rape, the first survivor may be asked to identify him as well. In a 1993 case in Minneapolis, four women were able to identify two men who had raped them, and DNA matches were able to link these same two men to a total of seventeen rapes in two counties over one and one-half years. Some of the earlier cases had become inactive before evidence from the later cases tied them all together.

In the last instance, the police have enough evidence and the case is cleared by arrest. To arrest a suspect, they must make the summary of the case and evidence available to the prosecutor. If the prosecutor also believes there is enough evidence for the state to prosecute successfully, a complaint or a warrant for the suspect's arrest is issued. Then the police can make an arrest. Prior to issuing the warrant, the prosecutor may insist the police get additional specific evidence. Sometimes they are able to do so, sometimes they are not. If they cannot, the case may become inactive.

Cases reported "cleared by arrest" can be misleading. The Uniform Crime Report, a report of national statistics for rape and other crimes, indicates that 52 percent of all reported rapes are "cleared by arrest." Unfortunately in this report, cases are classified "cleared by arrest" if a suspect was arrested, or if the case was closed exceptionally (as when the victim was uncooperative—did not return phone calls or could not be contacted, the defendant died, or there was a change in jurisdiction). Frazier found that in Minneapolis, in 1991, 69 percent of all rapes were reported cleared by arrest, using the Uniform Crime Report's definition. However, in reality only 27 percent were cleared by the arrest of an actual suspect, 39 percent were classified cleared due to lack of survivor cooperation, and 3 percent were cleared for other unspecified reasons.

The time during the investigation prior to the arrest may be a very frustrating period for you, especially if you know the assailant. You may live near him, work together, or go to the same school. Unfortunately, there are risks involved in arresting someone immediately. Sometimes a suspect is arrested right away on "probable-cause evidence." This means that the police have good reason to believe he is responsible but do not yet have sufficient evidence for a warrant. The police may make a probable-cause arrest if they catch the suspect at or near the scene of the crime or if they know who he is and are afraid he may leave the state.

When a suspect is arrested on probable-cause evidence, he can be held for only thirty-six hours without a complaint being issued by the county attorney. This means that if sufficient evidence is not obtained within that time period, he must be set free. Only in the most extreme cases will the prosecuting attorney order the suspect held for another thirty-six hours without issuing this complaint.

Before the complaint can be issued, the police must gather the necessary evidence, and you must go down to the police station and make a formal statement. If the police cannot locate you, or you do not return phone calls or contact them within thirty-six hours of when they arrest a suspect, they will be forced to set the assailant free. It is crucial that you maintain constant contact with the police and that you keep them up-to-date on how and where they can contact you during these initial stages of the investigation. The initial report is *not* sufficient; you also must make a formal statement, which will be typed up and which you will sign. You may ask for a copy of this report, and it is a good idea to do so, so that you can review it prior to going to court. Don't assume you can wait a week to contact the police, after you return from your friend's summer cabin, for instance. It may be too late by then. Seeing an assailant walk free because you could not be contacted is extremely disappointing and difficult for everyone. Lack of contact is one more of the many reasons very few rapists are ever convicted and sent to jail.

Still another factor may prevent the police from arresting the suspect.

I was so angry that the police did not arrest him. After the man who abducted me raped me, his two friends raped me in his garage. I thought they were going to kill me. They called him by name. There were even tracks in the snow from the garage to his house when the police went back to investigate. I still don't understand why he's home, safe, and I'm here in fear for my life.

He was safe because the Supreme Court has ruled that a person cannot be arrested in his own home on probable-cause evidence. The only exception is when the police are in "hot pursuit," a reason that also has been challenged in court. A "man's house is his castle," even if he is suspected of rape. Any evidence obtained under these circumstances, without a search warrant, no matter how conclusive, could and probably would be thrown out of court.

After making your initial report, you may go home expecting to hear from the police and not be called. If that occurs, do not hesitate to call and ask to speak to the investigator who has been assigned your case. Ask him what the status of your case is and what else you can do to help. Let him know you're interested. He probably gets one hundred or more cases each year. That's a lot of investigative work. Realistically, the more certain he feels you are willing to follow through with the case rather than change your mind and ask to have the charges dropped, the more willing he may be to spend the extra time and energy trying to get the evidence necessary to make an arrest.

Once the suspect is arrested, you may need to go down to the police station to view a lineup. This involves viewing the suspect in addition to four or five other men through one-way glass. They will not be able to see you. The purpose is to see if you can pick him out and make a positive identification. You can ask to have the men in the lineup repeat something said during the assault so that you can make a voice identification. If you think you see the man, even if you are not positive, mark the piece of paper the police have given you. If there are any scars or other marks or details you feel would help identify him, let the police know now, if you did not remember to tell them earlier.

After the lineup is over, you can talk with the police about any concerns you have about your identification. If the rapist had a beard or mustache when he assaulted you, tell the police. If he appears to have gained or lost weight, tell them that too. They can then check with neighbors or employers. Corroboration of this type may make the case an even better one.

Seeing the assailant again can be frightening. If you have a rape crisis counselor, you may want to ask her to accompany you to the police station. She will not be able to be present during the actual lineup, but she can provide support before and after. If you are not working with anyone, you may want to ask a friend to go with you.

If you knew the man, a lineup will not be necessary. Even if you did not know him well, a photo lineup may be possible instead of viewing him in person. If you do identify a suspect, from now on your primary contact will be with the office of the prosecuting attorney assigned to the case.

The Court System

Civil Court

You do have an alternative if the criminal charges are denied. You can press civil charges, or you can press civil charges in addition to the criminal charges; it is not an either/or situation. More and more women are pressing civil charges. To do this you must talk with a private attorney to see if you have a "good" civil case. In a civil lawsuit you need not prove your case "beyond a reasonable doubt," as is required to win in criminal cases. Civil cases require that a "preponderance of the evidence" be in your favor, so they are easier to win.

Civil charges may be filed against individuals or companies who are responsible for causing the damage—the rape—by not protecting you from a harm that was foreseeable, that they should reasonably have expected could occur. Some survivors have pressed civil charges against the assailant; his place of employment, if the assault was in any way work-related; the company in whose parking lot the rape occurred; or the apartment building or hotel that did not have sufficient security. Most typically you will sue in civil court for a dollar amount to cover physical and emotional injury as well as any property damage. That also means that no attorney will be willing to take the case if the assailant does not have any money or property of value, and if there is no company with assets to take that is responsible, so there is nothing to recover.

When filing a civil case, you usually do not pay an attorney ahead of time. The attorney will receive one-third of whatever money is recovered. Some law firms ask you to sign an agreement giving them a higher percentage, possibly 40 percent. They do this when they believe they will incur a lot of unusual expenses in preparing the case. Others may want you to pay certain expenses as they occur. You should ask about this and negotiate ahead of time. You do not have to agree to a higher fee. If one firm won't take the case for the usual one-third, you may want to check with other attorneys before signing an agreement.

Unfortunately, even if you win a civil suit, the assailant will not be punished by a prison term or have a felony on his record. But to some people a large monetary loss may hurt almost as much.

Criminal Court

Most prosecuting attorneys do not have written criteria by which they judge how "good" a case is and whether or not they should issue a complaint or warrant. They essentially rely upon two criteria: The attorney must believe sexual contact occurred against the woman's will, and there must be enough evidence to prove this and win the case in court. Often the most salient criterion in the attorney's decision to charge a case, that is, to press criminal charges against the assailant, seems to be the likelihood of winning the case in court. (To "deny" a case is to refuse to press charges.) The attorney's judgment, based on personal past experiences and biases, thus plays an important role in the outcome of your case. The attorney's willingness to take the risk of charging a marginal case is also important.

If the attorney denies the case when the police initially present it, you have the right to meet and discuss the reasons for denial. At this time you may provide additional information and explain why you believe a warrant should be issued. Do not assume the attorney has all the information.

You will be the most important evidence should the attorney decide to take the case to court. Marginal cases initially denied have been taken to court because the survivor met with the attorney and convinced him or her that she would follow through with the case and make a good witness. Other similar cases have been less successful. You must be convincing. It's the prosecutor's decision in the end, but you do have the right to have your feelings and concerns heard and to have any decisions explained in terms you can understand.

You have a right to know what is happening and a responsibility to cooperate as best you can. To do this, it's essential that you understand what unfamiliar legal terms mean; don't be embarrassed to ask to have them explained.

If you don't hear from anyone after a warrant has been issued, call and ask to talk to the attorney assigned to your case. In some areas, usually large cities, a legal advocate is assigned to keep you posted as to the progress of your case. Some states now have a Victim's Bill of Rights. This requires that you be notified at important points, such as plea bargaining and sentencing. While you still have no decision-making rights, you are allowed to make your feelings and desires known and to be present at the hearings, if you like. As mentioned before, it is your responsibility to ensure that the police have a current phone number and address to contact you. If they do not, the process will occur anyway, or worse yet, the charges may be dropped and the assailant may be let free.

By now you probably have been screened, or questioned, at least three times: by the police officer who took the initial report; by the police investigator; and by the prosecuting attorney. If you have made it this far, they all probably believe that a criminal rape occurred and that there is enough evidence to have a good chance to win in court. Now the prosecuting attorney must develop a strategy to show "beyond a reasonable doubt" in court that there was a rape and that the suspect is the man who raped you.

The Preliminary Hearing

The next court day or within thirty-six hours after the warrant has been issued and the suspect arrested and charged, a preliminary hearing will take place. You do not need to be present. At this hearing, the suspect will appear in court and the charges against him will be read. If he does not have an attorney, a public defender will be assigned at this time and bail will be set.

The Arraignment

The next step is arraignment before a judge in the courthouse. You need not be present here either, though you may attend. Many survivors find it empowering to attend the preliminary hearing and/or the arraignment. Now you are free and in control and he is not. He will arrive wearing jail clothes, if he hasn't been able to post bail, and even if his handcuffs are taken off for the courtroom, you can be assured he wore them to court. This is a good time to see him, to face him before the trial to see that he no longer has any power over you. Many survivors express a sense of accomplishment at being able to stare at him, focusing all the anger and disgust they can in his direction.

The suspect's attorney will be present to enter a plea of guilty or not guilty at this time. If the suspect pleads guilty, he will be asked to sign a formal sworn testimony of guilt and a date will be set for sentencing. A guilty plea is rare so early in the process. If he pleads not guilty, a date will be set for an omnibus hearing and for trial.

Plea Bargaining

The prosecuting attorney working with you will meet with the assailant's attorney prior to the trial to "plea bargain." Plea bargaining involves a complex process of negotiations. Each attorney evaluates the evidence available and determines his or her likelihood of winning the case. In return for the client's "cooperation" with the prosecution, the defense attorney will attempt to negotiate a charge of less serious degree of criminal sexual conduct and a lighter sentence for an assailant who agrees to plead guilty. In a 1992 review of records for Hennepin County, in Minnesota, Frazier found that assailants who plead guilty do indeed get lighter sentences than those who are found guilty by a jury. If the assailant does not have a strong defense, he is more likely to want to plea bargain. By going to trial, however, the assailant is offered the possibility of complete exoneration. Assailants with a stronger defense or who believe you have little evidence or that you will not be willing to testify in court may choose this option. If you do not show up in court to testify, all charges likely will be dropped and he will go free. If you do not want to go to court, you should let the prosecuting attorney know and strongly encourage him or her to accept a plea at this time.

The Omnibus Hearing

Shortly before the trial, there will be a preliminary, or omnibus, hearing. Once again you need not be present, although you may attend if you wish. The police involved probably will be present. The primary purpose of this hearing is to determine whether there is probable cause to believe a crime was committed by the suspect and to determine if his constitutional rights were violated. If probable cause exists and the defendant's consitutional rights were not violated, he may be held for trial. At this time both attorneys tell the judge what evidence they wish to introduce. The judge then rules on which evidence can and cannot be submitted during the trial. This avoids wasting time in court. For instance, if the prosecuting attorney wants to introduce a torn, bloody blouse, he will say so. The other attorney may object, asking "How do we know whose blouse or whose blood it is?" Your attorney would qualify the "chain of custody" explaining that the blouse was taken from you in the emergency department by the nurse who completed the evidentiary exam, given to the police officer, who gave it to him. Your name is also on the bag that blouse was taken from, which was sealed with evidence tape. (This evidence is often crucial to your case. That is why it is important that it be examined as soon as possible after the assault and that you bring along the other clothes you were wearing—especially your underclothes—at the time of the assault.)

The Pretrial Period

Typically it takes two or three months for a trial to begin. *During
this time you can and probably should refuse to talk to the defense
attorney or investigator unless the prosecuting attorney is present.*
This includes phone conversations. Generally the defense is contacting you only to try to find discrepancies between what you said in
your statement and what you are saying now. It is not uncommon
for you to remember something new, forget some details, or remember
something differently. You probably won't want the defense to have
access to this information. Be certain you know to whom you are
speaking before giving out any information about your case over the
phone. If in doubt, refuse to speak to anyone until you can check
with your attorney, even if the individual claims to be on your side.
Investigators for the defense attorney sometimes say they are "working on your case"; this is true, only they are working for the other
side.

Should you get any harassing letters or phone calls, report them
to the prosecuting attorney and the police immediately. Survivors have
received letters and phone calls from assailants' mothers and wives
begging them to drop the charges, "or you will ruin all our lives."
Remember: He is the one who decided to rape you, and he is the one
who is hurting them, not you, and you're probably not his first victim.
Give these letters to your attorney.

Work closely with a victim advocate if one is available during this
pretrial period. She or he is there to keep you informed of the progress
of your case, to help you understand the system, and generally to
make the process less trying for you. Don't hesitate to use this valuable
resource. If you work with an advocate, you may meet with the attorney only once or twice before going to court.

If you have never been to court, visit a courtroom before the trial
to familiarize yourself with it. Your advocate can show you where the
prosecuting attorney will sit, where the assailant will sit, and where
you will be when you testify. Unlike on television, you will not sit up
front next to the attorney, and you cannot be present in the courtroom
except when you are testifying. Since you are a witness, the theory is

that if you hear the other witnesses testify it may bias your testimony. You can, however, sit in on another case to see what it's like to be in court.

If you are uncertain, ask your advocate or attorney how you should dress for court. Be sure to wear something you like and in which you will feel comfortable and good about yourself. Also remember that court is rather formal and dress conservatively. While slacks are fine in some areas, they are not in other areas of the country. Blue jeans or shorts are not a good choice. Don't wear anything that could be considered provocative or sexy. Especially avoid halter tops, low-cut necklines, or extra-short skirts. Too much makeup and jewelry could also create an unfavorable impression. Remember, the jurors do not know you, so, right or wrong, they will be basing their judgment of you on how you look as well as on what you say. A simple suit, skirt and blouse, or dress will do nicely.

Review your initial police statement just before going to court, paying particular attention to the details you may have forgotten over the past few months. Call your court advocate or your attorney's office the day before the trial to ensure there are no postponements. Unfortunately, the trial may be postponed a number of times before it actually takes place. Reasons for postponements include the inability of witnesses to appear, lack of an available judge, other cases taking longer to try than was anticipated, or illness, among others. While delays may be necessary, sometimes the defense seems to use them to extend the process in the hope that you will not be able to take it anymore and give up. Delays can be devastating. Each time you arrange your whole life around a new court date, only to have it postponed at the last minute, it can feel as if you are being told to put your life on hold once again, as if no one cares or understands the inconvenience it means. Each time you must get psychologically prepared for court, it seems a little harder to do. Usually it also feels as if you can't put the rape behind you and get on with your life, until the trial is over. The only good thing about delays is that if you are in counseling, at least you will be in a stronger position to deal with the stresses of court because you've had more time to recover from the trauma of the rape.

Jury Selection

The day the trial is scheduled to begin actually is the first day of jury selection. This seldom takes more than one day, two at the most, except in very high-profile cases. Both attorneys will ask each potential juror one or two questions and accept or disqualify him or her on the basis of their response. The prosecuting attorney is allowed to excuse three people, and the defense attorney, seven people, without cause. After that they must state why they feel a particular person may be prejudiced against their client.

Many prosecuting attorneys used to believe that they should select young women if the victim was young, because in other criminal cases they found that the more the juror was like the victim, the more they identified with her and the harsher they were with the defendant. When juror selection was investigated more thoroughly in relationship to sexual assault cases, however, this tendency was found not to be true. Jurors, too, needed to believe in their own invulnerability. As a result, the more they were like the victim, the more they tended to blame her and find the defendant not guilty.

Though the evidence is often contradictory, for the most part studies have found that men are more likely to judge the assailant harshly, especially in recommending punishment. However, white males are more likely to assume that the survivor's actions were contributory. Men are most punitive toward the rapist and most likely to find him guilty when they themselves do not adhere strongly to sex-role stereotypes and are not coercive or violent in their relationships with women. Women with daughters who are routinely in the same type of circumstances as the survivor was when assaulted are likely to be more punitive toward the assailant. Women who know someone who has been raped are more likely to show empathy toward the survivor. Older women are also more likely to be more punitive and suggest harsher sentences for the assailant.

Your Day in Court

After the jurors have been selected, opening statements will be made by both attorneys, then witnesses will be called and evidence introduced as the state's attorney builds your case and the defense attorney builds the defendant's case. Though instructed to focus on facts, the defense attorney will attempt to make the jury empathize with the defendant. Neither you nor the assailant is required to take the stand to testify. You almost always will be needed to testify, however, because your testimony is the most important part of the state's case. When you do testify, the prosecuting attorney will question you first. You will need to tell the events of the assault in detail. The courtroom is usually open to the public; however, in most cases not more than a very few people who are not involved in the proceedings attend. You may find it difficult to retell the intimate details of the assault in court, especially with the assailant present. Don't be worried if you become emotional or cry. If you need more time, stop a moment, then continue. Some survivors find it helpful to imagine that the area where the assailant is sitting is nothing more than an empty black hole in the universe, and avoid any eye contact with him. Others will look him in the eye and refer to him as "the rapist" or "the man who raped me," not by his name.

When the prosecuting attorney has finished, the defense attorney will cross-examine you. This will likely be an unpleasant experience. You may be asked seemingly insignificant details, such as a description of where all the furniture was in the room, in an attempt to find a small discrepancy or error to use to discredit the accuracy of your recall. Sound as confident and sure of yourself as you can when you do know the answers. If you are unsure, say so. "I don't know" and "I don't remember" are perfectly acceptable answers when true. If you did not hear the question or did not understand it, ask the attorney to repeat it. Your responsibility is to answer the questions to the best of your ability.

Try to prepare for the unexpected. One defense attorney even "accidentally" called the survivor by her first name and the defendant's last name. The survivor corrected him. The defense attorney might ask you if you enjoyed the rape. In one such instance, the survivor responded, "If you really think I enjoyed being beaten, stran-gled, and raped, you're not very bright." You need not answer such an offensive question, however. The prosecuting attorney should object.

Most states now have rape shield laws that do not allow the wom-an's past sexual history to be brought into the courtroom *unless* she had a sexual relationship with the defendant prior to the rape; she had consenting sex with someone else within seventy-two hours prior to the assault, so it could be his seminal fluid that was collected during the evidentiary exam; her past sexual relationships establish a pattern similar to the incident with the assailant; or she has a history of "false" reports of rape, in which case the judge may rule that her past sexual history is admissible evidence. Clever defense attorneys still ask leading questions, such as "Isn't it true that on a number of occasions you have been known to meet men in bars and later willingly engage in sex with them?" Your attorney will object. The objection will be sustained, and the jury will be instructed to pretend they did not hear the statement—an impossible task, of course. Attacks on your character are especially painful to endure. Remember what you are there to do, and try to keep your composure so that you will be an effective witness. Angry outbursts will not help your case.

You may want to have someone supportive in the courtroom who is not on the witness list to listen to the testimony, especially when you or the assailant testifies. The most unbiased observer is often your legal advocate or a rape crisis counselor. If a friend or relative has been particularly supportive and wants to attend the trial, be aware that you may be very uncomfortable recounting the details of the attack in front of him or her, if you haven't already done so. Just remember, even though most trials are public, you can decide who is present from your family and circle of friends. If you don't want them to attend and are having trouble asking them not to or you feel they won't respect your wishes, ask your attorney to put them on the witness list so they won't be permitted in the courtroom unless they are testifying. Your attorney need not call them to the stand. The benefit of this tactic is that they will be in the waiting room with you and can offer you support.

Many survivors find the "story" the defendant relates in court frustrating and infuriating, even when the story is so ridiculous it would be funny under other circumstances. One observer told a survivor:

> The rapist testified, "She came back to my apartment willingly to have sex. She wanted it too." When asked about the survivor's bruises and vaginal lacerations, he answered, "Well, while I was in the bathroom undressing, I peeked out the keyhole and saw her stealing my money. She stuck it up inside her. That's how she got the cuts there. I had to beat her and tear her clothes off to get my money back. She ran into the hallway screaming."

The assailant probably will use one of two defenses: mistaken identity or consent. The first is by far the easiest on you in court. In the first instance, he will claim that while you may have been raped, he is not the person who did it. He may try to prove he was elsewhere or just that you cannot identify him beyond a reasonable doubt. He may have lost or gained weight, grown or shaved off facial hair. Usually he will be dressed very differently. One defense attorney had another man who looked very similar to the defendant sit beside him during the trial. The defendant sat behind them with a hat pulled down over his forehead. Unfortunately, the survivor did not look closely and identified the wrong man. The case was lost. Few assailants use this plea today, because the medical evidence collected, especially DNA, even though not conclusive, is so valuable in making an identificaiton.

If the assailant claims you consented to have sex with him, it will be your word against his, especially when there are no witnesses and no signs of force. It is difficult to provide clear corroborative evidence showing a lack of consent. In this case his attorney will try to defame your character by implying that you asked for it or should have known what would happen, or that you are in some way nonconventional and do not conform to "normal" female behavior. The defense attorney may ask you where you live and if you have a male roommate, or may ask, "This wasn't the first time you were out drinking alone or left the bar with a strange man, is it? You asked him to dance first, didn't you?" One defense attorney even tried to make a survivor "look bad" through the use of a condescending voice when he asked her why she was wearing a plain shirt, "like men wear," and not carrying a purse. The defendant may go so far as to make up a story that you were really prostituting and got angry over what he was willing to pay you or feared being discovered by a friend, so you cried rape. He may also claim you were exchanging sex for drugs. Remember, it's his word against yours.

> Jeanette took the bus home from a city street festival about ten o'clock at night. She was a secretary for a local employment agency and had moved to the Twin Cities from a farm community in Iowa. She felt uncomfortable, but had to transfer and was waiting at a deserted bus stop when a man jumped her, threatened her with a knife, dragged her into some bushes, then beat her brutally and raped her both orally and anally. When the assailant took the stand, he claimed he had met her on the corner many times in the past to sell her drugs. She hadn't had any money that night, probably having spent it all at the festival, so he had agreed to give her the drugs she wanted in exchange for sex. She had wanted more than he thought she was worth and attacked him. He was acquitted.

One tactic the police sometimes will use when consent is an issue is to get both parties to take a lie detector test and to agree to announce the results in court, before the outcome is known. However, few defendants and their attorneys will agree to this. While sometimes useful, lie detectors are not infallible. If you still believe you are at fault because you left your door unlocked or accepted a ride home from the rapist, you may appear to be lying.

At the end of the trial, in states that still require corroborating evidence, the judge warns the jury of the danger of convicting the defendant on the word of the victim alone, "because human experience has shown that girls and women do sometimes tell an entirely false story that is easy to make up, but extremely difficult to disprove." In no other type of criminal case is the jury warned in a similar way.

Unfortunately, juries are not instructed that it is still rape if the woman is married to the defendant or if she left a bar willingly with him. They are not warned of the danger of letting rapists back out on the streets, free to rape other women.

When the jury returns from deliberating its verdict, if the defendant is found guilty, a date will be set for sentencing. If he is found not guilty, he is released immediately. You must remember that even if he is acquitted, it does not necessarily mean that some of the jurors don't believe he raped you. The whole jury must agree on his guilt, beyond a reasonable doubt, to get a conviction.

Sentencing

In most areas, a presentencing investigation is completed by a parole officer, who should contact you to determine how you feel the rape has affected your life and what you see as an acceptable outcome. Your input is included in a report to the judge, who decides on the sentence. If there is no investigation or if you are not contacted, you still have the right, and a responsibility, to make the effort to express your opinion to the judge. Take advantage of this opportunity. Write to the judge and let him or her know how the rape has affected you. Now you have the opportunity to better educate the judge about how seriously the assault has affected your life and your family. It is also a chance to ask that the sentencing guidelines be exceeded, for instance, and your assailant given a harsher sentence because of the trauma he caused you. Family and friends may want to write impact statements as well. You can send these statements to the judge before the sentencing and/or ask to read them at the time of sentencing, in front of the assailant and his family. The judge considers your letter, the seriousness of the crime, and the assailant's past record in setting the sentence. Rape sentences have ranged from suspended sentences with no time in prison to 1,500 years in prison. In 1984 a Baltimore, Maryland, grand jury recommended castration as the only effective deterrent for repeat offenders. A bill was introduced in the Georgia Senate in the mid-1980s proposing castration of repeat offenders. It was defeated 33 to 19.

In states that have passed the Victim's Bill of Rights, you should be notified when the sentencing will occur so you can be present if you choose. Check your state's policy. If you are not notified automatically, you still can call and ask the date. If you don't want to be present, you can ask to be notified of the results.

Many individuals, even survivors of rape themselves, feel sorry for the rapist and want him put into a treatment program instead of prison. Since we seldom can keep rapists in jail forever, it would be wonderful if we could rely on treatment programs to "cure" sex offenders and ensure they would not rape again. In an extensive review of reports on all the currently used treatment methods from all around the world published in 1991, William L. Marshall and colleagues concluded that while some treatment programs have been effective with child molesters and exhibitionists, *none* have been effective with rapists. They found that for repeat offenders who completed treatment programs, 33 to 71 percent raped again and were caught and convicted of a new sexual offense. Results with first-time offenders were better; only 10 to 21 percent of them were convicted of another sex offense. It is important to remember, however, that only 2 percent of rapists are convicted in the first place. While indeed past rapists may be watched more closely, it is hard to believe that there is even the possibility of 100 percent identification of repeat offenders. Also, few studies exceed six years of follow-up and some are for as little as two years after release from prison. Marshall and colleagues also found that the combined cost to the hospital, police, courts, and corrections in dealing with a single offense amounts to $180,000. It's hard to believe that effective treatment programs for sex offenders can't be developed that would be much less costly to taxpayers.

Once the assailant is found guilty, you also can request that he be ordered by the court to pay you restitution for losses that resulted from the rape. This could include money to replace clothes or other personal property damaged in the assault; lost wages; child care expenses during trial; and counseling expenses. Talk to your victim advocate or county attorney about the policy in your area.

The Outcome

In Hennepin County, Minnesota, in 1990, about 60 percent of the sexual assault cases taken to trial were found guilty by the jury. In 1991 the figure rose to nearly 90 percent. About the same number of cases were taken to court each year, so it does not appear that the rise in conviction rates resulted from better screening of cases. Instead, wide media coverage of sexual assault issues appears to have resulted in juries being more likely to convict. However, in both 1990 and 1991, five times the number of assailants pled guilty as went to trial, so if a case was charged by the county attorney, a survivor knew there was only about a 20 percent chance she would have to testify in court.

A Senate Judiciary committee reported in May of 1993 that almost half of all rape cases that are charged nationally are dismissed, and charges are dropped before the case goes to trial. Accused robbers and murderers, the report said, are much more likely to be tried and convicted. The committee found that only about one in ten reported rapes result in time served in prison. Of the men convicted, 21 percent are released on probation and 24 percent sentenced to local jails where they spend eleven months or less behind bars.

Your case may proceed smoothly, your credibility and motives may not be challenged, and you may not need to fight for your rights within the court system. But whatever the outcome of your case, even if a suspect was never identified, or if you went to court and he got off, you need to remind yourself that you did the best that you could do under your circumstances. That is all anyone can expect of herself.

While only a small number of cases get to court, more of those cases are being won each year. We need to continue to better educate the public, as well as individuals within the court system, to dispel myths about rape and further reform our justice system, so that everyone gets just treatment.

TO THE SIGNIFICANT OTHER

Helping Her Through the Legal System

When personnel within the legal system appear not to believe the survivor, or when they insinuate that somehow she deserved what happened, the situation may be especially difficult for both you and her. If this occurs, it is important for you to reassure her again that you believe her and that you know she is not to blame. Your support will make going through the whole process much easier for her.

If her case is not charged by the prosecuting attorney, or if the defendant is not found guilty in court, she will need your support in dealing with her disappointment. It is normal for her to feel angry, helpless, and depressed. You too may experience these feelings. Allow her to go through the process without having to pretend that she feels better than she actually does. Remind her that the rapist's acquittal does not mean he was found innocent. It means there wasn't enough evidence to convict him. It also says much more about our legal system, with its prejudice and injustice, than it says about his lack of guilt.

You may want to discuss the possibility of a civil suit with her. Consult an attorney to get advice on the feasibility of this alternative.

Instead of assuming that you should attend the trial, ask the survivor what she would prefer you do. It may be more difficult for her to retell her story in full if you are there to hear the humiliation she endured and to hear the defendant's lies. She may fear you will believe him. It may be more helpful to her if you are outside the courtroom, where she will be most of the time. Don't feel hurt or rejected if she doesn't want you there at all. Don't make her use the little energy she may have left to take care of you. If she doesn't already have one, a legal advocate could provide the help she needs at this time. Call your county attorney's office and ask if legal advocacy services are available.

Delays in trial may be devastating. The stress of court will be draining. You will help her immensely if you can assume some of the responsibilities she normally carries, such as cooking, housework, and especially child care. If you cannot assume these responsibilities yourself, perhaps you can find someone else who can. If feasible, take some time off work to be with her or plan some time to relax with her in the evening.

It probably is not a good time to plan activities for you both with other people, unless they are very close friends. Ask her how she feels. If she is preoccupied with the court process and needs to talk about her concerns, social engagements and conversations with other people could be too distracting or unnerving.

What If You Know the Assailant?

Things may be especially difficult for you if the survivor was raped by an acquaintance you both know. You may have ambivalent feelings about the rape and wonder how much is true and how much she is to blame.

These doubts are especially likely to occur if the assailant does not fit your stereotype of a rapist. Remember, however, that even the least likely man could be a rapist. Looks can be deceptive. They all say "It's not true. I didn't do it." Ministers, successful businessmen, grandfathers, choir leaders, doctors, lawyers, the neighbor next door, the star quarterback, boys and men from all occupations and walks of life have committed and will commit rape. Dr. Margaret Aiken, author of *False Accusations*, reported in 1993 that estimates from police, attorneys, and rape crisis centers indicate only 1 to 6 percent of reported rapes are false. Therefore, if you believe the victim, you are more likely to be right.

If you are experiencing a lot of ambivalence, talk with a rape crisis counselor as soon as possible. He or she may be able to help you resolve your concerns. Only then will you be able to provide the survivor with the help she needs and deserves.

Knowing the assailant and the type of person he is may make you doubt the survivor less. You may wonder why she trusted him at all. But we all want to trust people and believe we are safe when out with friends.

You may feel as if you never will really know for certain what happened. Maybe it doesn't matter. What really matters the most now is that the survivor needs your support. You need to let her know how much you care about her. She doesn't need you to judge her too. There are enough other people doing that.

9

Who Rapes?

I am my choices.
—Jean-Paul Sartre

Unfortunately, there is no clear answer to why men rape women, and why they are doing so in ever-increasing numbers in the United States. The motivations are complex and often hard to understand.

While police records indicate that the majority of reported rapists are between sixteen and twenty-five years old, the range is from eight to seventy. Those apprehended and imprisoned usually come from lower socioeconomic groups, have little education, and frequently already have a criminal record of arrests or convictions for minor offenses.

Due to many biases operating within the criminal justice system, apprehended rapists are, however, a select group. These biases largely determine which rapes are reported; which rapes the police believe, thoroughly investigate, and then forward to the prosecuting attorney to charge; and which men go to court and are found guilty. These biases are likely to result in an overrepresentation of poor, uneducated minorities among apprehended rapists compared to the number found in the general population. This minority overrepresentation also occurs in other categories of violent crimes. Ruth's case is a good example of how these biases operate.

Seventeen-year-old Ruth was waiting for her girlfriend after class at the university one evening when a well-dressed man drove up and asked her for a light. As she approached his car, he grabbed her and forced her inside. He drove her to a deserted area and raped her, after beating and strangling her. In the struggle, a card fell out of his shirt pocket onto the floor of the car. She grabbed it without his knowing. As he drove off, she also got his license plate number.

She ran home and told her mother, who immediately called the police and took her to the hospital for an evidentiary exam. Although she was not seriously hurt, she had several bruises on her neck. The card turned out to be his insurance card, complete with his name and address. Ruth and her mother gave the card to the police.

The mother became concerned when several days had passed without the police officer calling for further information, as he had said he would, so she called him. He told her that he had gone and talked to the man in question. However, he said, "He's a respectable salesman with a new baby. He's got a lot more to lose than your daughter. Besides, there are a lot of prostitutes working the area where your daughter was." He had decided not to proceed with the case.

Biological Explanations of Rape

At one time it was believed that men with an extra male chromosome (XYY) were more aggressive and more likely to become violent than men without the extra Y chromosome. More sophisticated research later showed this was not true. While there were indeed a large number of men with an extra Y chromosome in jails, there were many in the normal population as well. When these men committed crimes, they were not necessarily more violent either.

Biological factors, such as a higher level of the male hormone, testosterone, also have received attention as a possible explanation for rape. Men with a higher level of testosterone have been described as "sexually supercharged individuals," unable to control their biologically triggered sexual desires. People who believe this theory encourage injecting convicted rapists with a female hormone to lower their sex drive. The assumption is also congruent with the old myth that only men have a strong sex drive, not women. However, research conducted by Ursula Laschet in 1973 showed that, while it is possible to lower the level of testosterone in sex offenders using medications, such treatment has no effect on their likelihood of offending again. The study concluded that rape is not motivated by higher levels of testosterone and an uncontrollable sex urge but by a desire for dominance and control. Laschet did find that the most violent rapists had higher testosterone levels than the less violent rapists, and she concluded that while men with higher levels of testosterone were not more likely to rape, they were more likely to be more violent when they did rape. Apparently testosterone is more highly correlated with violence than it is with sex drive.

Some attorneys are now using this correlation as a defense to keep their clients out of jail if they will agree to take female hormone shots. Unfortunately, a 1981 study at Johns Hopkins University found that 91 percent of individuals who started this type of treatment and then dropped out committed further sex crimes. And the dropout rate for this form of treatment is nearly 50 percent. Even among those who completed treatment, 30 percent reoffended. Therapists administering female hormone treatment do not expect it to eliminate sexual offending behavior; rather they hope to reduce it to a manageable level. The University of Texas Medical Branch in Galveston has extensive experience in the use of hormone therapy. Researchers there have concluded that it is useful only with those men whose sex offenses are clearly related to sexual arousal by children. As a result, they refused to administer the female hormone Depo-provera to a convicted rapist who did not fit this picture, even though the drug treatment was a condition of his parole. They knew it would not deter him.

Rape is not biologically programmed. Rape-free societies do exist and will be considered in greater detail in chapter 10. Rape is socially programmed in cultures such as ours where women are seen as unequal, in cultures that generally accept interpersonal violence and in which male dominance of women in social, business, and sexual encounters is expected and allowed. Rape is only an extension of the overall pattern of violence in interpersonal relationships in which women are expected to be submissive and to comply, and are often thought of as the property of men. To a great extent the rapist is only acting out the broader social script.

The Role of Sex and Aggression

During a rape, sex is used as a weapon to intimidate, control, and humiliate the victim. If rape was simply sexually motivated, Las Vegas, which is surrounded by legalized prostitution, would not have one of the highest rape rates in the nation. However, according to police statistics, it does.

There is clear evidence that at least one-third of rapists are sexually dysfunctional. Premature ejaculation or ejaculating immediately upon penetration are reported frequently, as is retarded ejaculation, in which the man takes a long time to ejaculate. Some survivors indicate that the rapist forced them to try numerous methods to get him to ejaculate. In a few cases, even after thirty minutes to one hour of steady penetration, he was unable to climax. The rapist often blames his inability to ejaculate on the survivor, on her inadequacy, as he probably blamed it on his past sexual partners. According to researchers such as Ann Burgess and Nicholas Groth, retarded ejaculation seems to occur in rapists with much greater frequency than in the population at large.

Rapists undergoing treatment often report encountering erectile inadequacy. In these cases they experience partial or complete failure to achieve and sustain an erection. The problem sometimes is resolved when they force the victim to stimulate them orally or manually. Other rapists become sexually stimulated by their own violence or by the victim's struggle to get away.

A study completed in 1988 at the University of California confirmed a link between sex and aggression, though the mechanism is not well understood. It was found that painful stimulation can evoke sexual as well as aggressive response selectively in both men and women. Exposure to sexual stimuli was shown to increase aggressiveness as well as sexual responsiveness. Thus in some people there appears to be a reciprocal relationship where anger may lead to sexual arousal and sexual arousal to aggressiveness. This link may not be direct, however. Both forms of arousal instead may be the result of a rise in the individual's general level of arousal.

The Role of Pornography

Pornography, like other social factors and conditions, contributes to the second-class status of women. It is naive, at best, to assume that pornography entertains an individual without affecting his or her perceptions of sexuality and what is acceptable, appropriate behavior toward members of the opposite sex. Pornography has become much more explicit in the past ten years, and research has shown there are certainly adverse effects.

In the male fantasy world of pornography, the woman often is portrayed as a compliant sexual object—an anonymous, panting plaything. While she initially may object to the male's advances, she soon invites the powerful, masterful man to use her sexually and appears to enjoy even the most gruesome torture. Pornography depicts forms of sexuality and aggression in which men derive pleasure at the expense of women, who are degraded and humiliated in the process, all the while smiling compliantly.

There are many documented cases in which men have forced or coerced women to try assorted sexual techniques or activities that they saw in pornographic films or magazines. Since many women have been taught to be submissive and comply with male sexual demands, they may try to meet these sexual "needs" for fear of rejection and at the expense of humiliation. Otherwise the men will feel justified in looking elsewhere for sex, and the women feel it is their fault, because they did not meet their mate's needs. Women often take the brunt of this porno-inspired experimentation, and perfectly sensitive women are then accused of being frigid when they, unlike the women in pornography, do not enjoy the roughness.

A research study completed in 1982 at Indiana University was designed to explore the consequences of continued exposure to "soft" pornography on the individual's beliefs about sexuality in general and disposition toward women in particular. Researchers found that people who were frequently exposed to pornography believed that unusual sexual practices were more common in real life than did those *not* exposed, even though the films did not include unusual sexual practices. The subjects exposed to pornography also greatly overestimated the number of people who are sexually active. Most disturbing, the research showed that both men and women in the former group later trivialized rape and were less compassionate toward rape victims. However, the women in each group still saw rape as more serious and acted more punitively toward rapists than the men in their group. The researchers found it interesting that people exposed to common sexual acts in erotic films would then come to view uncommon acts as occurring more frequently and rape as less serious. If this occurs, what impact does frequent exposure to sadomasochistic pornography have on people?

Another study conducted in 1981 in Canada by Neil Malamuth found that exposure to rape movies resulted in more violent sexual fantasies. The researchers questioned the potential role of such media in the development of antisocial attitudes and behavior.

Pornography is no longer limited to books, movies, and live sex acts on stage. Unfortunately, cartoons such as *The Rape of Sleeping Beauty* are now available for rental on videotape. Even cartoons on television often traditionally portray women as pieces of property. In *Popeye*, Popeye and Brutus constantly fight over Olive Oyl. In the process, she is beaten over the head and dragged around screaming and protesting. She survives only by manipulation and pleading for mercy, a poor example for our sons and daughters. Now that we have moved into the computer age, so has pornography. Pornographic computer games are now available where the player gets points for raping. The longer the rape and assault continues, the higher the "score." Here too, the victim smiles while being assaulted.

As a society we cannot afford to tolerate treating rape and the degradation of women as a game. Like rape, pornography often is antifemale, defamatory, and libelous to women, who are depicted as compliant objects. Pornography is not an expression of sexual freedom; it is a powerful force undermining true sexual expression. Even nonviolent pornography appears to promote sexual callousness toward women, a growing dissatisfaction with sexual reality, and the trivialization of rape. We cannot continue to legitimize a form of "entertainment" with such antisocial consequences.

Motives for Rape

Motives for rape are indeed complex, often overlapping, and difficult at best to understand. As a first step in preventing rape, we must try to determine not only who rapists are, so we can avoid them and lock them behind bars, but also why they rape. Some men use rape as a form of social control; it is a way others meet their social expectations of being "a man"; some use it as a form of revenge; and some men see it as a man's right.

Researchers have learned from studying convicted rapists that most are from dysfunctional families and may have been physically or sexually abused themselves. Often assailants abuse children who are the age they were when they were first abused. It is important to note that not all abused male children become abusers—just as many do not abuse others. For the most part, rapists did not bond with positive adult figures as children, and they are thus unable to be intimate as adults. They have deep-seated feelings of inadequacy and rageful anger. Most became sexually active early, at about ten years of age. They are typically in and out of jail, at first for minor offenses such as burglary or indecent exposure. Once they begin to rape, they usually reoffend on an average of once a month. Consequently, until arrested, all rapists are serial rapists, but most are not identified as such.

Gang Rape

Studies indicate that a group situation can promote sex offenses in men who would not initiate such crimes on their own. While these men are as likely to have criminal records as men who rape as individuals, their records usually do not include past sex offenses. Gang rape is thus not rape by a number of rapists, but rather rape by a group that rapes. Psychologically, the man who rapes with a group of other men is reported to be more "normal" than the lone offender.

Neither sex nor injury is the motive in gang rape. The group uses sex to demonstrate its power and to validate its strength through group conquest. It is a way for the group to interact, compete, and develop camaraderie and cohesiveness. To refuse to join in would mean exclusion and loss of self-esteem and peer recognition within the group. The rape also may be an expression of group hostility, frustration, or an attempt to compensate for feelings of inadequacy. As several sensational court cases in 1992 and 1993 show, some fraternities and gangs actually consider rape a game, in which one member is charged with finding a woman and setting her up for the group. Rape is a common initiation rite of these male groups across the country. This fact typically comes out when an arrest is made and a police investigation results.

Police reports indicate that approximately 20 percent of all reported rapes involve more than one assailant. While there are usually two men involved in a group rape, ten or more can participate. Gang rape is most likely to occur on Friday or Saturday night. While the victim may be a stranger picked up off the street, more often she will have known or been acquainted with one member of the group, having met him that night at a party or a bar. The victim of gang rape is also more likely to have been drinking prior to the assault, which makes her more vulnerable. Gangs looking for a woman to rape generally look for one who seems vulnerable. Like the lone assailant, men who rape in groups use alcohol or drugs about half the time. Some violence, hitting, or kicking is likely to occur, resulting in minor injuries to the victim. Serious physical injury is uncommon.

Unfortunately, gang rape of young girls by teenage boys has been increasing rapidly in recent years. In areas of New Jersey, in the summer of 1993, mothers were hesitant to allow their daughters to go to community swimming pools because boys were surrounding the girls, removing their bathing suits, and fondling them. Teenage boys in pairs or groups are assaulting and raping in ever-growing numbers as part of their initiation into gangs. The victims of these assaults are usually selected at random, because they are available and vulnerable.

Marital Rape

If women are seen as the property of men—father or husband—then a man cannot be accused of taking what is already his. According to some, forced sex within a marriage is thus not rape, but the right of the man.

"Damn it," Senator Jeremiah Denton, a Republican from Alabama, told the Senate Judiciary Committee in 1990, "when you get married, you kind of expect you're going to get a little sex, one way or the other." Using this line of reasoning, seven states still exclude marital rape from their rape laws. A wife who is raped by her husband in one of these states has no legal recourse. Fortunately, these laws are now changing.

In 1977 Oregon became the first state to delete the marital exclusion from its rape laws. One year later John Rideout was indicted and became the first husband charged with marital rape.

In 1980 only eight states had abolished at least part of the marital exclusion: Oregon, Nebraska, New Jersey, California, Delaware, Hawaii, Minnesota, and Iowa. By 1990, however, only seven states— Kentucky, Missouri, New Mexico, North Carolina, Oklahoma, South Carolina, and Utah—still had a spousal exclusion law on the books. Even those states exclude situations in which the couple are legally separated, living apart, or have filed for divorce.

Profiles of Rapists

Profiles compiled by police sex crimes investigators show that there are four primary types of men who rape as individuals: power-reassurance rapists; power-assertive rapists; anger-retaliation rapists;

and anger-excitation rapists. By studying the types of rapes men commit, police have learned more about them, which sometimes has led to their apprehension.

Power-Reassurance Rapist

More than 80 percent of all rapists fit into the power-reassurance group. The goal for these rapists is to resolve their doubts about their manhood and feelings of sexual inadequacy. They select victims of about their own age and rape close to their own homes. These men most often walk to the scene of the crime and talk to the victim during the assault, possibly complimenting her. They are polite and reassuring to her; leading the police to refer to them sometimes as "gentleman rapists." They have the victim remove her own clothes, much as in consenting sex. They kiss the victim and ask a lot of questions about the sex, wanting reassurance from the victim that she is enjoying the sex and that they are good sexually. These men may even take the victim's phone number and ask for a date at another time or apologize after the rape and beg for forgiveness.

Typically they use little force, although they may carry a weapon to facilitate gaining control. If she fights they usually will not hurt her. However, they become more confident and more violent with each successive rape. They usually select vulnerable, easy targets and surprise their victims.

Many power-reassurance rapists keep records of the rapes and take a souvenir, usually the woman's underpants and sometimes a bra as well. They are likely to rape once every seven to fifteen days.

These men have low self-esteem, are of average intelligence, and are low achievers. They are usually nonathletic, single, with few friends—"loners." They usually have menial jobs and may rape near the job site, if not near their homes. Most often they drive older cars with high mileage and often burglarize in addition to raping. They think women have fantasies about being raped and thus believe their victims will really enjoy it too. They consider all women "sluts" and don't trust them. They are seldom in a relationship or even dating.

Power-Assertive Rapist

The goal of power-assertive rapists is to act out their anger and induce fear in the victim. About 10 to 12 percent of all rapists fit into this category. They are threatening and threaten to kill, they intentionally degrade the victim, and they use constant profanity. Such rapists are likely to start their criminal sexual activity with obscene, threatening phone calls or by exposing themselves. They are likely to be very outgoing, social, and self-confident, macho, smart, athletic with a good physique, and dress well. Often they drive a flashy car that is well maintained. They also are likely to participate in traditionally masculine activities, such as football, baseball, hockey, fishing, and hunting.

These rapists appear to like women and often meet their victims in singles' bars, where they spend a lot of time. They have a healthy sexual appetite, which is seldom satisfied, and many consenting sexual encounters. They are sexually selfish and will do whatever they want regardless of how much the victim fights. They tend to treat women as objects, taking "her" much as they would take a car or radio they wanted. These rapists rip the clothes off their victims and spend a lot of time with them, frequently because ejaculation is retarded. They will assault the victim in multiple orifices. Often they prefer to rape women anally, *then* orally to further degrade them.

The attacks of power-assertive rapists are likely to be sporadic with no set pattern. As they are intelligent, these offenders are better able to evade the police. They are very violent and also become more violent with each rape.

Anger-Retaliation Rapist

The goal of anger-retaliation rapists is to retaliate and express their anger against women. About 5 percent of all rapists fit into this category. Their targets are usually older women in their sixties or seventies, which suggests that the rapists' anger may be toward their mothers. They kick and beat their victims violently, leaving them bruised over much of their bodies. Like power-reassurance rapists, they too rape near their homes, but the rapes are not frequent, usually only once a year. Anger-retaliation rapes are the most spontaneous rapes, with the least forethought. It is believed that they occur as a result of a fight with a woman. They may occur at any time of the day or night. Usually the rapists have drunk some alcohol prior to the rape, but they are not drunk. They get drunk afterward. They have an explosive temper and are impulsive. They hate women and are usually divorced, renting their homes because they are unable to keep a job for any extended time.

Anger-Excitation Rapist

By far the most dangerous and, fortunately, the least prevalent, accounting for about 2 percent of rapists, are the sexual sadists, or anger-excitation rapists. Most of their victims are found murdered. These rapists are disappointed if their victims die too quickly, however, so they try to keep the victims alive, sometimes for days, before killing them. The goal of sexual sadists is terrifying the victims. These rapes are well planned. The rapists may plan for months before picking up each successive victim and have elaborate torture chambers that they bring the victims back to, usually in their homes. They are likely to utilize bondage and to have many devices, including electrical shocks, prods, and leather restraints. These rapists con their victims, usually young boys, into going with them and often drug the boys to keep them compliant. Such rapists are likely to have elaborate records with pictures, names, dates, and what they did to each victim, ending with the time each "checked out."

Most of these rapists are white outdoorsmen with gun or knife collections and are avid readers of detective and soldier-of-fortune magazines. They are smart and often are college graduates with no prior arrest record. They often have big dogs. Usually they start to attack in their late thirties when they become bored with fantasy. While their first victims are often women, once they begin with male victims, all subsequent victims are males. They receive a lot of media attention when discovered and are easier to prosecute because of the records they keep. Unfortunately, they often evade discovery for years.

Men Who Are Raped

It is impossible to estimate how many men are raped each year. While only one in ten women report rape, it is likely that many fewer men report being raped, because they do not want to admit to the humiliation and degradation and do not want to have their masculinity and sexuality questioned. The problem has been ignored for decades.

While men who are raped usually are raped by other men, a very small number of men (fewer than one-half of 1 percent) are raped by women. By far the majority of offenders are male.

Men Raped by Other Men

Many people assume incorrectly that the only males who become rape victims are male children, or that male rape occurs only in prisons or among homosexuals. While it is true that male victims are often young, the age range is as wide as that for female victims, a few months of age to over ninety years. The primary difference seems to be in the number of assailants and the amount of force used in the cases reported.

Male rape victims usually are attacked by groups of men and sustain more physical trauma than female victims. Those victims who come to the attention of the authorities may be a highly select group, however, since the physical trauma may be what precipitates their coming to a hospital. In a large number of these cases, the men first went to a hospital emergency department to have their injuries treated and did not report the rape. Skilled emergency department staff later identified the precipitating event.

Male rape is more common in settings where women are absent, such as male prisons. As with female victims, rapists attack men in an attempt to assert dominance and control. Prisoners have their own values and standards. For instance, inmates who have molested children are usually detested by other prisoners and may be raped as an "inside" form of punishment.

Male survivors face many of the same problems that female survivors face. Like female survivors, males often are not believed or are accused of being homosexuals who were asking for it. An article published in the *Southwestern Medical Journal* in 1980 advised physicians examining a male rape survivor to "maintain a high level of suspicion, since in some cases the 'victim' may have an ulterior motive in reporting an alleged attack. Even if the survivor is a child, the story may be fabricated in a bid for attention."

The most devastating problem the male survivor faces is having his masculinity and sexual preference questioned by other men. Most men protect themselves from feeling vulnerable by believing only "gay" men are raped, thus the survivor must "really be gay" and have wanted it, or "is not a real man anyway."

Men Raped by Women

Although it is highly unusual, women can and do rape men. The belief that it is impossible for a man to respond sexually when he does not choose to do so is incorrect. Recently research has indicated that male sexual response can occur in a variety of emotional states, including anger and terror.

In reported and corroborated cases, men have been forced by a single woman or a group of women to participate in sexual activity, including intercourse under threat of physical violence. The men reported being physically restrained, fearing not only for their safety but also for their lives. Despite the fear, anxiety, embarrassment, and terror, they reported having had erections even though they felt no sexual desire. In some cases they repeatedly were stimulated manually by their female captors and even ejaculated.

These men, much like men and women raped by other men, experienced significant emotional trauma, which often lasted for years following the assault. As they are more likely to hide the assault for fear of disbelief and ridicule, the problems are often aggravated. The most immediate impact is the disgrace and humiliation that makes a survivor feel he is less of a man.

While they usually come to the attention of therapists when seeking help for sexual dysfunction, the men may not associate the dysfunction with the rape, especially since years probably have passed. Once in treatment, they may be involved with a therapist for years before divulging the assault.

Another major problem for men who responded sexually during an assault is that they later feel abnormal—any "normal" man would have been unresponsive. This only adds to their feelings of inadequacy and may result in their questioning their own sexual preference, possibly changing their sexual gender preference, at least in experimentation. This is especially problematic with teenage boys assaulted by men. The anxiety coupled with their sexual dysfunction may make them fear they are becoming homosexual. Other post-trauma fears include most of those experienced by female victims: extreme depression, fear and anxiety, shock, disbelief, and disorganization. They may withdraw socially from friends and family and quit or lose their jobs.

While men are typically the aggressors, sometimes they too become victims of rape. If more men were aware that they are not invulnerable, perhaps they would be more understanding of the fear of rape with which many women live.

10

Preventing Rape

> *Experience has shown me that I am not going to solve anything in one stroke, at best I am going to chip away at it.*
>
> —HUGH PRATHER

Preventing rape means first knowing that this crime does not need to occur. Rape is not an inherent factor of our existence with which we must learn to cope. Rape is not only an individual problem that each woman must work to solve, it is also a family problem, a social problem, and a national problem that we all must work actively to resolve. Before we begin to prevent rape, we must first understand how we got to a point in our society where so many women are raped each year. We must understand what the threat of rape means, what its effects are, and what it reflects in our own and other cultures. We must understand how we differ from rape-free societies.

We must then create preventive strategies based on our understanding of the dynamics involved. There are measures you can take to make yourself less vulnerable to rape. There are also strategies your community, and our society, can employ to alter situations that facilitate, condone, or simply overlook rape. While you may choose, as an individual, to utilize avoidance or risk-reducing strategies to lower your vulnerability, in the long run, as a community, we must work together toward removing the threat. We must address and change those sociocultural factors that predispose us to be a rape-prone society.

Societies in which rape is absent or virtually unknown do exist. In 1982 Peggy Reeves Sanday, an anthropologist at the University of Pennsylvania, completed a review of data available on ninety-five tribal societies and found that half were rape free. The existence of these rape-free societies demonstrates that rape is not a biological force but a societal one. It is the result of specific sociocultural factors, attitudes, and motivations of individuals within these societies. Among the factors she found that distinguish these societies are the status of women, attitudes about violence, and the parent-child relationship.

Women who live in rape-free cultures are respected, influential members of the community. They contribute equally with men to the well-being of the group, and have equal status with men. In most cases, no division of labor based on sex occurs. Women are economically independent and experience no limits on their mobility or on the places where they are permitted.

Dominance of others is not valued in rape-free societies, nor do these societies strive to dominate nature. Instead they take what they need from nature for food and shelter in the least violent, least aggressive manner possible. Their goal is to live harmoniously with each other and with the environment.

While there are certain exceptions, for the most part the wife in a rape-prone society is responsible for the nurturance of the children, and the husband is the head of the household. He provides for the family, protects them, and controls them. He is sometimes cold, distant, aloof, and stern. His main role in child care is to punish. In many American families, misbehaving children are told by their mothers, "Just wait until Daddy gets home." Many boys who grow up in rape-prone societies are taught to be tough and aggressive, not "sissies." Competition, often violent, is a way for them to demonstrate their superiority and dominance over others and is the primary measure of their value and esteem. Rape serves as an illustration of this superiority.

Protecting Yourself

Some women remain safe by not going out of the house alone, especially at night; not going out without men to "protect" them; not making eye contact with passersby; never talking to strangers; inviting only men they know well to their homes; not living alone; and wearing clothing that could not be considered "provocative."

These are passive rather than active measures. They limit your life and your activities. They may isolate you, limiting your access to people and activities that could benefit you in your social life or on your job. This passive resistance places the responsibility and burden for preventing rape solely on women.

In a 1982 report on dealing with urban crime, Stephanie Riger indicated that this kind of avoidance behavior is used most often by people who see themselves as physically weak, helpless, and vulnerable. They are usually women or the elderly. They are also more likely to be poor, black, unemployed, and living in the inner city.

On the other hand, other strategies allow you to manage risk in the face of danger. You can learn to manipulate your environment instead of limiting your life. When you go out of the house alone, carry something that you could use as a weapon, such as keys, which you can hold between your fingers. Carry key rings that hold Mace containers or a whistle that will attract attention. Since an assailant can take a knife or gun away and use it against you, carrying these weapons is not a good idea. Your local police department can tell you what weapons are legal to carry in your area.

Look confident, as if you know where you are going (whether you really do or not), when you are walking down the street alone. Criminals often choose their victims by the way they carry themselves, not by their size, weight, or sex. When driving alone, keep the windows up and the car doors locked, especially the passenger door. Have your keys ready when you approach your car, even in the daytime, and be aware of strangers near your car or people who may be following you. Always lock your car, even if you just get out for a minute, and don't accept rides from or give rides to strangers. Even the most innocent-looking stranger may be dangerous.

> Sixteen-year-old Sarah had stopped at a large chain store to shop on her way home from her girlfriend's. When she came back to her car, an old woman was sitting in it. She told Sarah she was tired. "I need a ride to my daughter's. Won't you please help me?" Sarah felt uncomfortable, but the woman was insistent. Her mother had specifically told her never to give a stranger a ride. Was this an exception? She told the woman she had to make a quick phone call first. Sarah called her mother, who told her to call the police so that they could give the woman a ride.
>
> When the police came they had difficulty extracting the old woman from Sarah's car. When they finally did, a knife fell out from under her shirt, and the "woman" turned out to be a man.

If you have to wait at a bus stop at night, wear shoes that are easy to run in. Always be alert. Know what is going on around you, and don't be afraid to run away before danger becomes acute.

Your local police department will be able to tell you what parts of town have the lowest crime rates. You may decide not to live in a ground-floor apartment, especially one with sliding glass doors. If you do have sliding glass doors, use a bar to lock them. You should keep your ground-floor windows and doors locked at night. Doors should have dead-bolt locks. Don't be tempted to leave windows up, even on those hot summer nights. While rapists often cut a screen to gain entry, in the more than sixteen years I have been working with survivors, I have not heard of one case where an assailant broke a glass window to get inside. You may even want to install a security system. Many good systems are available, and with self-installation the price is reasonable. You also may decide to get a dog.

It's important to get to know your neighbors. You and your neighbors know who is in your area who does not belong there, much more so than the police. Call the police and then your neighbors if you see someone who looks suspicious, and ask them to do the same for you.

Even if you live alone, you need not identify yourself as a single woman. Instead of putting your full name on your mailbox, put only your first initial. Do the same in the telephone book. If you live in a security building, never buzz people in if you don't know who they are, and don't let a stranger walk in with you when you enter the building. Rapists repeatedly have gained access to locked buildings by using these two techniques. Insist that the entrance to your building and the parking area be well lighted if it is not. If you are looking for a new apartment, ask your prospective landlord if there have been any burglaries or assaults in the building or area, and ask the police as well.

If people come to your door and want to make a phone call, offer to make it for them while they wait outside. While there are certainly legitimate reasons for people to enter your home, you are the one who must decide whom to let inside. It is your right and responsibility to say no to people. If you did not call a repairman, don't let one inside. Before allowing him entrance, insist on talking with whoever called him. Even if a man is in uniform, ask to see a picture ID before unlocking the chain lock.

A fireman appeared in uniform at Suzette's home and wanted to inspect her apartment. Even though he was insistent, she felt uncomfortable and would not let him inside. As soon as he left she called the police. They caught him as he was leaving the building. Three women in the area had been raped recently by a man posing as a fire marshal in order to gain entrance. All three made a positive identification.

Instead of being afraid to take a nighttime job, walk to and from the parking area with a coworker. Many businesses have escort services, although many women are hesitant to use them. If you don't like the idea of having to wait for a man to walk with you, ask a female coworker to accompany you to your car, then drive her to hers. Don't drive off until she is safely inside with her car's motor running. (Cars don't always start.)

If your car should stall on the road, you need not accept a ride from a stranger. Stay in the car with your doors locked, and if someone stops, ask him or her to call the police. If you are on a major highway, the police will be along eventually. If you see someone stalled, instead of stopping, call the police and report the incident to them. If someone hits you from the rear and you feel uncomfortable getting out, pull forward enough to get the license plate number without leaving your locked car, then drive to a safe place and call the police. If you are unable to get the license number, remember or record as many details as possible about the car and its occupants.

You also may decide to take a self-defense course. Such courses are especially helpful in promoting the attitude that you are capable of taking care of yourself. They teach you that there are many ways to get out of situations safely before they become dangerous or threatening to you. Many women report that after taking self-defense courses, they feel stronger, braver, more in control, more cautious, and more confident. They have learned to assess potentially dangerous situations and take control if attacked, without being too timid to make a move, if necessary. They have learned to get angry instead of freezing with fear. Your fear is an attacker's most powerful weapon.

Dealing with sexual harassment and not accepting it is another important part of prevention. Managing situations before they escalate may prevent problems in the future. You must learn to distinguish between friendly behavior and behavior that is overly friendly. Use your instincts: If you are at all uncomfortable, it's not okay. If you don't like the way someone touches you or puts his arm around you, ask him politely not to do so. It is not rude to maintain your privacy. Even comments that appear to be compliments on the outside are harassment when they are inappropriately familiar. Tell the person, "It makes me uncomfortable when you say that. Please don't." Don't be intimidated. Not allowing behavior that makes you uncomfortable to continue is one way of maintaining control. Let people know your boundaries. If you don't really want to have coffee or go out with a man, tell him, "Thank you, I'm not interested." If his response is "What's wrong? Don't you trust me?" a red flag should go up. You probably should *not* trust him. Don't be afraid to say no, or "That's not the point. I'm just not interested." Then don't feel guilty if he is hurt or upset that you would not do what he wanted you to do. What you want is just as important as what he wants, and your safety is more important than his ego.

Learn to deal with sexual harassment yourself. If it is difficult, practice the things you want to say in front of a mirror or with a friend. *Don't smile* when you ask someone not to touch you or when you say no. Doing so makes you look weak and gives a double message.

Instead of being afraid to talk to all strangers on the street, choose the people you want to talk to. Don't feel as if you have to say hello or talk with everyone who addresses you on the street or in any public place.

Another way to protect yourself is to lower your vulnerability by not going out alone when you plan to drink. Remember, as many as 26 percent of women who are raped are legally intoxicated, with impaired judgment. If you are out with a friend who is drinking, look out for her best interests also. If it appears that someone is attempting to get her very drunk, don't leave her alone; instead offer her a ride home. Discourage her from leaving with a man neither of you know. Set up some type of signal with your friends before you go out drinking that you all agree means "It's time to go," then stick to it.

Resisting Rape

It is extremely important to remember that every rape is different. Even if you were raped in a situation that sounds very similar to one in which someone else escaped being raped, it does not mean that you did anything wrong that caused your rape or that you could have done anything different to have prevented it. You made the best decision you could in determining what was possible and wise to risk in that particular situation, with that particular assailant, at that particular time. The most important thing is that you lived through the rape.

It also is important to remember that, for the most part, our information about resisters is quite biased. While many women successfully free themselves from a man intent on rape, most of these women do not make a police report. Many do call rape crisis centers or see counselors later as a result of the fear, anxiety, and anger they experience. However, the numbers are still significantly lower than the actual number of attempted assaults. Most survivors of attempted rapes continue life as usual, feeling relief at their escape though aware of a newly gained sense of vulnerability. This feeling is accompanied by varied degrees of fear. The more threatening the attempted rape, the stronger the resulting fear. Some women may even wonder days or weeks later, "Could he really have planned to rape me? Maybe I overreacted and only imagined he was after me."

The resisters who do report are more likely to be those who were physically hurt when resisting. As a result, a common misbelief is that rape resisters are more likely to be hurt or even killed, when many more are not hurt and successfully escape. We seldom hear from this latter group. In addition, women who make no attempt to resist often are hurt. Of the survivors interviewed in a 1984 Minneapolis study, approximately 25 percent of the women harmed did not resist in any way, and over 20 percent of those who resisted were not harmed. In a 1993 survey of its readers, *Glamour* magazine found that only 19 percent of women who had resisted a rape felt it had made the situation worse. Another 39 percent felt their resistance allowed them to avoid injury, or greater injury; 37 percent escaped as a result of the resistance; and 21 percent scared off their would-be attacker.

To determine in which situations resistance is most likely to be successful, researchers have compared information provided by survivors who escaped rape and survivors who were raped. However, this is not intended to provide general advice on how, when, or whom to resist. No one can tell if you will escape successfully, be seriously hurt, or be killed. You can only trust your instincts at the time.

A study completed in Chicago in 1981 found that women who successfully resisted rapists were usually attacked by a stranger. They were more likely to be attacked outside, where they and the rapist could flee more easily. Attacks that occur outside are also more likely to be interrupted by a passerby who may accidentally come upon the assault or hear screams or struggling. A young boy in St. Louis received national attention when he called the police, who then stopped two other boys who were raping a young girl in a city park. Shortly after that incident, a group of women came to the rescue of another woman who had been stripped by a man intent on rape. Incredibly enough, this last attack occurred in the early afternoon on a busy sidewalk of another large midwestern city—Minneapolis.

Resisters were more likely to try a number of different strategies to get free. These women were also more likely to use active forms of resistance, such as biting, kicking, hitting, struggling, and screaming. A Denver study found resisters are younger, and those who don't resist older. In our culture physical forms of resistance are more acceptable for children and teens than for mature women. The former have not yet been taught the importance of acting like ladies; as a result, they are more likely to kick and bite, and run away, certainly not "ladylike" behavior. The likelihood of resistance diminishes significantly among girls sixteen or older and is even less likely among those nearly twenty. In the Denver study, black women, however, were found to physically resist attackers at a somewhat older age than white women.

A study conducted in Israel in 1977 asked a group of convicted rapists what their victims could have done to make them stop the rape. The overwhelming response was to make them see her as a real person with real feelings and to make them understand that what they were going to do was going to ruin her life. These rapists reported that it was important for them to maintain emotional distance from their victim and to see her as a nameless, faceless object. They did not relate to her suffering. Over 50 percent denied harming the victim emotionally or physically and expressed no regret for the rape. They reported feeling emotions for their victims only when they did not complete the rape. When they could not depersonalize the victim as insignificant, when she told them about her problems or somehow aroused personal feelings in the assailants, they did not rape.

Talk alone won't necessarily prevent rape. The 1981 Chicago study just cited also found that women who were raped were more likely to use fewer and more passive forms of resistance, such as pleading or talking their way out. They more likely knew the assailant and were attacked in their home with fewer avenues of escape for themselves and the rapist. In some cases they were awakened from their sleep and were confused or disoriented. They usually were threatened with force and were afraid of being killed. Their initial response when attacked was fear rather than anger, and their primary concern was in staying alive and living through the experience without being mutilated.

The timing of resistance appears to be an important factor in its success. So is maintaining control. Escaping before the situation becomes physical is always preferable. There is usually an ambiguous period during which you're really not sure what he wants and he is not really sure what his next move will be. This is your chance to take control by making the first move. Don't wait until you "know" he plans to hurt you. Why give him the benefit of the doubt? If you feel uncomfortable, it's time to take action. Many women let this initial chance for escape pass by because they are afraid of looking silly or appearing rude when no real harm was meant. The alternative is too serious to worry about possible embarrassment. It is better to make a scene than to be raped. If you even think you hear someone following you, don't be afraid to run away or turn and face the person if escape does not seem possible. One woman who had just taken her first self-defense lesson found herself in such a situation.

Carla started taking the self-defense class because she had been raped a year before in her home. One night while walking home from the bus, she heard footsteps behind her. "I crossed the street. He did too. He was getting closer. It was almost midnight and the street was deserted. There was nowhere to run. My heart was pounding and my knees weak from fear. 'No,' I said to myself, 'I will not let it happen again.' My fear turned to anger. I stopped, turned around, quickly yelled as loudly as I could, and assumed a karate stance. Fortunately, he turned and ran away, because that was as far as my first class had gone."

Carla had caught him off guard and thwarted a potential rape. Rapists, like other criminals, usually have one scenario that they repeat. This man's was probably to grab the woman from behind. He was afraid to attack a woman face to face, especially one who looked so strong and sure of herself. Although Carla's fear soon returned, she had been powerful and in control when necessary.

> While on her first date with Andy, Lucy began to get uncomfortable as he drove away from the restaurant and became insistent that she accompany him to his apartment. The more angry and insistent he became, the more frightened she became. He locked the doors so she could not get out of his car. She pretended to change her attitude and affectionately moved over beside him as he stopped at a light. As she did so, she put her foot down hard on the accelerator and rammed into the car stopped in front of them. As the driver of the car they had hit came back to talk to Andy, she unlocked her door and got out.

If a stranger enters your home uninvited, order him out—loudly. You'd be surprised how many leave. To maintain control of the situation, you need to react with authority and sound forceful and commanding—angry instead of afraid. You need to look self-assured and confident on the outside no matter how anxious you are inside. He is counting on your being afraid and doing what he wants.

Remember, though, only you can decide if attempts at resisting are appropriate. The most important thing is to stay in control and be alert for the right moment to resist, if one should come along. Your success will depend on the situation and the assailant as well as on you. Not everyone has the opportunity to get away.

Community Preventive Strategies

Rape is a crime against the community, not just the individual. The community has both an opportunity and a responsibility to play an active role in effecting change through political, legal, and neighborhood organizations.

Politicization of Women

Individual women in positions of power and influence and groups of women have a responsibility to become politically astute and actively demand change to benefit women in general. These concerned individuals need to develop public pressure groups with task forces and to initiate legislative lobbying efforts. They must demand accountability from private and public boards, businesses and organizations, and become familiar with the voting record of elected officials on women's rights issues. Hillary Clinton, a powerful first lady, is setting an excellent example for the young women of this country by being more concerned about health care and welfare reform than about redecorating the White House.

Uncooperative businesses, such as those selling rape video games, should be picketed, and press releases sent out that clearly state the objections to these businesses. Environmental groups have been employing these techniques successfully for years. The nationwide tuna boycott is a good example of how this strategy can impact businesses. Women Against Pornography in New York City exerted political pressure over the video game *Custer's Revenge,* in which a cowboy rapes an Indian maiden to "score." The end result, which is far from adequate, is that the game is still on the market, but the woman now smiles when raped and is not bound. Not giving up, the activists decided to put pressure on the legislature to pass ordinances banning the distribution of the game. Oklahoma City did so.

Due to persistent efforts on the part of professional and citizen's groups of both men and women, the U.S. Congress mandated in 1976 the National Center for the Prevention and Control of Rape. Money was specifically allocated through the center for funding rape crisis centers and rape research across the country. These centers were the beginning of active community change in large and small communities.

The state and federal legislatures, as a result of political pressure and the entrance of more women into the legal profession, also have changed laws related to rape. As discussed earlier, these laws now make it easier to prosecute rapists. However, the changes in the laws have not been sufficient. Laws alone won't stop rape. Laws are only as good as the people who enforce them. Myths, biases, and stereo-types about rape held by individuals within the criminal justice system and within the pool of prospective jurors limit the enforcement of these laws and the prosecution of rapists.

When the government decided it was time to stop Americans from littering, an active campaign was launched across the country and littering was greatly reduced. Groups and individuals even "adopted" stretches of highways to keep them litter free. When San Francisco elected a female mayor who took an interest in stopping rape, there was significantly less rape.

It is indeed tragic that Anita Hill had to endure the attempted defamation of her character and credibility at the hands of an all-male board of inquiry after speaking out about the sexual harassment she had already endured at the hands of Clarence Thomas, then a nominee to the U.S. Supreme Court. The result was, however, that women in Congress decided they could no longer quietly sit back. This travesty of justice spurred them on. Perhaps when more women are sitting in the House and Senate, preventing rape will become as important as curtailing litter.

Neighborhood Activism

Neighborhood organizations can play an effective role in lowering the incidence of rape by establishing neighborhood watches. The neighborhood watch program, which the police have introduced in many areas, is an effective way in which people can look out for each other by reporting any suspicious activity to the police. Participation in neighborhood organizations to fight crime and remove drug dealers from your neighborhood is also important and has been effective. It is also a good way to get to know the people in your community and enlist their help in dealing with the threat of rape. As a group you may be able to remove signs of neighborhood decay and improve the general feeling of safety.

Communities have held meetings in churches or schools to ensure that everyone is aware of a rapist in the area, so everyone can take precautions. Fliers may go out publicizing the assaults and speakers may be brought in to talk about preventive strategies. Some communities have begun "Take Back the Night" rallies, or campaigns for the neighbors to keep their lights on at night, on porches and in yards.

Safety-awareness programs should be targeted at teenagers and women under thirty, who make up the large majority of potential victims. Reporting should be encouraged to help catch rapists and spare other women from victimization. Education to dispel myths and stereotypes should be directed at people within the criminal justice system—police, attorneys, judges, clerks—who interact with survivors and who make decisions about which cases are prosecuted. Most important, this education must include the general population, those people who may one day be part of the jury of a rape case.

Sociocultural Preventive Strategies

In order to stop rape, not just deflect the rapist to another individual or another community, rape prevention must occur within the sociocultural context and include the assurance of equality for women, nontolerance of interpersonal violence, and a change in our childrearing practices.

Men and women do not need to share the same bathroom to be equal, although that was one of the scare tactics used to defeat the Equal Rights Amendment. Women and men can remain different though equal. Women can function effectively in combat military positions, and did so during the Gulf War. There was even a female B-52 bomber pilot during World War II, a well-kept military secret.

True equality for women will be achieved only when sexual oppression is removed from our laws, our institutions, our family structure, and our psyches. Equal status means that the separation of jobs and decision making must occur on the basis of ability, not sex. It means that sex-role stereotyping must be eliminated from the attitudes and perceptions of the expected and appropriate behavior of both men and women. It means that sex biases must be eliminated from hiring practices, from organizational boards of directors, from businesses, and from religious institutions.

Equal rights also means assuming equal responsibility and contributing equally to the social welfare. It means no longer devaluing women's work or women's art, as has been done for generations by both men and women. When the first woman climbed Mount Everest, a prominent male guest on a television talk show commented, "If a woman can do it, it must not be that hard." Women's work is devalued openly in the amount of money many industries pay women in comparison to men. Many government agencies have recently implemented "equal value, equal pay" systems where job worth is being reevaluated and salaries adjusted accordingly.

Sex-role stereotypes and women's dependence on men are burdensome and limit men as well as women. With so many expectations and limitations based solely on gender, neither sex is able to reach its full potential. Women must let go of the false security that dependence provides and affirm their own worth. Dependence on someone else relieves fear and conflict for only a brief period, it does not resolve it. Only self-reliance will do that. While men may act benevolently toward women who submit willingly to their control, some may quickly justify violence when the women are not grateful. You cannot be "protected" and independent at the same time. As long as someone else is responsible for you, you are not in control.

It is possible to be feminine and still be independently successful, forthright, and equal to men. Yet many women who achieve career success and equality in the business world are insecure in their femininity in social relationships because of traditional stereotypes perpetuated by both sexes. Men also can be masculine and nurturing at the same time.

Instead of trying to stop rape by restricting women's activities and thus further victimizing them, women must become actively involved with the problem of rape and in deciding appropriate solutions. As Golda Meir proclaimed when the Israeli government suggested putting a curfew on women to "protect" them from rape: "Put a curfew on the men."

Each of us must be a party to the resolution of this problem. Rape is an affront to the civilized standards of all members of humanity. It is a socioeconomic problem of grave magnitude. It is not something that is going to be resolved overnight. Before rape stops, a sociocultural change must occur. The result must be a new social order with true gender equality, a new way of life—more fulfilling and rewarding—with a new freedom for all involved. In the process of bringing about this change, we must not establish a new adversarial system pitting women against men. Both men and women must work together to stop rape. Women must assume their place as equals to men—strong, independent, self-reliant, and in control of their lives and bodies.

Rape Crisis Centers
in the United States

What follows is a representative listing of centers around the country. It is not an exhaustive list. If your town is not shown here you may be able to find a local center by looking in your telephone directory under "Rape." In the listings, the first telephone number is a twenty-four-hour hot line, unless indicated by an *.

ALABAMA

BIRMINGHAM

Rape Response Program
3600 Eighth Avenue South
Birmingham, AL 35222
(205) 323-7273

DOTHAN

Wiregrass Comprehensive
  Mental Health Center
104 Prevatt Road
P.O. Drawer 1245
Dothan, AL 36302
(205) 794-0300
(205) 794-0731

MONTGOMERY

Council Against Rape—
  Lighthouse
1415 East South Boulevard
Montgomery, AL 36116
(205) 286-5987
(205) 286-5980

ALASKA

ANCHORAGE

Standing Together Against
  Rape
360 West Benson
  Boulevard, Suite 201
Anchorage, AK 99503
(907) 563-7273
(907) 563-9981

FAIRBANKS

Women in Crisis—
  Counseling &
  Assistance, Inc.
717 9th Avenue
Fairbanks, AK 99701
(907) 452-2293

KENAI

Rape Intervention Program
Women's Resource Center
325 Spruce Street
Kenai, AK 99611

(907) 283-7257
(907) 283-9479 (office)

NOME

Bering Sea Women's
  Group
P.O. Box 1596
Nome, AK 99762
(907) 443-5444

ARIZONA

PHOENIX

Center Against Sexual
  Assault (CASA)
5555 N. Seventh Avenue
Phoenix, AZ 85013
(602) 257-8095
(602) 956-1163

PRESCOTT

Faith House, Inc.
1535 Private Road
Prescott, AZ 86301

(602) 445-4673
(602) 445-4705

TUCSON

Tucson Rape Crisis Center,
Inc.
P.O. Box 40306
Tucson, AZ 85717
(602) 623-7273
(602) 327-1171

ARKANSAS

FORT SMITH

Rape Crisis Service
P.O. Box 2887, Station A
3111 S. Seventieth Street
Fort Smith, AR 72913
(501) 452-6650

PINE BLUFF

Volunteers in Courts/Rape
Crisis Counseling
Program
512 Pine Street, Suite 427
Pine Bluff, AR 71601
(501) 535-6770

CALIFORNIA

BAKERSFIELD

Rape Hotline Kern County
Kern Medical Center
Bakersfield, CA 93305
(805) 324-7273

BERKELEY

Bay Area Women Against
Rape
357 MacArthur Boulevard
Oakland, CA 94610
(510) 845-7273
(510) 465-3890

CHICO

Rape Crisis Intervention of
North Central California
2889 Cohasset Road,
No. 2
(916) 342-7273

CLAREMONT

Project Sister Rape Crisis
Service
P.O. Box 621
Claremont, CA 91711
(714) 623-4357
(714) 623-1619 (office)

CONCORD

Rape Crisis Service of
Concord
1760 Clayton Road
Concord, CA 94520
(415) 798-7273

DAVIS

Sexual Assault and
Domestic Violence
Center
927 Main Street
Woodland, CA 95695
(916) 662-1133
(916) 758-8400
(916) 661-6336 (office)
(916) 371-1907

FORT BRAGG

Project Sanctuary
200 B-S Franklin Street
P.O. Box 1224
Fort Bragg, CA 95437
(707) 964-4357
(707) 961-1507 (office)

FRESNO

Rape Counseling Service
1551 E. Shaw, Suite 130
Fresno, CA 93710
(209) 222-7273
(209) 227-1800 (office)

LAGUNA BEACH

Rape Crisis Unit
460 Ocean Avenue
Laguna Beach, CA 92651
1 (800) 564-8448
(714) 494-0761

LOMPOC

Lompoc Rape Crisis
Center
P.O. Box 148
Lompoc, CA 93438
(805) 736-8913
(805) 736-7273
(805) 928-5818

LOS ANGELES

Los Angeles Rape and
Battering Hotline
6043 Hollywood
Boulevard, Suite 200
Los Angeles, CA 90028
(310) 392-8381
(310) 626-3393 (office)

Rape Response Program
8730 Alden Drive, Room
C301
Los Angeles, CA 90048
(310) 855-3506
(310) 855-3530 (office)

MONTEREY

Monterey Rape Crisis
Center
P.O. Box 2630
Monterey, CA 93940
(408) 633-5900

ORANGE

Rape Crisis Hotline
17200 Jamboree Road,
Suite D
Irvine, CA 92714
(714) 831-9110

PALO ALTO

Mid-Peninsula Rape Crisis
Center
4161 Alma Street
Palo Alto, CA 94306
(415) 493-7273
(415) 494-0993 (office)

PASADENA

Pasadena YWCA Rape
Crisis Center

78 N. Marengo Avenue
Pasadena, CA 91101
(818) 793-3385

RIVERSIDE

Riverside Area Rape Crisis
Center
2060 University, Suite 203
Riverside, CA 92507
(909) 686-7273

SAN BERNARDINO

San Bernardino Sexual
Assault Service
1875 North D Street
San Bernardino, CA 92405
(909) 882-5291
(909) 883-8689 (office)
1 (800) 222-7273

SAN DIEGO

Center for Women's Study
and Services
2467 E. Street
San Diego, CA 92102
(619) 233-8984

SAN FRANCISCO

San Francisco Women
Against Rape
3543 Eighteenth Street,
Box 7
San Francisco, CA 94110
(415) 647-7273

University of California
Rape Treatment Center
500 Parnassus Avenue
San Francisco, CA 94143
(415) 666-9000

SAN JOSE

YWCA Assault and
Prevention Services
375 S. Third Street
San Jose, CA 95112
(408) 287-3000
(408) 295-4011 (office)

SAN LUIS REY

Women's Resource Center
4070 Mission Avenue
P.O. Box 499
San Luis Rey, CA 92068
(619) 757-3500

SAN MATEO

San Mateo Women Against
Rape
P.O. Box 6299
San Mateo, CA 94403
(415) 349-7273

SAN PABLO

Rape Crisis Center of West
Contra Costa
c/o Brookside Hospital
2000 Vale Road
San Pablo, CA 94806
(415) 236-7273

SAN RAFAEL

Marin Rape Crisis Center
24 H Street
San Rafael, CA 94901
(415) 924-2100

SANTA BARBARA

Santa Barbara Rape Crisis
Center
700 N. Milpas Street
Santa Barbara, CA 93103
(805) 569-2255
(805) 963-6832 (office)

SANTA CRUZ

Santa Cruz Women
Against Rape
P.O. Box 711
Santa Cruz, CA 95061
(408) 426-7273

SANTA MONICA

Rape Treatment Center
Santa Monica Hospital
Medical Center
1225 Fifteenth Street

Santa Monica, CA 90404
(213) 319-4000

SANTA ROSA

Sonoma County Women
Against Rape
P.O. Box 1426
Santa Rosa, CA 95402
(707) 545-7273
(707) 545-7270 (office)

STOCKTON

Sexual Assault Center of
San Joaquin County
930 N. Commerce
Stockton, CA 95202
(209) 465-4997
(209) 941-2611

COLORADO

ASPEN

Aspen Couseling Center
P.O. Box 1340
Aspen, CO 81612
(303) 920-5555

BOULDER

Mental Health Center
Rape Crisis Team
1333 Iris
Boulder, CO 80302
(303) 443-7300

COLORADO SPRINGS

Colorado Springs Police
Department
705 E. Vernijo
Colorado Springs, CO
80903
(303) 444-7700

DENVER

Rape Assistance Awareness
Program
P.O. Box 18951
Denver, CO 80218
(303) 322-7273
(303) 329-9922 (office)

DURANGO

Rape Intervention Team
P.O. Box 2723
Durango, CO 81302
(303) 247-5400
(303) 247-4311

GRAND JUNCTION

Rape Crisis Center
1129 Colorado Avenue
Grand Junction, CO
  81501
(303) 243-0190

GREELEY

Weld County Sexual
  Assault Support Team
Box 240
Greeley, CO 80632
(303) 352-7273

CONNECTICUT

BRIDGEPORT

Rape Crisis Service
753 Fairfield Avenue
Bridgeport, CT 06604
(203) 333-2233
(203) 334-6154 (office)

HARTFORD

Sexual Assault Crisis
  Service/YWCA
135 Broad Street
Hartford, CT 06105
(203) 522-6666
(203) 525-1163 ext. 205
  (office)

MIDDLETOWN

Middlesex County Sexual
  Assault Crisis Service
P.O. Box 1514
Middletown, CT 06457
(203) 346-7233

MILFORD

Milford Rape Crisis Center
70 W. River Street

P.O. Box 521
Milford, CT 06460
(203) 878-1212

NEW HAVEN

Rape Counseling Team
Yale-New Haven Hospital
20 York Street,
  Room 1-218
New Haven, CT 06504
(203) 785-2222

Rape Crisis Center/YWCA
48 Howe Street
New Haven, CT 06511
(203) 624-2273

NEW LONDON

Women's Center Rape
  Crisis Service
16 Jay Street
New London, CT 06320
(203) 442-4357

STAMFORD

Rape Crisis Center of
  Stamford
1845 Summer Street, 2nd
  floor
Stamford, CT 06905
(203) 329-2929

DELAWARE

MILFORD

Rape Crisis Service
P.O. Box 61
Milford, DE 19963
1 (800) 262-9800
(302) 422-2078 (office)

DISTRICT OF COLUMBIA

D.C. Rape Crisis Center
P.O. Box 21409
Washington, DC 20009
(202) 232-0202

FLORIDA

GAINESVILLE

Rape/Crime Victim
  Advocate Program
730 N. Waldo Road,
  Building "B"
Suite 100
Gainesville, FL 32601
(904) 377-7273
(904) 372-3659 (office)

MIAMI

Rape Treatment Center
1611 N.W. Twelfth Avenue
Miami, FL 33136
(305) 585-7273
(305) 585-6949

OCALA

Creative Services/Rape
  Crisis/Spouse Abuse
P.O. Box 2193
Ocala, FL 34478
(904) 622-8495

ORLANDO

Rape Response
719 Irma Avenue
Orlando, FL 32803
(407) 740-5408
(407) 246-8007

PENSACOLA

Rape Crisis Center of
  Northwest Florida
Lakeview Center
1221 W. Lakeview Avenue
Pensacola, FL 32501
(904) 433-7273

SARASOTA

SPARCC—Safe Place and
  Rape Crisis Center of
  Sarasota, INC.
1750 17th Street,
  Building G
Sarasota, FL 34234
(813) 365-1976
(813) 365-0208 (office)

TAMPA

Hillsborough County
Crisis Center
2214 E. Henry Avenue
Tampa, FL 33610
(813) 238-7273
(813) 238-8411 (office)

GEORGIA

ATLANTA

Rape Crisis Center
Grady Health System
P.O. Box 26049
80 Butler Street S.E.
Atlanta, GA 30335-3801
(404) 659-7273

MARIETTA

YWCA Rape Crisis Center
48 Henderson Street
Marietta, GA 30364
(404) 428-2666

SAVANNAH

Rape Crisis Center of the
Coastal Empire, Inc.
P.O. Box 8492
Savannah, GA 31412
(912) 233-7273
(912) 354-6742

HAWAII

HONOLULU

Sex Abuse Treatment
Center
1415 Kalakaua Avenue,
Suite 201
Honolulu, HI 96826
(808) 524-7273

IDAHO

BOISE

Rape Crisis Alliance
720 W. Washington Street
Boise, ID 83702
(208) 345-7273

NAMPA

Mercy House
Box 558
Nampa, ID 83653
(208) 465-5011

MOSCOW

Alternatives to Violence of
the Palouse
P.O. Box 8517
Moscow, ID 83843
(208) 883-4357
(509) 332-4357
(509) 332-0552 (office)

POCATELLO

Pocatello Women's
Advocates
454 N. Garfield
Pocatello, ID 83204
(208) 232-9169
(208) 232-0799 (office)

TWIN FALLS

Volunteers Against
Violence, Inc.
P.O. Box 2444
Twin Falls, ID 83303
(208) 733-0100

ILLINOIS

BELLEVILLE

Rape Team/Call for Help,
Inc.
9400 Lebannon Road
Edgemont, IL 62203
(618) 397-0963

CHICAGO

Rape Hotline
Department of Human
Services
510 N. Prestigo Court
Chicago, IL 60611
(312) 744-8418
(312) 744-5829

Chicago Women Against
Rape

Loop YWCA—Women's
Services
180 N. Wabash
Chicago IL 60601
*(312) 372-6600, ext. 301
(9:00 A.M.–5:00 P.M.)

JOLIET

Will County Rape Crisis
Center
P.O. Box 2354
Joliet, IL 60434-9998
(815) 722-3344
(815) 744-5280 (office)

MOLINE

Rape Crisis Line
111 19th Avenue
Moline, IL 61265
(309) 326-9191
(309) 797-1777

ROCKFORD

Rockford Rape Counseling
Center
P.O. Box 1976
Rockford, IL 61110
(815) 964-4044
(815) 964-2991

SPRINGFIELD

Rape Information and
Counseling Service
(RICS)
110 W. Laurel
Springfield, IL 62704
(217) 703-8081
(217) 744-2560 (office)

INDIANA

COLUMBUS

Turning Point
P.O. Box 103
Columbus, IN 47202
1 (800) 221-6311
(812) 379-9844 (office)

EVANSVILLE

Crisis Line
1018 Lincoln Avenue

Evansville, IN 47714
(812) 425-4355

FORT WAYNE

Rape Awareness
P.O. Box 10554
Fort Wayne, IN 46853
(219) 426-7273

WARSAW

Protective Services for
    Sexual Assault
Otis R. Bowen Center for
    Human Services
850 N. Harrison Street
Warsaw, IN 46580
1 (800) 342-5652
(219) 267-7169

LAWRENCEBURG

Rape Crisis Intervention
    Team
Community Mental Health
    Center
285 Bielby Road
Lawrenceburg, IN 47025
1 (800) 832-5378
(812) 537-1302

IOWA

AMES

Access
P.O. Box 1965
Ames, IA 50010
(515) 232-2303

CEDAR RAPIDS

Rape Crisis Services/
    YWCA
318 Fifth Street SE
Cedar Rapids, IA 52401
(319) 363-5490
(319) 365-1458 (YWCA)

DAVENPORT

Rape/Sexual Assault
    Counseling Center of
    Scott and Rock Island
    Counties

115 W. 6th Street
Davenport, IA 52803
(319) 326-9191

FORT DODGE

Domestic/Sexual Assault
    Outreach Center
P.O. Box 173
Fort Dodge, IA 50501
(515) 573-8000
(515) 955-2273 (office)

IOWA CITY

Rape Victim Advocacy
    Program (RVAP)
17 W. Prentiss
Iowa City, IA 52240
(319) 335-6000
(319) 335-6001 (office)

KANSAS

HAYES

Family Shelter, Inc.
P.O. Box 284
Hayes, KS 67601
(913) 625-3055
(913) 625-4202 (office)

HUMBOLDT

Rape Counseling Service
Southeast Kansas Mental
    Health Center
1106 S. Ninth Street
Humboldt, KS 66748
(316) 473-2241

HUTCHINSON

Sexual Assault/Domestic
    Violence Center
1 East 9th
Hutchinson, KS 67501
(316) 663-2522
(316) 665-3630 (office)

JUNCTION CITY

Junction City-Geary
    County Rape Victim
    Support Team

1102 St. Mary's Road
Junction City, KS 66441
(913) 238-4131

LAWRENCE

Rape Victim Support
    Service
1419 Massachusetts
Lawrence, KS 66044
(913) 841-2345
(913) 843-8985

MANHATTAN

Crisis Center Inc.
P.O. Box 1526
Manhattan, KS 66502
1 (800) 727-2785

WICHITA

Wichita Area Sexual
    Assault Center Inc.
215 N. St. Francis, Suite 1
Wichita, KS 67214
(316) 263-3002
(316) 263-0185 (office)

KENTUCKY

LEXINGTON

Lexington Rape Crisis
    Center
P.O. Box 1603
Lexington, KY 40592
(606) 253-2511
(606) 253-2615 (office)

OWENSBORO

Green River
    Comprehensive Care/
    Crisis Line
P.O. Box 950
Owensboro, KY 42302-
    0950
(502) 684-9466
(502) 684-0696 (office)

Rape Victims Services
    Project
2010 Triplate Street

Owensboro, KY 42301
(502) 926-7273

LOUISVILLE

YWCA Rape Relief Center
226 W. Breckenridge Street
Louisville, KY 40203
(502) 581-7273

NEWPORT

Women's Crisis Center of
  Northern Kentucky
321 York Street
Newport, KY 41071
1 (800) 928-3335
(606) 491-3335

LOUISIANA

ALEXANDRIA

Turning Point Shelter
HELP LINE
1404 Murray Street
Alexandria, LA 71301
(318) 445-2022
(318) 448-0284

BATON ROUGE

Stop Rape Crisis Center
233 St. Ferdinands, No.
  205
Baton Rouge, LA 70801
(504) 383-7273
(504) 389-3456

NEW ORLEANS

YWCA Rape Crisis Service
601 S. Jefferson Davis
  Parkway
New Orleans, LA 70119
(504) 483-8888
(504) 482-9922 (office)

MAINE

PORTLAND

The Rape Crisis Center of
  Greater Portland
P.O. Box 1371

Portland, ME 04104
(207) 774-3613

WATERVILLE

Rape Crisis Assistance
P.O. Box 924
Waterville, ME 04903
1 (800) 525-4441
(207) 872-0601

MARYLAND

BALTIMORE

Sexual Assault Recovery
  Center
2225 N. Charles Street,
  5th floor
Baltimore, MD 21218
(410) 366-7273

CHEVERLY

Prince George's County
  Sexual Assault Center
3001 Hospital Drive
Cheverly, MD 20785
(410) 341-4942
(410) 341-2005 (office)

COLUMBIA

Howard County Sexual
  Assault Center
8950 Route 108, Suite 124
Columbia, MD 21045
(410) 997-3292
(410) 964-0504

MASSACHUSETTS

AMHERST

Counselors/Advocates
  Against Rape
Everywoman's Center
Wilder Hall, University of
  Massachusetts
Amherst, MA 01002
(413) 545-0800
(413) 545-3474 (office)

BOSTON

Rape Crisis Intervention
  Program

Beth Israel Hospital
330 Brookline Avenue
Boston, MA 02115
(617) 735-3337
(617) 735-4645

CAMBRIDGE

Boston Area Rape Crisis
  Center
99 Bishop Richard Allen
  Drive
Cambridge, MA 02139
(617) 492-7273
(617) 492-8306

DEDHAM

Norfolk County Rape Unit
360 Washington Street
Dedham, MA 02026
(617) 326-1111

HYANNIS

Independence House
22 Main Street
Hyannis, MA 02601
1 (800) 439-6507
(508) 771-6507

LYNN

Atlantic Care Medical
  Center
Rape Crisis Services
212 Boston Street
Lynn, MA 01904
(617) 477-5385

WORCESTER

Rape Crisis Program
100 Grove Street
Worcester, MA 01519
(508) 799-5700
(508) 791-9546

MICHIGAN

ANN ARBOR

Assault Crisis Center
2340 E. Stadium
  Boulevard

Ann Arbor, MI 48197
(313) 994-1616

YPSILANTI

Assault Crisis Center
1866 Packard Road
Ypsilanti, MI 48197
(313) 483-7273
(313) 483-7942

BAY CITY

Bay County Women's
Center for Rape and
Assault
P.O. Box 1458
Bay City, MI 48706
(517) 686-4551

DETROIT

Rape Counseling Center
Detroit Police Department
4201 St. Antoine
Detroit, MI 48201
(313) 833-1660

EAST LANSING

Sexual Assault Counseling
of the Listening Ear
423 Albert
East Lansing, MI 48823
(517) 337-1717

GRAND RAPIDS

Cornerstone Sexual
Assault Services
240 Cherry Street,
9th floor
Grand Rapids, MI 49503
(616) 336-3535

KALAMAZOO

Kalamazoo Sexual Assault
Program
YWCA
353 East Michigan Avenue
Kalamazoo, MI 49007
(616) 345-3036

MUSKEGON

Rape/Spouse Assault Crisis
Center of EveryWomen's
Place
425 W. Western
Muskegon, MI 49440
(616) 722-3333
(616) 726-4493 (office)

PONTIAC

Oakland Crisis Center for
Rape and Sexual Abuse
YWCA of Pontiac-North
Oakland
92 Whittemore Street
Pontiac, MI 48058
(313) 334-1274
(313) 334-1284

PORT HURON

St. Clair County Domestic
Assault and Rape
Elimination Services
Task Force (DARES)
P.O. Box 610968
Port Huron, MI 48061-
0968
(313) 985-5538

SAGINAW

Saginaw County Sexual
Assault Center
1226 N. Michigan Avenue
Saginaw, MI 48602
(517) 755-6565

MINNESOTA

BRAINERD

Sexual Assault Services
P.O. Box 602
Brainerd, MN 56401
(218) 828-1216

DULUTH

Aid to Victims of Sexual
Assault
2 E. Fifth Street
Duluth, MN 55085
(218) 727-4353

MINNEAPOLIS

Sexual Assault Resource
Service
525 Portland Avenue,
7th level
Minneapolis, MN 55415
*(612) 347-5832 (Monday
through Friday, 9:00
A.M. to 5:00 P.M.)

Sexual Violence Center
2100 Pillsbury
Minneapolis, MN 55404
(612) 871-5111
(612) 871-5100

Rape and Sexual Assault
Center
2431 Hennepin Avenue
South
Minneapolis, MN 55405
*(612) 825-4357 (9:00
A.M. to 7:30 P.M.)

ROCHESTER

Rapeline Program
151 S.E. 4th Street
Rochester, MN 55904-
3711
(507) 289-0636

St. CLOUD

Central Minnesota Sexual
Assault Center
601½ Mall Germain Street
St. Cloud, MN 56301
(612) 251-4357

St. PAUL

Sexual Offense Services of
Ramsey County (SOS)
1619 Dayton Avenue
St. Paul, MN 55104
(612) 298-5898

WINONA

Women's Resource Service
77 East Fifth Street
Winona, MN 55987
(507) 452-4440

MISSISSIPPI

BILOXI

Gulf Coast Women's
Center
P.O. Box 333
Biloxi, MS 39533
(601) 435-1968
(601) 436-3809

JACKSON

Jackson Rape Crisis Center
P.O. Box 2248
Jackson, MS 39225-2248
(601) 366-3880

MISSOURI

COLUMBIA

The Shelter
800 N. Providence, Suite 2
Columbia, MO 65201
(314) 875-1370
(314) 875-1369

KANSAS CITY

MOCSA
3515 Broadway, Suite 301
Kansas City, MO 64111
(816) 531-0233
(816) 931-4527

MONTANA

BILLINGS

Billings Rape Task Force
1245 N. Twenty-ninth
Street, Room 218
Billings, MT 59101
(406) 259-6506

KALISPELL

Kalispell Rape Crisis Line
Box 1385
Kalispell, MT 59903-1385
(406) 752-7273

NEBRASKA

LINCOLN

Rape/Spouse Abuse Crisis
Center

2545 Nancy
Lincoln, NE 68510
(402) 475-7273
(402) 476-2110

OMAHA

Women Against Violence
YWCA
222 S. 29th Street
Omaha, NE 68131
(402) 345-7273

NEVADA

LAS VEGAS

Community Action
Against Rape
749 Veterans Memorial
Drive
Las Vegas, NV 89101
(702) 366-1640
(702) 385-2153 (office)

NEW HAMPSHIRE

MANCHESTER

Women's Crisis Service
YWCA
72 Concord Street
Manchester, NH 03101
(603) 668-2299

NASHUA

Rape and Assault Support
Services
10 Prospect Street
P.O. Box 271
Nashua, NH 03060
(603) 883-3044

NEW JERSEY

FLEMINGTON

Women's Crisis Services
47 E. Main
Flemington, NJ 08822
(908) 788-4044

NEWARK

Sexual Assault Rape
Analysis Unit (SARA)

1 Lincoln Avenue
Newark, NJ 07104
(201) 733-7273

NEW MEXICO

ALAMOGORDO

HELPline Rape Crisis
Team
Otero County Mental
Health Association
1408 Eighth Street
Alamogordo, NM 88310
(505) 437-8680
*(505) 437-7404 (8:00
A.M. to 5:00 P.M.)

ALBUQUERQUE

Albuquerque Rape Crisis
Center
1025 Hermosa S.E.
Albuquerque, NM 87108
(505) 266-7711

ARTESIA

Artesia Rape Crisis Team
Artesia Council for
Human Services, Inc.
801 Bush Avenue
Artesia, NM 88210
(505) 746-9848

CARLSBAD

Carlsbad Mental Health
Association
918 N. Canal
Carlsbad, NM 88220
(505) 885-8888
(505) 885-4836

DEMING

Rape Crisis Program
P.O. Box 1132
Deming, NM 88031
(505) 546-2174 (office)

FARMINGTON

Community Counseling
Center

724 W. Animus
Farmington, NM 87401
(505) 325-1906
(505) 325-0238

GRANTS

Rape Crisis
The Resource Center, Inc.
P.O. Drawer 966
Grants, NM 87020
(505) 287-7985

HOBBS

Rape Crisis Center
Lea County Crisis Center,
Inc.
920 W. Broadway
Hobbs, NM 88240
(505) 393-6633
(505) 393-3168

LAS VEGAS

Rape Crisis Services
Sangre De Cristo Mental
Health Service
116 Bridge Street
Las Vegas, NM 87701
(505) 425-3558

PORTALES

Roosevelt County Rape
Crisis Advocacy
Mental Health Resources,
Inc.
300 E. First Street
Portales, NM 88130
(505) 432-2159
(505) 359-1221 (office)

ROSWELL

Counseling Association
Box 1978
Roswell, NM 88201
(505) 623-1480

SANTA FE

Santa Fe Rape Crisis
Center
P.O. Box 16346

Santa Fe, NM 87506
(505) 986-9111

NEW YORK

BINGHAMTON

Rape Crisis Center
P.O. Box 836
Binghamton, NY 13902
(607) 722-4256

BROOKLYN

Brooklyn Women's Anti-
Rape Exchange
30 3rd Avenue
Brooklyn, NY 11217
(718) 330-0310

BUFFALO

Advocate Program for
Victims of Sexual
Assault
2964 Main Street
Buffalo, NY 14214
(716) 834-3131

NEW YORK CITY

Rape Crisis Intervention
Program
622 W. 168th Street
New York, NY 10032
(212) 305-9060

Mount Sinai Medical
Center Rape Crisis
Intervention Program
1 Gustave L. Levy Place
Box 1170
New York, NY 10029
(212) 241-5461

ONEONTA

Oneonta Rape Crisis
Network
c/o Opportunities for
Otsego
3 West Broadway
Oneonta, NY 13820
(607) 432-8088

PLATTSBURGH

Crime Victim/Sexual
Assault Program
36 Brinkerhoff Street
Plattsburgh, NY 12901
(518) 561-2330

ROCHESTER

Rape Crisis Service of
Planned Parenthood of
Rochester and Monroe
County
114 University Avenue
Rochester, NY 14605
(716) 546-2595

SCHENECTADY

Rape Crisis Service of
Schenectady, Inc.
c/o Planned Parenthood
414 Union Street
Schenectady, NY 12305
(518) 346-2266

SYRACUSE

Rape Crisis Center of
Syracuse, Inc.
423 W. Onondaga Street
Syracuse, NY 13202
(315) 422-7273

NORTH CAROLINA

ASHEVILLE

Rape Crisis Center of
Asheville
P.O. Box 7453
Asheville, NC 28802
(704) 255-7576

BURLINGTON

Rape Crisis Alliance of
Alamance County
Box 2573
Burlington, NC 27216
(919) 227-6220

CHAPEL HILL

Orange County Women's
Center

P.O. Box 871
Chapel Hill, NC 27514
(919) 967-7273
(919) 968-4647

CHARLOTTE

Victim Assistance/Rape
Crisis
901 Elizabeth Avenue,
Suite 500
Charlotte, NC 28204
(704) 375-9900

CONCORD

Cabarrus Rape Crisis Help
Line
301 S. Brevard
Charlotte, NC 28202
*(704) 788-1156 (8:00
A.M.–5:00 P.M., 7:00
P.M.–11:00 P.M.)

GREENVILLE

Rape Victim Companion
Program
REAL Crisis Prevention,
Inc.
312 E. Tenth Street
Greenville, NC 27858
(919) 758-4357

MORGANTON

Foothills Rape Crisis
Service
Burke County Human
Resources Center
700 East Parker Road
Morganton, NC 28655
(704) 438-6226

SALISBURY

The Rape, Child and
Family Abuse Crises
Council
131 W. Council Street
Salisbury, NC 28144
(704) 636-9222
(704) 636-4718

STATESVILLE

Rape and Abuse
Prevention Group of
Statesville/Iredell
County, Inc.
1400 Fifth Street
Statesville, NC 28677
(704) 872-7638
(704) 872-3403

NORTH DAKOTA

FARGO

Rape and Abuse Crisis
Center of Fargo-
Moorhead
P.O. Box 2984
Fargo, ND 58108
(701) 293-7273

GRAND FORKS

Abuse and Rape Crisis
Center
111 S. 4th Street
Grand Forks, ND 58201
(701) 746-8900

OHIO

AKRON

Akron Rape Crisis Center
670 W. Exchange Street
YWCA Building
Akron, OH 44308
(216) 434-7273

CANTON

Rape Crisis Center
American Red Cross
618 Second Street, NW
Canton, OH 44703
(216) 452-1111

COLUMBUS

Women Against Rape
P.O. Box 02084
Columbus, OH 43202
(614) 221-4447
(614) 291-9751 (office)

WARREN

Rape Crisis Team
c/o Contact Community
Connection
1569 Woodland Avenue
NE
Warren, OH 44483-5646
(216) 393-1565
(216) 395-5255

OKLAHOMA

ENID

Rape Crisis Center
525 S. Quincy
P.O. Box 3165
Enid, OK 73701
(405) 234-7644
(405) 234-7581

NORMAN

Women's Resource Center
P.O. Box 5089
Norman, OK 73070
(405) 360-0590

TULSA

Rape Crisis Line
2121 Columbia
Lower Level 6
Tulsa, OK 77114
(918) 744-7273
(918) 744-7361

OREGON

CORVALLIS

Center Against Rape and
Domestic Violence
P.O. Box 914
Corvallis, OR 97339
(503) 754-0110
1 (800) 927-0197 TTD
*(503) 758-0219 (office;
Monday through Friday,
9:00 A.M. to 5:00 P.M.)

OREGON CITY

Victim Assistance Program
708 Main Street

Oregon City, OR 97045
(503) 655-8616

PORTLAND

Women's Crisis Line
P.O. Box 42610
Portland, OR 97242-0610
(503) 235-5333
(503) 232-9751 (office)

PENNSYLVANIA

ALLENTOWN

Rape Crisis Council of
  Lehigh Valley, Inc.
509 N. 7th Street
Allentown, PA 18103
(215) 437-6611
(215) 437-6610 (office)

ALTOONA

Sexual Assault Volunteer
  Effort (SAVE)
2022 Broad Avenue
Altoona, PA 16601
(814) 944-3585
(814) 944-3583

BLOOMSBURG

Bloomsburg Women's
  Center
111 N. Market Street
Bloomsburg, PA 17815
(717) 784-6631

BUTLER

Irene Stacy Community
  Mental Health Center
112 Hillvue Drive
Butler, PA 16001
(412) 287-0791

DOYLESTOWN

Doylestown Network of
  Victim Assitance
30 W. Oakland Avenue
Doylestown, PA 18901
1 (800) 675-6900
(215) 348-5664

STROUDSBURG

Women's Resources
400 Main Street
Stroudsburg, PA 18360
(717) 421-4200
*(717) 424-2093 (Monday
  through Friday, 9:00
  A.M. to 5:00 P.M.)

ERIE

Erie County Rape Crisis
  Center, Inc.
125 W. 18th Street
Erie, PA 16501
(814) 870-7087

HARRISBURG

Harrisburg Area Rape
  Crisis Center
215 Market Street
Harrisburg, PA 17101
(717) 238-7273

LANCASTER

Lancaster Rape Aid and
  Prevention
501 W. James Street
Lancaster, PA 17603
(717) 392-7273

MEADVILLE

Crisis Line
1034 Grove Street
Meadville, PA 16335
(814) 724-2732

MEDIA

Delaware County Women
  Against Rape, Inc.
P.O. Box 211
Media, PA 19063
(215) 566-4342

NORRISTOWN

Victim Services Center of
  Montgomery County,
  Inc.
70 E. Penn Street
Norristown, PA 19401
(215) 277-5200

PITTSBURGH

Pittsburgh Action Against
  Rape (PAAR)
815 19th Street
Pittsburgh, PA 15203
(412) 765-2731
(412) 431-5665 (office)

STATE COLLEGE

Women's Resource Center
Rape Abuse Services
140 W. Nittany Avenue
State College, PA 16801
(814) 234-5050
(814) 234-5222
  (information and
  referral)

WEST CHESTER

Crime Victims Rape Crisis
  Center
236 W. Market Street
West Chester, PA 19382
(215) 692-7273
(215) 692-7420

WILKES-BARRE

Victims Resource Center
68 S. Franklin
Wilkes-Barre, PA 18702-
  1409
(717) 823-0765

YORK

Rape and Victim
  Assistance Center of
  York
P.O. Box 892
York, PA 17405
(717) 854-3131

RHODE ISLAND

PROVIDENCE

Rhode Island Rape Crisis
  Center, Inc.
300 Richmond Street
Providence, RI 02903
(401) 421-4100

SOUTH CAROLINA

CHARLESTON

People Against Rape
15 Hutson Street,
Room 233
Old Citadel Annex
Charleston, SC 29403
(803) 722-7273

GREENVILLE

Rape Crisis
104 Chapman Street
Greenville, SC 29605
(803) 467-3633

SOUTH DAKOTA

ABERDEEN

Women's Resource Center
317 South Kline
Aberdeen, SD 57401
(605) 226-1212

RAPID CITY

Women Against Violence,
Inc.
P.O. Box 3042
Rapid City, SD 57709
(605) 341-4808
(605) 341-3292

TENNESSEE

KNOXVILLE

Knoxville Rape Crisis
Center
P.O. Box 11523
Knoxville, TN 37939-1523
(615) 522-7273
(615) 558-9040

MEMPHIS

Comprehensive Rape Crisis
Program
2600 Poplar Street,
Suite 300
Memphis, TN 38122
(901) 528-2161

NASHVILLE

Rape and Sexual Abuse
Center of Davidson
County
56 Lindsley Avenue
Nashville, TN 37210
(615) 259-9055
1 (800) 879-1999
*(615) 256-8526 (8:00
A.M. to 6:00 P.M.)

TEXAS

ABILENE

Abilene Rape Crisis Center
P.O. Box 122
Abilene, TX 79604
(915) 677-7895

AMARILLO

Rape Crisis and Sexual
Abuse Service
900 S. Lincoln
Amarillo, TX 79101
(806) 373-8022

BEAUMONT

Rape Crisis Center of
Southeast Texas, Inc.
P.O. Box 5011
Beaumont, TX 77706
(409) 835-3355

DALLAS

Dallas County Rape Crisis
Center
P.O. Box 35728
Dallas, TX 75235
(214) 653-8740

EL PASO

Rape Crisis Service
5250 El Paso Drive
El Paso, TX 79905
(915) 779-1800

FORT WORTH

Rape Crisis Program
1723 Hemphill

Forth Worth, TX 76110
(817) 927-2737
(817) 927-4039

KILLEEN

Rape Crisis Center
P.O. Box 25
Killeen, TX 76540
(817) 634-8309
(817) 634-1134

LUBBOCK

Lubbock Rape Crisis
Center
P.O. Box 2000
Lubbock, TX 79457
(806) 763-7273
(806) 763-3232

ROUND ROCK

Rape Crisis Center
211 Commerce Street,
No. 103
Round Rock, TX 78664
(512) 255-1212

SAN ANTONIO

Rape Crisis Line
P.O. Box 27802
San Antonio, TX 78227
(512) 349-7273

TYLER

Rape Crisis Center
3027 SSE Loop, No. 323
Tyler, TX 75701
1 (800) 333-0358
(903) 595-3199

UTAH

SALT LAKE CITY

Salt Lake Rape Crisis
Center
2035 S. 1300 E
Salt Lake City, UT 84105
(801) 467-7273
(801) 467-7282

VERMONT

BURLINGTON

Women's Rape Crisis
Center
P.O. Box 92
Burlington, VT 05402
(802) 863-1236

RUTLAND

Women's Network and
Shelter
P.O. Box 313
Rutland, VT 05702
(802) 775-3232

VIRGINIA

ARLINGTON

Rape and Domestic
Violence Services of
Arlington
1725 N. George Mason
Drive
Arlington, VA 12205
(703) 358-5150
(703) 527-4077

CHARLOTTESVILLE

Charlottesville Rape Crisis
Group
P.O. Box 6705
Charlottesville, VA 22906
(804) 977-7273
(804) 295-7273

NORFOLK

YWCA Women in Crisis
Program
253 W. Freemason Street
Norfolk, VA 23510
(804) 625-5570
(804) 625-4248

RICHMOND

Crisis Intervention
Program
501 N. Ninth Street
Richmond, VA 23219
(804) 648-9224

WASHINGTON

BELLINGHAM

Whatcom County Crisis
Services/Rape Relief
124 E. Holly
Bellingham, WA 98225
(206) 734-7271
(206) 671-5714

BREMERTON

Kilsap Sexual Assault
Center/Rape Response
P.O. Box 1327
Bremerton, WA 98310
(206) 479-8500
(206) 479-1788

EVERETT

Providence Sexual Assault
Center
P.O. Box 1067
Everett, WA 98206
(206) 252-4800
(206) 258-7844

OLYMPIA

Safe Place
P.O. Box 1605
Olympia, WA 98507
(206) 754-6300
(206) 786-8754

RENTON

Sexual Assault Service
304 Main Street
Renton, WA 98055
(206) 226-7273
(206) 226-5062

RICHLAND

Benton Franklin Rape
Relief and Sexual
Assault Program
P.O. Box 9
Richland, WA 99352
(509) 946-2377

SEATTLE

Seattle Rape Relief
1825 S. Jackson, Suite 102
Seattle, WA 98144
(206) 632-7273
(206) 325-5531

Sexual Assault Center
Harborview Medical
Center
325 Ninth Avenue ZA-07
Seattle, WA 98104
*(206) 521-1800 (days:
8:30 A.M. to 5:00 P.M.;
recording after 5:00
P.M.)
*(206) 223-3000 (nights,
weekends: ask for social
worker)

SPOKANE

Rape Crisis Network
S. 7 Howard, Suite 200
Spokane, WA 99201
(509) 624-7273

TACOMA

Pierce County Rape Relief
Allenmore Medical Center
Building A, Suite A 302
1901 S. 19th
Tacoma, WA 98405
(206) 474-7273
(206) 597-6424

WENATCHEE

Wenatchee Rape Crisis
Center
P.O. Box 2704
Wenatchee, WA 98801
(509) 663-7446

YAKIMA

Sexual Assault Unit
P.O. Box 959
Yakima, WA 98907
1 (800) 572-8122
(509) 575-4200

WEST VIRGINIA

MORGANTOWN

Rape and Domestic
Violence
Information Center
P.O. Box 4228
Morgantown, WV 26505
(304) 292-5100

WISCONSIN

GREEN BAY

Sexual Assault Center &
Family Service
Association

132 S. Madison
Green Bay, WI 54301
(414) 433-0584

MADISON

Rape Crisis Center, Inc.
128 E. Olin, Suite 202
Madison, WI 53701
(608) 251-7273

OSHKOSH

Sexual Abuse Services
201 Zeape Avenue
Oshkosh, WI 54901
(414) 426-1460 (office)

KENOSHA

Kenoshans Youth
Development Services
5407 8th Avenue
Kenosha, WI 53140
(414) 657-7188

WYOMING

CHEYENNE

Safe House/Sexual Assault
Services, Inc.
P.O. Box 1885
Cheyenne, WY 82003
(307) 637-7233
(307) 634-8655

Suggested Readings

GENERAL

Dowling, Colette. *The Cinderella Complex*. New York: Pocket Books, 1981.

Griffin, Susan. *Pornography and Silence*. New York: Harper and Row, 1981.

Gubar, Susan, and Joan Hoff. *For Adult Users Only: The Dilemma of Violent Pornography*. Bloomington: Indiana University Press, 1989.

Kivel, Paul. *How to Stop the Violence That Tears Our Lives Apart*. Center City, Minn.: Hazelden Educational Materials, 1992.

Lovelace, Linda. *Ordeal*. New York: Berkley Books, 1980.

Sanday, Peggy Reeves, and Ruth Gallagher Goodenough. *Beyond the Second Sex: New Directions in the Anthropology of Gender*. New York: New York University Press, 1990.

Schaef, Anne Wilson. *Women's Reality*. Minneapolis: Winston Press, 1981.

Tarvis, Carol. *The Mismeasure of Woman*. New York: Simon and Schuster, 1992.

Thorne, Barrie. *Gender Play: Girls and Boys in School*. New Brunswick, N.J.: Rutgers University Press, 1993.

Wolf, Naomi. *The Beauty Myth: How Images of Beauty Are Used Against Women*. New York: Anchor Books, 1991.

RAPE

Beneke, Timothy. *Men on Rape*. New York: St. Martin's Press, 1982.

Brownmiller, Susan. *Against Our Will*. New York: Simon and Schuster, 1975.

Burgess, Ann W., ed. *Rape and Sexual Assault: A Research Handbook*. New York: Garland Publishing, 1985.

Burt, Pauline, and Patricia O'Brien. *Stopping Rape: Successful Survival Strategies*. New York: Pergamon Press, 1985.

Fairstein, Linda, ed. *Sexual Violence: A War Against Rape*. New York: William Morrow and Company, 1993.

Groth, Nicholas. *Men Who Rape*. New York: Plenum Press, 1979.

Maltz, Wendy. *The Sexual Healing Journey: A Guide for Survivors of Sexual Abuse*. New York: HarperCollins, 1991.

Russell, Diane. *Rape in Marriage*. New York: Macmillan Publishing Co., 1982.

Warshaw, Robin. *I Never Called It Rape*. New York: Harper and Row, 1988.

CHILDREN

Brady, Katherine. *Father's Day*. New York: Dell, 1979.

Geiser, Robert L. *Hidden Victims: The Sexual Abuse of Children*. Beacon Press, 1979.

Russell, Diane. *Sexual Exploitation: Child Sexual Abuse and Workplace Harassment*. Beverly Hills: Sage Publications, 1984.

Index